The Girl IN THE Italian Bakery

A
MEMOIR

The *Girl* IN THE
Italian Bakery

Kenneth Tingle

dedication

Dedicated to Andy Puglisi and Ron June.
Put a good word in for me in heaven.

Thank you, God, for granting me the time, wisdom,
and perseverance to write this book.
In spite of my foolishness, you always did look out for me.

A special thanks to Candace Sinclair and J.D. Byrum
for all their hard work and excellent advice.

Every time a family falls apart, it is the death of a small civilization.

author unknown

introduction

We all have a story to tell, every single one of us. Some people will tell you their story whether you want to hear it or not, and they will probably tell it to you more than once. Other people keep their story to themselves, live with it their entire life, and then quietly take it to the grave with them. Never having shared it with anyone, never giving others the benefit of their experience; the mistakes they made, the things they did right, gone forever with them. Often the stories that went untold are the ones we needed to hear the most.

As my fortieth birthday approaches soon, I am suddenly looking back at my life and thinking about all the mistakes I made and the things I actually got right. I didn't plan this self-examination. It just came upon me suddenly, like some kind of built-in mechanism that clicks in when you turn forty. It is almost as though Chapter One of my life is now concluding, and before I can start Chapter Two, I need to review the first one. My life thus far has been anything but ordinary. I remember at age thirteen my grandmother saying, "My

God, it's a wonder your head is still screwed on right with all you have been through." And there was still plenty left to come.

So here I am, looking back over forty years and trying to make some sense of things that make no sense. Old feelings have come creeping back—insecurity, fear, anger, resentment, confusion, and hope. Some of the memories I try to forget; others I want to hold on to forever. More than anything else, I remember the girl in the Italian bakery and the foolish mistake I made. I have never told anyone my story before. But it is now time to tell it. I don't know why—but I need to tell you my story.

1

The kitten stood trembling, his legs buckling from the pain. He had a bewildered, mournful look on his little face. Three large German Shepherds stood around him in a ring and they took turns picking him up in their teeth, biting as hard as they could, shaking him violently side to side, and then hurling him against the pavement. They growled viciously and drool dripped from their teeth.

I stood there shivering, paralyzed with fear, crying and screaming for help, "Somebody do something. Help him!"

There were other kids there and some of them seemed to be enjoying the show.

"No, let them go. He's almost dead!" they shouted back.

The dogs were only about twenty feet away between a row of garbage cans and a large clothesline section. They bit into the helpless kitten one last time, shook him from side to side and dropped him. He lay limp and motionless on the concrete.

I turned and ran around the corner and up the short hill to our apartment, bursting through the front door with tears streaming. "Mom, Mom! They killed the kitty, they killed the kitty!"

My mother was in the kitchen and she ran into the living room to meet me.

"Who killed the kitty? What kitty?"

"A ... a cute little kitty; the bad dogs killed him," I cried, choking on tears.

"What happened?" my mother yelled, alarmed at my distress.

"He didn't do anything ... he was just a cute little baby. They kept biting him and he died. Those dogs are bad dogs!"

I was crying even harder now.

My mother hugged me.

"There, there, Ken, honey, everything is going to be all right," she comforted as I turned and walked up the stairs with my head down.

I wondered how those dogs could be so evil. How could they do something like that to a cute, helpless little kitten? The world wasn't supposed to be like this. Kittens were supposed to be held and cuddled; dogs were supposed to wag their tails and fetch sticks. I went into my room and lay on the bed face down. I cried for the kitten and wondered if it was in heaven, thinking something so innocent surely must be. Or maybe he was in some kind of cat heaven, made up entirely of catnip with balls of yarn everywhere, tuna and milk served three times a day. I hugged Bunny, my stuffed rabbit that I had found in the garbage with a torn leg, that my mom had sewn up good as new, and took comfort in the idea that the kitten was having the time of his life in cat heaven.

No mother wants her five-year-old son to see a kitten torn to shreds and she was upset. She was angry that the kitten was killed and even angrier that I saw it. When my mother moved to America from Scotland several years back, she never thought she would wind up in a housing project in a tough city like Lawrence, Massachusetts. But here she was with three kids and no husband, in one of the worst places to raise a family. The Stadium Project was bad, but there were worse neighborhoods in Lawrence—the Hancock Projects, where a cab driver was shot in the head during a robbery, the Essex Projects where the police were afraid to go, and some areas with row after row of three-story tenements and gangs of youths roaming the streets. The Stadium Projects was its own little isolated world, many little gray or yellow buildings with eight apartments each, spread out and expansive over a large area. They were originally built for military families, but had been converted to low-income housing years ago. The only hint of its military past was an army reserve station at the bottom of the hill. It was full of military vehicles and surrounded by a tall chain-link fence, which gave it a forbidden atmosphere. There was a single large building that was painted a drab yellow color and you rarely saw anyone in the compound.

After awhile my mother called up the stairs, "Ken, honey, dinner is ready."

I made my way slowly down the stairs and walked into the kitchen where my two brothers were already waiting. Tommy was the oldest and everyone said he wasn't normal; sometimes he would laugh to himself when nothing funny happened, or laugh when he wasn't supposed to, like in church or in his classroom when the teacher was talking. He usually kept to himself, partly because he was a loner, but mostly because he didn't have any friends. Kids in the project picked on him constantly. Sometimes a whole gang of kids chased and taunted him. Fortunately, Tommy was an extremely fast runner and was nicknamed "LTTT" by the kids in the neighborhood, which stood for "Light Toes Tommy Tingle." That's our last name, Tingle, as if we didn't have enough problems. My mother nicknamed Tommy, "The Bone" because he was thin as a rail and as he ran he looked like a gazelle rocketing across a field, his speed saving him from a lot of beatings. I sometimes heard adults whisper to my mother, "What a shame, such a handsome boy. He has such beautiful teeth and wavy dark hair, such a shame." He was four years older than me.

My other brother Gary was the middle child and he had a way about him that always got under my mother's skin. She could be in a great mood, but after a few moments with Gary she would be screaming, "You're going to be the death of me!" Gary had rusty brown hair and was thin like Tommy and me. He was already taller than Tommy and you could tell he would be a big man when he grew up. Gary was in a bad position when it came to the bullies in the project—he had a brother who wasn't normal and attracted trouble, like a wounded fish becomes the prey, another brother three years younger who was too young to help, and a last name like Tingle. I looked up to him; he was my big brother. We spent a lot of time together and my mother used to say, "Wild horses couldn't drag those two apart." My mother nicknamed him, "Guggi," pronounced "Guh-gee," and he did not like it one bit.

"We can eat in the living room tonight while we watch TV," my mom said in a soft voice, trying to make me forget the kitten.

This was usually my favorite time of day—the Flintstones, Gilligan's Island, and Lost in Space would come on, one after another, and we would sit together as a family and watch them.

"Mom, I'm not really that hungry," I said, feeling a knot in my stomach.

"You have to eat something. You can't go to bed hungry."

I put a bite of mashed potatoes and gravy in my mouth, chewing slowly, and when I swallowed I felt it go halfway down and it almost came right back up, making me feel slightly nauseous. I tried to clear my mind and concentrate on keeping my food down. The Flintstones started and after a few minutes of Fred and Barney in some ridiculous situation, I felt a little better. I worked slowly on my mashed potatoes and peas. There was no way I could eat any meat tonight, wondering if I could ever again. Gilligan and company discovered there were headhunters on the island and the spoof of it almost made me laugh. But I couldn't. On Lost in Space someone pulled out the robot's power pack, as usual, and he collapsed forward while saying "Dangerrrrr," only to have it reinserted in the nick of time to save the Robinsons. At least on TV the good guys always won, and there was always a happy ending. The world worked the way it was supposed to on TV. The families were always together, with a mother and father who never yelled, and little kittens weren't torn to shreds. Every night after dinner, I would escape with my mother and brothers to that perfect world. Ten feet away, outside the front door, was the real world where the rules didn't always matter. But here on the couch with my mother and the Flintstones I was safe.

I dozed off and my mom carried me upstairs to my room, tucked me in with Bunny beside me, and gave me a kiss on the forehead. "Good night, honey."

I looked up at her and asked, "Mom, is the kitten in heaven?"

"Of course, honey, of course."

If my mom said the kitten was in heaven then it had to be true. Moms didn't lie.

The next morning I awoke to my brother Gary standing over me.

"Hey, PJ Timmons is at the door."

I focused on his blurry face. "It's early. What does he want?" I asked, rubbing my eyes.

"It's Saturday. He probably wants you to go out and play."

"Tell him I'll be out in a few minutes."

I put Bunny to the side, put on my clothes, and ran down the stairs toward the front door, only to be stopped abruptly at the bottom of the stairs by my mother grabbing my arm.

"I don't want you playing with that boy. He has lice in his hair."

My mother didn't like PJ. She said he was dirty. But I liked PJ a lot; he was one of the friendliest kids in the project, an athletic kid who always knew how to have fun, and there was always a smile on his freckled face. PJ didn't have nice clothes, but neither did I.

"He does not have bugs," I protested.

"Yes, he does. I saw them."

"He does not!"

My mother opened the front door and PJ was standing there patiently, with his hands in his pockets and a smile on his face.

"Hi, Mrs. Tingle, is Kenny home?"

"Yes, PJ, could you come here a second?" my mom said as she stepped out onto the porch.

She reached down and ran her fingers through his red curly hair, looking for the evidence to prove her point.

"Hold still, PJ," she said impatiently, not finding it.

PJ was six years old but he knew what was going on, and his face flushed red with embarrassment.

My mother mumbled, "Well, maybe it was some other kid." She turned to me. "Eat your cereal, brush your teeth, and then you can go. PJ, you can come back in a few minutes."

I did as my mother asked and I sprinted out the front door with PJ. The autumn air was cool, especially in the morning, and as I came out the door, it felt like someone had splashed cold water against my face.

"What do you want to do?" PJ asked, breathing slightly hard as we ran across an area of clotheslines and up a hill to the parking lot.

"I don't care," I answered, with a certain tone that said you figure it out.

PJ stopped in the parking lot.

"Wait, wait," he said, surveying the area.

Down the hill was the stadium where the high school practiced all their sports and held their home games for football, baseball, and track meets. We played there a lot when the students were away.

"Want to go to the stadium?" I suggested, because I had no other ideas.

"Nah, too early."

PJ turned and looked down the other hill toward the town dump.

"Wanna go to the dump?" he asked, as he pointed in that direction.

"What for?"

"I don't know, there's lots of cool stuff there," he said, trying to convince me with enthusiasm in his voice.

"I have a better idea. Let's catch grasshoppers in the woods," I said, as I crossed the street toward the tall grass on the other side.

It wasn't really what you would consider "woods," as it only extended a mile or less before you hit the highway, and in the other direction maybe a little bigger, but to us it was a vast forest full of uncertainty and adventure, possible danger behind every tree.

I walked a short distance into the tall grass and onto the embankment that looked over the military reserve station.

"We need something to catch them in," I said, looking around on the ground for anything that would possibly hold a grasshopper captive.

We spent several minutes scanning the area, and then PJ walked by the side of the road.

"I found something!" he yelled, holding up a paper cup like he had just found a twenty-dollar bill.

We tromped through the tall grass, being as disruptive as we could in order to stir them from their safe havens. A grasshopper shot out of the grass a few feet into the air and then down to a new hiding spot.

"There's one!"

"Get him!"

PJ made his way quietly through the grass, holding the cup down with its open mouth toward the grasshopper. He carefully put the cup over it and closed off the top with his free hand.

"Let me see! Let me see!" I screeched, like I had never seen a grasshopper before.

He slowly pulled his hand back, and the grasshopper shot out of the cup and deep into the grass.

He took a second leap and then a third, well out of sight.

"Look what you did," PJ said with frustration.

"I just wanted to see it."

"Well, now we have to find another one."

We slowly made our way through the tall grass again, this time trying a different method of attack. Instead of stirring them up, we decided on the element of surprise. After awhile, when I felt it was now hopeless, I came across an odd looking creature that was unlike anything I had ever seen before. It was bright green with a big head and its front arms were folded forward.

"PJ, PJ, what the heck kind of grasshopper is this?"

He ran over and crouched down beside me.

"It's one of those praying manta things. Don't touch it! It can kill you!"

I backed off quickly, startled. "No way," I said, trying to convince myself that something so small couldn't hurt me.

"Yah way," PJ said, with the tone of an expert, "and if you hurt it the police will come and take you to jail."

I was scared but I didn't want PJ to know, so I acted bored with the entire situation and suggested we do something else.

"Let's go into the woods," I said, trying to disguise the fear in my voice.

"Yeah, okay, I'm tired of this anyways."

We ran together, side by side, into the woods and down a winding trail that led toward the dump. Even though we were only a hundred yards into the woods, it became darker, and I felt like I was miles from home. The shadows created by the sun as it shone down between the trees only enhanced a surreal and eerie appearance. Bushes became crouching figures; the larger trees cast odd shadows that suggested a person might be behind them; the sudden cawing of birds seemed to signal an alarm that only they could see from up high. I knew my mother would be worried if she was aware that I was in the woods and I began to miss her. I was a momma's boy.

PJ pointed a short way into the woods. "Look," he said, and in the distance I could see a homemade tent.

We approached slowly, cautiously, tip-toeing as we came closer, expecting a person to jump out at any time. When we got there we could see it was made out of a blanket with two sticks supporting it.

"Look inside," PJ said, trying to get me to go first.

"No way. You do it," I countered.

"Okay, we'll do it at the same time."

We each grabbed a flap and pulled them back to look inside—a sleeping bag, some magazines, and an old wool sweater. Someone had slept here the night before.

"What if he comes back?" I said, fear shooting from my toes to my head. Then, with no warning to PJ, I turned and began to run away as fast as I could. My imagination was running wild and I could envision a large bearded man coming back and going into a rage when he saw us looking into his tent, and this made me run even faster.

It wasn't long before PJ was running alongside me, and then he passed me. "Let's get out of here!" he gasped. We emerged out of the woods and crossed the street into the parking lot, doubled over and tried to catch our breath.

"Wanna do something else?" PJ asked, panting heavily.

"Nah, I have to go home and check in with my mother. Maybe after lunch."

PJ headed off toward his house on the other side of the project and I went the other way; down the hill, through the clothesline section, and on the path toward my house. Up ahead I saw Kathy Horrigan and I didn't want to walk past her. She was a stocky girl with short blonde hair and she was more of a bully than most of the boys her age. She had given several of them a bloody nose or two. She had a foul mouth and never backed down from an argument or fight, which she usually started. She was a few years older than me.

I tried to walk by unnoticed, but she turned to me, "Hey, Kenny, my father said he is sick of that noise coming from your house."

"What noise?"

"Don't act stupid, you know what noise!"

And I did. There was a large gray radiator in my mother's bedroom that wasn't working right. It stood about three-feet tall and was made up of vertical coils with a black screw-on cap on the top. Every fifteen minutes or so it would repeat the same irritating cycle—first a buildup of steamy pressure, *hisssss*, followed by a loud clanking of pipes, *clunk, caclunk, caclunk*, then it would finish off in a grand finale of screeching steam, *phhhhhwwwweeeeee*, so loud that it traveled through the wall into the Horrigan's apartment and they would bang on the wall with a broom. The banging broom actually became a part of the cycle; as soon as the radiator finished you could count on a couple of thumps from the other side of the wall.

Maintenance had been called numerous times, but never came to fix it.

"Okay, I'll tell her," I said, happy she wasn't starting a fight with me.

I walked through the back door, which led directly into the kitchen. "Mom, I'm home!" I shouted.

My mother was in the living room reading a book on the couch. "Where did you go?" she asked, closing the book.

"I was catching grasshoppers with PJ. Then we went into the woods for a little while."

"The woods! I told you I don't want you going into the woods unless you're with someone older! This is why you can't play with PJ anymore."

"It was my idea, not PJ's."

"Well, the next time you go in the woods you can spend the rest of the day in your room. Do you understand me?"

"Yes," I answered, looking down at the floor, avoiding eye contact.

"It better not happen again. I'm going next door to visit Peggy and you can come."

"No, please, I don't want to go to Peggy's. It's boring!"

I knew if I went I would be stuck sitting there and listening to them talk about a bunch of grown-up stuff. Peggy was a notorious gossip, skilled at her craft, with a wagging tongue that could clean the gravy out of a pot from ten feet away. She rarely left her apartment and how she got dirty details on everyone was a mystery. I couldn't understand grown-ups; my mother would visit Peggy one day and the next she would be calling her a flat-ass gossip. My mother always said that Peggy had a flat ass because she never got off the couch.

I protested all I could but it was no use. I was going to Peggy's for at least an hour of torture. My brothers were out playing and had escaped this cruelty. "Can I at least bring a toy?" I asked, defeated.

"Bring whatever you want. But make it fast." I went upstairs and grabbed my GI Joe doll and came back down. We walked out the front door and took a few steps to our left and knocked on Peggy's door.

She opened the door wearing the same old tan, polyester pants and knit sweater.

"Well, hello," she said, red lipstick visible on her teeth. "Come in, sit down."

Peggy had a big fluffy couch and whenever she entertained she would sit on one end and her guest would sit on the other. It was Peggy's lair, a trap of sorts, because as people would sit and listen to her gossiping about everyone else, she was slowly and carefully extracting information from them to be used in her next session with someone else. It was like a psychiatrist's couch; a functional tool for a distinct purpose. She took great pride in her couch and had it arranged the exact same way every time I went there—a fluffed pillow on each side against the arm, and on each side of the back sat a stuffed monkey with long legs and exaggerated big lips. I once tried to take one of the monkeys to play with and Peggy quickly let me know they were "off limits."

"Glad you could come, Frances, sit down."

My mom sat on one end and Peggy sat on the other. I sat on the floor and created an adventure for GI Joe. He had his machine gun that fit in his left hand and in my adventure he was fighting off throngs of well-armed men, the story unfolding as unrealistic as only a five-year-old could create. I tried to ignore the conversation between my mother and Peggy, but every once in awhile I picked up bits and pieces against my will—"Oh, that Bill, big drinker you know, blah blah blah. Oh, that Barbara, getting all dolled up for a night on the town and leaving those kids alone, blah blah blah. Would you like some more tea, Frances? Tell me, what's been going on with you and the kids? Blah blah blah." When Peggy stood up and leaned forward to get something on the far side of the coffee table, I noticed that my mother was absolutely right; her butt was completely flat! It was a strange and unique sight to see, wide and flat. It had followed a basic principle of evolution—adaptation, she was always on the couch and her butt had adapted to that fact, had

anatomically changed its very shape to contour to the couch, like a
key fitting a lock.

Finally, after what seemed like eternity and Peggy was done tearing everyone we knew to shreds, they promised to get together for
tea again and we left. As we walked out Peggy's door Mr. Horrigan
was walking out of our door with a large plumbing wrench in his
hand. My mother almost walked right into him and was completely
startled, her jaw dropping down, unable to muster a word for a few
good seconds. Mr. Horrigan was a big man. Big in height and girth;
he had gray hair that could only be described as disheveled, always
wore a tight white T-shirt that made his stomach look even bigger, and he was always hunched over a little as he walked. I never
saw Mr. Horrigan happy. "How dare you go into my house when
I'm not there!" my mother barked, finally getting her bearings back
and no longer startled. Mr. Horrigan's face turned red as he was
embarrassed at being caught. He thought he would slip in and out
unnoticed and didn't plan on this sudden confrontation.

"I'm sick and tired of that damn radiator of yours. All day,
all night! We can't even get a good night's sleep!" Mr. Horrigan
screamed at my mother, but she wasn't backing down.

"Well, I called maintenance several times and no one comes!
How would you like it if I called the police and told them you went
into our house when we weren't home?"

"Listen, lady, you ought to be thanking me," he said, holding
up the wrench. "I fixed the damned thing!" Then he stormed off
the porch and took a few steps down the path to his own door and
slammed it as he went inside. My mother stood there for a few
seconds, not knowing if she should be angry or grateful. The noise
had been driving her crazy, too. Then she went into our apartment
without saying anything.

I stood on the porch for a moment. As I was ready to follow my
mother inside, I saw Gary Ching running to his house, which was
a few doors down from the Horrigans. He was crying and being
chased by the Paquette brothers—some of the worst bullies in the
project. There were four of them and they all looked different.

Timmy, the oldest, had red hair and freckles with a stocky build and a permanent sneer on his face. Mike was the second oldest and he had brown hair with a similar stocky build, then came Kevin who had blond hair and the same sneer on his face as Timmy, and last was skinny little Doug who had dark black hair. They were laughing as they chased him and yelling sexual and racial slurs. Gary made it to his door and turned around to look at them, wanting to say something back, but realizing that he would pay for it the next time they caught him alone. I felt bad seeing him cry; he was the only Asian kid in the project and the Paquettes never let him forget it. I wished I were like those superheroes in the comic books that my brothers and I collected. Superman, the Hulk, Batman, any of them, so I could go over to every bully in the project and knock them over like bowling pins, swing them around by their ankles, make them feel the same embarrassment and anger that they so enjoyed making other kids feel. But I also had a sense of relief that they were bothering him and not me and my brothers, which they often did. Taunting us, "Tingle, Tingle, shit on a shingle," or, "Tingle bells, Tingle bells, Tingle all the way." They often did it in front of my mother, having no fear of grown-ups. The only thing they understood or feared was someone bigger and tougher than them. There were few kids in the project tougher than the Paquettes, and even if they were they knew they would have to fight all four of them. Jerry Horrigan, Kathy's teenage brother, was one of the kids they didn't mess with. Jerry was a muscular teenager and they didn't usually come around our block because of him. But he was gone often, and when he was they would feel emboldened to come our way.

I went in the house and my mom was back on the couch reading her book. "Where's Gary and Tommy?" I asked.

"Tommy is off somewhere running around. Gary is sweeping the sidewalk out front," she answered, without looking up from her book. I walked through the kitchen and out the front door where Gary was sweeping the sidewalk, half-hearted strokes and a disgruntled look on his face, brushing little piles of dirt into the grass on the edge of the sidewalk.

"Where's Tommy?"

"I don't know. He went down the other side of the project, by the Alicon's house. I told him he was stupid. Where were you?"

"I was at Peggy's house with Mom."

"Ha, ha, you had to go to boring Peggy's house!"

"Ha, ha to you. At least I don't have to sweep the sidewalk!" Gary stopped sweeping, picked up a small rock, and motioned as though to throw it but stopped himself when he realized he could hit the window.

"You don't have the guts," I taunted. With a quick flick of his wrist the rock soared by me and ricocheted off the side of the house with a loud bang. "Ha, ha, you missed, ha, ha, you mi—."

I stopped mid-sentence, seeing Tommy coming around the corner of the next block like a jack rabbit, eyes wide open and yelling, "They're coming after me! Help!" Right behind him, running as fast as he could and trying to reach out and grab Tommy's back was Sean Alicon, the older of two brothers, both bigger than the Paquettes and every bit as mean. They lived on the other side of the project and almost never came around our way. As Tommy passed Gary on the sidewalk and headed for our porch, and just as Sean Alicon was making his final lunge at Tommy, Gary swung the broom and it made a loud crack as it struck him in the rear end.

Sean stopped suddenly, shocked and holding his rear end in pain. He turned to Gary with a scowl. "You're dead, Tinglebell!"

"Leave my brother alone," Gary said, taking up a defensive posture with the broom cocked back and ready to strike. Sean lunged toward the broom hoping to get it out of Gary's hand, and as he did, Gary swung low and caught him on the thigh with a significant blow.

His leg buckled, "Ahhhhhh, my leg. You're dead, you're dead!" He started toward Gary and Gary cocked the broom again and headed toward him fully intending to defend himself and Tommy at all costs. Sean saw the determination in Gary's eyes and knew he would take a beating with this broom if he didn't retreat. He turned suddenly and started to run away, and Gary chased him with the broom for a good distance until he knew he would not come back. I was proud of Gary for standing up to one of the toughest kids in the project, but I was also afraid for him. Kids in the project had long memories and would settle a score when you least expected it.

My mother heard the commotion and had come out on the porch just as Gary was chasing him away. I thought she was going to scream at Gary, but she took a look at Tommy's terrified face and grumbled, "The little son-of-a-bitch got what he deserved! I want all three of you to come inside. You can play inside for the rest of the afternoon."

"Ah, c'mon, Mom, let us stay outside. Please?" Tommy whined.

"No, you can stay inside and that's it."

"But we didn't start it, he did," Gary joined in.

"I said you're playing inside and that's the end of it. Go upstairs to your rooms and find something to do." We marched in the door, a column of three, silently and angrily going through the kitchen, the living room, and tromping up the stairs as loud as we could to show our dissatisfaction with this afternoon-destroying judgment. Gary and Tommy shared a room and slammed the door behind them as they went in. I knocked on the door.

"Can I play with you guys?"

"No!" came through the door muffled. I turned and went into my room directly across the hall. The only thing between their bedroom and mine was the bathroom. I looked around my room for something to do. There was my collection of stuffed animals: Baboon, who lay in a homemade hammock that my brothers and I had made, Bunny, who went with me almost everywhere, and a large stuffed snake that I didn't particularly care for. I had already played with GI Joe at Peggy's, and had already defeated several armies with just him.

Sometimes my brothers and I would take Baboon out of his hammock and sing the song, "Did you happen to see the most beautiful girl in the world, if you did, tell her I'm sorry, tell her I need my baby," but we changed the lyrics to, "Did you happen to see the most beautiful baboon in the world, if you did, tell her I'm sorry, tell her I need my banana, na na na." But there would be none of that today. They had gone to their room to play and I was closed out.

After a few minutes their door swung open and Tommy went to the top of the stairs, "Mom, Gary won't let me play with his toys!"

Gary followed right behind. "He's lying. He wants to read my comic books and I said no."

"Gary's lying!"

"No, Tommy is!"

I came out into the hallway, found a spot to yell down myself, "Mom, they won't let me play with them!"

"We don't want to play with stupid GI Joe!"

"I didn't say I wanted to play with GI Joe!"

My mother came to the foot of the stairs with her opened book in her hand. "I can't get a minute's peace with you three. I'm damn well fed up! I'm going to the supermarket to get some odds and ends. If you three can't play together then you can go with me and carry the bags."

The day was getting worse and worse. It started out with an escaping grasshopper, then an hour of torture at Peggy's house, the brawl with Sean Alicon, now a long walk to the supermarket, and then back carrying heavy bags. What a miserable Saturday.

We walked down the hill in front of our house and got on the sidewalk and headed toward the supermarket, passing all the different blocks of apartments, sometimes a group of kids playing outside. When we passed a particular one we heard, "Tingle bells, Tingle bells" in a familiar, aggravating voice. It was Bobby Poole. He and Gary were constantly getting into fights; nasty, kicking and punching, hair-pulling, head-locking, bloody-nose fights. He had a younger brother my age named Ricky and sometimes I would get pulled into it, although at our age Ricky and I did little more than push each other.

"Shut up, Poole, stupid-looking goof," Gary shot back.

"I can take you, Tinglebell!" Poole said, sticking his chest out.

"Gary, don't bother with him. He's just a little punk!" my mother said, loud enough so Bobby could hear it.

"Ha, ha, Tingle bells, Tingle bells," he continued to taunt as we kept walking, his voice fading more with each step until it was only an indecipherable noise in the distance, then gone completely. We came to the road that divided the project in half; if you went left you would go to the stadium, if you went right you would eventually come to a dead end, but there was a left you could take first that brought you into the south end of the city.

We crossed the street and climbed a set of stairs that brought us into the other side of the project, following a long, straight path that went directly in between all the different apartments. Tommy was laughing to himself about some secret joke that only he understood. In the distance loud rock-n-roll music blared out of an open window, "Smoke on the water, fire in the air . . ." To me it seemed an entirely different housing development. The buildings looked the same, but with the exception of PJ I didn't know anyone here, making it seem foreign and a little scary. We came out the other side of the project and crossed another road, then through a parking lot, and down a short dirt path that led between Riley's Roast Beef and Baker's Dozen donut shop.

"Mom, can we have Riley's for supper tonight?" Gary asked.

"No, I don't have enough money. I only have enough for the supermarket."

I turned to Baker's Dozen and looked up at my mother.

"Can we get a donut? They're just five cents."

It was as if my mother felt a little guilty about denying us Riley's, so she bought the three of us a honey dipped donut. We gobbled them quickly as we crossed the busy road between Riley's and the First National Supermarket, my mom holding my hand and hurrying me across.

As we walked through the automatic door of First National we were greeted with that smell that is particular to supermarkets; a produce smell, a deli smell, a seafood smell, a cardboard box smell, all blending together to form a unique vapor. Right inside the door,

I saw the gumball machines, and in one of them a rubber Gumby toy for five cents. Gumby was my absolute favorite, followed by Scooby Doo, and I would get up early on Saturdays and keep turning the channel of the TV hoping to catch the Gumby show. For some reason it was only on once in awhile and I rarely caught it when it was. "Gumby!" I screamed, pointing at the machines. "Please, Mom, please!"

My mother knew I loved Gumby and gave me a nickel to buy it; she took out three nickels knowing that Tommy and Gary would not be cheated, and a second later both their cheeks were sticking way out as they worked on giant gumballs. I got my two-inch rubber Gumby and proudly stuck him in my pocket. My mother worked her way through the aisles, stopping here and there for an item or two, and we got in line at the cash register. When it was time to pay my mother looked around self-consciously and took out some funny-looking money. It had pictures of people on it like regular money, but it was white and said something about food on the front. My mother handed it to the cashier with it cupped in her hand and looked over her shoulder a few times; an awkward look on her face that I didn't recognize. The cashier sort of looked at her differently and said, "Have a nice day."

My mom handed some of the bags to us and carried a few herself as we walked out into the darkening sky, the days growing shorter as winter approached. She was quiet the whole walk home. When we got there we put our bags down in the kitchen.

"Boys, go upstairs and play for awhile. I'll call you when dinner is ready."

"Can I have a Ring-Ding?" Tommy asked.

"It will ruin your dinner. You can have one after dinner. Now go."

Tommy picked up a jar of mayonnaise and started laughing uncontrollably, "A ha ha ha, ahh haa haa haa."

"What's so funny?" Gary said, grinning.

"Look at the name on the mayonnaise." Gary and I looked at the jar and didn't see anything worth laughing about. "You don't think it's funny?" Tommy said, barely able to stop laughing long enough to put a sentence together.

"No, I don't. Do you Kenny?"

I shook my head back and forth, "Nope."

He pointed at the jar, frustrated that we just didn't get it. "Look, Hellman's mayonnaise. Hell-Man mayonnaise. Ahh, ha ha ha ha."

My mother rolled her eyes and could not help but laugh a little. "Tommy, Tommy, Tommy, what am I going to do with you?"

It was so late when we got around to eating that the ABC Saturday night movie was starting. We turned to Channel 5 and waited to see what it was, all three of us unaware that the Wizard of Oz was on tonight, and all three of us happy as clams when we found out.

"Mom! Mom! The Wizard of Oz is on tonight, come watch it with us."

"You kids go ahead. I've seen it a bunch of times. I'm going to have a few glasses of wine and listen to a record or two," she said, putting her record album player on the table and plugging it in; a bottle of wine in front of her.

We had our pajamas on and were in our favorite seats when the movie started, each with a Ring-Ding we had saved for tonight. I watched wide eyed as Dorothy was caught in the tornado, the house spinning in circles and cows flying by, and at last the house crashed down on one of the wicked witches to the delight of the little midget people. Every so often my mom's music could be heard over the movie and we asked her to turn it down. Every so often I heard her mumbling to herself, like she was arguing with someone, or replaying an old argument from the past. "So I said to him, why you son-of-a-bitch, the nerve of you," and then her tone would go quiet enough that I couldn't make out the words anymore, just faint mumbling mixed in with the music. The music was always a broken-hearted crooning about better times, "Oh we have to say goodbye for the summer, but darling I promise you this, I'll send you all my love, every day in a letter, sealed with a kiss." Or a song I could not understand, "Why, why, why, Delilah, na na na, they've come to break down the door, forgive me Delilah I just couldn't take anymore."

I walked into the kitchen and my mom was sitting there with glassy eyes staring out the window into the dark. The bottle of wine was almost empty, and my mom began to mutter something again, but stopped when she saw I had come into the kitchen.

"Who are you talking to, Mom?" I asked.

"No one, honey, just thinking out loud," she answered, slurring her words a little.

"Oh," I said, not really understanding. I went back into the living room and wondered why moms drank wine sometimes and listened to sad people sing. And the music played on, "When the rain beats against my window pane, I think of summer days again, and dream of you."

2

One bright and sunny spring morning, shortly after my eighth birthday, I looked out my bedroom window and saw the Horrigan's black station wagon pulling out of the parking lot. The whole family was crammed in amongst housewares, blankets, clothes, and a ten-speed bike was tied down to the roof. They drove off slowly, taking a left and going down the hill out of sight. I walked downstairs and found my mother in the kitchen.

"Mom, where are the Horrigans going?"

"They decided to move to Florida," she said, stirring some beans on the stove and flipping some eggs in a frying pan.

"I didn't even get a chance to say goodbye to Jerry." I was devastated. I looked up to Jerry, thought he was cool, and wanted to be just like him.

"Well, they were in a hurry I guess. It's a long drive to Florida.

Now tell your brothers to get down here and eat breakfast." After we finished, and Gary licked his plate clean, we walked outside and stood on the sidewalk in front of the Horrigan's now vacant apartment. The kitchen door had been left open, and we could see all the way through into the living room.

The rooms looked so empty with no furniture, kitchen cabinets left open, and on the floor a few small piles of dirt that someone had swept up but neglected to throw away. It seemed so strange that a place could be full of life one minute, and then desolate and quiet the next. Like a soul leaving its body. A maintenance worker walked into the kitchen from the living room and glanced at my brothers and me for a brief second before he continued his inspection, checking things off on a clipboard as he went along. As long as I could remember this was the Horrigan's house, and I couldn't imagine it ever being anything else. Anyone who moved here, in this apartment, would be staying in the Horrigan's house.

After a few minutes of looking in and digesting this change, my brothers and I went back to our house to get ready for church. We put on our Sunday best and walked into the parking lot to wait for a ride from a guy named Butch. We waited in the warm spring sun, my turtleneck shirt becoming uncomfortable, Tommy and Gary becoming impatient and complaining.

"When's Butch going to be here? When's Butch going to be here?"

My mom ran out of patience with them. "Ask me again and I'll slap the two of you silly!"

"Butch is always late," Tommy griped, drawing pictures in a patch of sand with a stick he had found. He drew a picture of the Statue of Liberty. As long as I could remember Tommy had a fixation with skeletons, the Statue of Liberty, and a little model town he had put together named Riverton, complete with buildings, trees, bridges and, of course, a river running through the middle.

I looked across the street to the new swimming pool that the state of Massachusetts had built in the last couple of years. Everyone called it the "State pool," but its official name was the

"Higgins Memorial Pool." We weren't even aware that the state had planned on building one there. Then one day bulldozers were tearing through the woods, knocking down trees, and digging giant holes deep into the earth. At first there was great speculation amongst the kids as we played near the construction site, everyone with a different explanation of what they were doing, what the plan was. When we found out it was indeed a swimming pool, a wave of excitement swept through the entire project. Each phase of construction was followed closely, anticipation building. When they poured the cement foundation and it looked like a pool, I thought I would burst waiting for it to open.

It was an enormous pool that a hundred people could use at the same time. At the deep end there were two diving boards: one the regular height of about three feet, and another for the brave that was a good ten feet tall. There were lifeguard chairs at various points looking down over the water. There were two big locker rooms and a snack bar over by a little kid's pool that was about two feet deep. It was only spring and the pool wouldn't open until school got out in mid-June, but standing there with my hot turtleneck on, I wished I could jump in right now.

Butch finally pulled up in his yellow Mustang and stepped out so we could all squeeze into the back. I had to sit on my mother's lap and it was crowded and awkward. Butch had on a plaid suit coat and he always kept a thick beard, and I wondered if he was more uncomfortable than I was. Fortunately, it was a short ride, my mother making small talk with Butch's wife in the front seat the entire time. When we got there people mingled for a little while and then everyone took their seats and the service started. I tried to follow along, but the adults would turn to different pages often, and most of the sermon went over my head and I grew bored. Every so often my mother pinched Gary or me for making funny faces at each other.

About halfway through the service there was a loud thud on the wall and one of the church elders ran outside, the preacher continuing his message uninterrupted. When the elder returned there was whispering in the pews that some kids had thrown a rock at the building and needed to be chased away. I found this shocking, that anyone could be bold enough to throw a rock at a church. I was sure some kind of curse would befall them, some harsh judgment, and I could envision them crashing their bikes into something or taking a terrible fall.

After the service, there was a little more mingling and then Butch dropped us off at the project. I ran upstairs and changed out of that miserable turtleneck as quick as I could, and put on some comfortable clothes. After lunch, Gary and I walked out front and saw that the Horrigan's door was now closed. The maintenance man had finished his inspection and left, everything locked up tight. There was a strange quietness to which I was unaccustomed. No noises coming from the Horrigan's kitchen, no Kathy Horrigan yelling out front, and no Mr. Horrigan yelling inside the house.

"Mom, we're going to the stadium," Gary yelled in the kitchen door.

Amongst the clatter of pots and pans being put away I heard my mom answer, "Stay out of trouble and be back before dinner."

Gary turned to me, got into a sprinter's stance, and said, "I'll race you there. Last one there is a rotten egg!"

"Eat my dust!" I screamed, taking off before he had a chance to start running.

"You're a cheater!" he called out, laughing as he chased me.

I sprinted as fast as I could around the corner, down across the basketball court that had no rims for playing, laughing as I went along. Gary was laughing too, knowing he could catch me if he really wanted. I gave everything I had as I crossed a wide lawn between two buildings, running out of breath as the stadium was only 100 feet away. I struck a victorious pose as I arrived there first.

"Oh, man." he faked, pretending that I had legitimately beat him.

"Ha, I'm the champion!" I said, putting my arms up to an imaginary crowd of cheering people.

He stomped his foot. "Damn," he said, with an exaggerated disappointment. I knew he could really have beaten me if he wanted, but he let me win because I was his little brother, and I took advantage of that fact. Gary was my favorite friend in the world.

"Let's go up on the bleachers," he said, walking in that direction. We climbed all the rows of seats, and at the top we could see over the fields and well into the project. These weren't your typical aluminum bleachers, like you see at most high school stadiums. These were cement and colossal. There was a booth at the top for the announcers to call the games, and from up there you had a view of the entire stadium, all its fields, the clubhouse with locker rooms, and down the other way you could see the bowling alley and movie cinema. We stomped down the rows of seats, jumping from one bench to the next, until we reached the bottom. Then we ran across the football field and past a smaller set of wood and iron bleachers where the opposing fans sit. Past that was a wide-open area that led to the baseball field, grassless and uninviting, and we stopped at the dugout that was covered in obscene graffiti. Every filthy word known found its way into a sentence or two.

We no sooner got there when Timmy Paquette stepped out from behind the dugout with another punk his age, smoking a cigarette, with troublesome grins on their faces. I could see Gary's whole body tense up and I felt mine tense up as well. Timmy was several years older than Gary and he was a big, stocky teenager, a toughened street punk; we didn't have a prayer of getting out of this.

"Hey, look, it's Gary Tinglebell and little Tinglebell." They both laughed, and then Timmy grabbed Gary by the shirt and pushed him hard against a chain-link fence. Gary winced from the pain. "What are you going to do about it, Tinglebell?"

"I didn't do anything to you," Gary pleaded, his voice cracking, like he wanted to cry.

"*I didn't do anything to you,*" Timmy mocked, trying to make his voice sound like Gary's. Then, he brought his knee up hard into Gary's stomach and Gary doubled over breathless, his eyes bulging out, gasping for air. I stood there motionless, powerless, hate burning inside me. If I made a feeble attempt to help him it would just make things worse, give them a reason to hurt him even more, and that's what these punks lived for.

Then Timmy's friend took his lit cigarette and put it against the bare skin of Gary's arm and he writhed away in pain. Timmy held his arm so that he couldn't pull it away, and I could see the pain in Gary's eyes as they became watery. I felt mine become watery too, and then I felt warm tears running down my face. "Leave him alone!" I screamed. Gary would not let himself cry, that would just encourage them more, but I could see he wanted to.

Then Timmy threw him down into the dirt, "Go home and cry to your mother, Tinglebell, ha ha ha." Gary got to his feet as quick as he could and we ran out of the stadium and back into the project to our house.

Gary never told my mother what happened. If he did, she might go to the Paquettes' house, as she had before. Their mother would probably promise to do something about it, but she wouldn't, and Timmy would just make Gary pay for it the next time he saw him. That's the way the projects worked—tell on someone and pay later. So Gary just hid the burn on his arm and kept his mouth shut, keeping his anger inside, me keeping my anger inside, and both of us went to bed.

In the morning, I made the short walk to my school, the John Breen Elementary School, in the cool spring air. The sun was just coming up over the horizon, announcing the start of a beautiful day. Spring was always my favorite time of year. After the long and bitter winters of New England—that seemed to go on forever, refusing to loosen their icy hold, the days short and the nights long—spring would finally emerge like a reward for all your patience, and there was nothing as radiant as spring in New England. Things blossoming everywhere, flocks of birds singing as they flew overhead, the scents in the air—damp earth, lilac bushes, and everything else that grows and gives off a fragrance.

I was unmoved by all this new life and new possibility. I was deep in my mind, dealing with my anger the only way I knew how. I imagined I was like a superhero in my comic books, the Hulk.

When those punks burned my brother with a cigarette, I grew into a muscle-bound monster and grabbed their terrified faces and clobbered them. This made me feel a little better. And I kept on imagining this scenario, thrashing them as I made my way through the crowds of kids, making them pay as I walked up the stairs, humiliating them as I walked into my classroom and took my seat.

My daydreaming ended quickly when Mrs. Jackson walked into the classroom. She was a square-shouldered woman with short curly hair, glasses, and she was all business. She was the toughest second grade teacher in the school, possibly the world, and she had no tolerance for gum chewing, talking, or anything that could be considered fun. She had superhuman hearing ability; anytime a student thought they could lean over and whisper something to a friend, her loud voice would boom from the front. "You can come up here right now, Mister!"

We started our days with our phonics lessons. I actually liked this part of the day, reading a short story from a collection of books you could choose from, and then answering the questions at the back of the book. When finished, your answers would go in a box up front for Mrs. Jackson to correct, and you would sign a sheet on the wall above to let her know you were done. She wasn't always quick in grading them. As I finished a lesson and signed the sheet, I saw that someone had written, "I'm steel waiting" across the top.

When Mrs. Jackson walked over and saw it, she was enraged, saying, "Who wrote this? How dare you! And look how you spelled still … S, T, E, E, L! Well, who wrote it?"

There was complete silence, and I held in my laughter as my face grew red, amused at how angry this simple spelling error had made her. Then her eyes turned to my red face.

"You think this is funny, Kenneth? Did you write that?"

"No, Mrs. Jackson, I just finished mine," I said, relieved that mine would be on the top of the pile to prove it.

After math and science, the lunch people came and delivered our meals to the class. There was no cafeteria in elementary school, and we sat at our desks and opened the little aluminum trays. We peeled back the cardboard cover to see what lay underneath. Would it be Salisbury steak, or one of those metallic tasting hamburgers with a side of fries, or the infamous sloppy Joe? There were muted groans scattered across the classroom at the site of the Salisbury steak; no one liked it. Every class got something different. The kids who brought bagged lunch were spied on with envy, and there were several negotiations going on around me.

"Hey, Brian, I'll trade you this yummy Salisbury steak for your peanut butter and jelly."

"No way!" Brian answered, too smart to fall for this unbalanced trade.

"I'll give you this tennis ball for your baloney and cheese," met a similar fate in the back of the room.

There were looks of repulsion between two girls as they cut a piece and put it in their mouths, "Ugghhhh, this is so gross!" I knew I couldn't trade out of this, so I ate the mashed potatoes and very little of the steak.

After lunch, I asked to use the bathroom and I ran down the two flights of stairs to the basement. There in the hall, right before the bathroom door, was a pile of sawdust with a wet circle in the middle; a common site in this elementary school. Some kid from another class got the wrong sloppy Joe, made a valiant effort to reach the bathroom, but lost the battle just short of his destination. And some disgruntled janitor had followed the vomit protocol of sawdust, became disgusted, and left the job unfinished. It was a double failure—the student failing to reach the bathroom, and the janitor failing to finish the job. I walked around the pile, used the bathroom, and walked around it again holding my nose as I ran to the stairs and back to my class.

The rest of the afternoon was spent on social studies and finally the dismissal bell rang. It was a loud, shrieking bell, more like a fire alarm than a school bell. I didn't care what it sounded like. I just knew I could get out of here. I walked home the same way I came, making sure I made a large loop around the Paquette's house, avoiding them at all costs, going through the parking lot and then cutting down through the clothesline section to my house.

When I got there I saw a couple of movers heaving a couch through the door of the Horrigan's old apartment, their faces red in the warm afternoon weather, with little beads of sweat on their forehead. I hung around to see if I could get a look at the new tenants. I saw a mother, a boy who looked about my age, another boy who looked several years younger than me, and a little girl who was maybe one or two. I didn't see a man so I figured they had no father like me. The boy who looked my age was standing out front and he looked my way, and I thought maybe I could make a friend. I walked over to him.

"Hey, I guess you guys are moving in?"

"Yup," was his only answer, as he looked at me, sizing me up. I was sizing him up, too; he was the same height as me, the same kind of build, about the same weight, the biggest difference being that his hair was brown and mine was blond. I wondered if he would be like us, or if he would become friends with the Paquettes or kids like them. I hoped he would be a friend.

"My name is Kenny," I said with a smile.

"My name is Andy," he said smiling back. I felt a sense of relief. At least he was being polite, and the punks were never polite so I figured he probably wouldn't be like them.

"How old are you?" I asked.

"Nine."

"Oh, I'm only eight. But my brothers are eleven and twelve."

"You're the youngest?"

"Yup."

"I'm the oldest. I have a brother and a sister," he said proudly.

"I don't have a sister, just two brothers. My oldest brother Tommy isn't normal."

"What's wrong with him?"

"I don't know," I said, shrugging, regretting that I had brought this up.

"Well, I have to help my mom put things away. Maybe I'll see you around."

"Maybe we can hang around sometime. I can show you the project or something," I said to him as he was walking away.

"Yah, okay," and he gave me a big, friendly smile while he walked into the house. I was sure I had made a friend.

I ran into the house and found Gary and Tommy sitting in the living room watching cartoons. "Hey, you guys, someone is moving in the Horrigan's house. There's a kid who is just a year older than me," I said, excited. Gary was sprawled out on the couch and barely acknowledged what I said.

"Yah, I saw them," he said, with little enthusiasm, not looking up from the TV. Tommy chuckled to himself as a mouse took a giant hammer and clobbered a cat over the head with it, completely absorbed in the cartoon, oblivious to what I had just said.

I spent the afternoon doing homework that Mrs. Jackson had assigned, my mom helping me with the more difficult math problems and always using apples as her instrument. "If I had ten apples, and I took away four apples, how many apples would be left? How much is two apples times four apples?" She had done this as long as I could remember, in kindergarten sitting me on her lap and asking, "How much is one apple plus one apple?"

"Two apples," I said, giggling.

When the sun went down and the sky turned to dusk, I heard some of the kids in the neighborhood playing hide and seek and I asked my mom if I could go out and join them, promising not to go too far. Gary came with me, but Tommy went off on his own as usual.

We could hear them over by the next block, by Kevin Wilson's house, and we walked over toward the sound of their voices. Kevin was the kind of kid you wished you looked like, with black wavy hair that never needed to be combed, and his skin naturally tan year round. He was tall for his age and a lot of the girls in school liked him.

"Hey, Kevin, can we play?" Gary shouted as we approached.

"Ya, but you're it," he shouted back. It was growing dark quickly, and that made the game easier to play, being able to hide in places that were impossible in daylight. I knew most of the kids there, a few unfamiliar faces of kids who didn't live in the project, and had been invited by someone who did.

In the dark, I could make out PJ Timmons.

"Hey, PJ, hide with me."

"Okay, but you follow me. I have a good place."

"Where am I supposed to count?" Gary asked.

"Go over to the building, turn around, and count to twenty, you know how... one Mississippi, two Mississippi," Kevin answered, pointing to the side of his apartment building.

"Everyone scatter!" Gary shouted, and there was the sound of feet slapping against the pavement as we all scrambled to find a good spot, two kids colliding with each other and getting up laughing.

And as always one kid telling another, "Find your own spot," or "Quit following me!"

I followed PJ as he ran behind a row of garbage cans and we ducked down. Gary wasn't far away so we spoke in hushed whispers. "PJ, this is your good spot?"

"Ya, what's wrong with it?"

"Someone threw some fish in this barrel and it really stinks. You can't smell it?"

PJ lifted his head and sniffed the air, and made an exaggerated gagging sound, "Uhhhyuck!"

"Be quiet," I whispered while squeezing his arm for emphasis. "Nineteen Mississippi, twenty Mississippi, ready or not here I come!" Gary screamed, and he turned to scan the area for anyone who had hidden poorly. From between two garbage cans I could see him heading in the opposite direction from where we were.

"PJ, he's going the other way. Let's find someplace else."

"You're not supposed to move after he's done counting. That's cheating."

"It stinks over here. That's not cheating."

In the distance, around the corner of Kevin's building, we heard Gary yelling, "I see you behind that porch, come out!"

"Oh, man, how did you see me?"

"PJ, he's gonna be over here in one minute, let's go."

"All right... on three. Ready, one, two, three, go!" We sprinted out from behind the cans, staying hunched over as much as possible, being our quietest as we ran up the short grass hill into the parking lot and slid underneath a car.

"This is cool. He'll never find us under here," PJ boasted proudly.

It only took Gary a few minutes to find everyone else, but he was becoming more and more frustrated as time went by and he still couldn't find us, "Where the heck are they?" he asked rhetorically, not really expecting another kid to rat us out, if they even knew where we were, which they didn't. It wasn't just Gary who was angry now. Everyone was getting sick of standing around and waiting for him to find us. Then Gary let out a loud call, one that is specific to hide and seek and means that wherever you are you have to come out. "*Olly Olly Entrafee*," his voice bellowed, and we slid out from under the car like snakes climbing out of the basket at the command of the snake charmer.

One of the kids saw us coming out and screamed, "Hey, they were up in the parking lot. I thought that was out of bounds?"

"You guys can't do that," Kevin said, turning to us as we came down the short hill to where everyone was waiting. There was a general irritation with us, with our illegal delay, and there was universal agreement that the two of us would be it. We went over to the building and stood with our backs turned and counted to twenty. "Ready or not, here we come!"

"Hey, Kenny," PJ whispered, "there's two of us so this should be easy. You go one way and I'll go the other."

"Good idea, this should be quick," I said, chuckling, like we were really getting the last laugh on them. We had played this game a dozen times before and if there was a hiding spot then we knew about it. PJ and I worked our way around, hitting all the hot spots with great efficiency, two sets of eyes finding them with ease, and they quickly realized the error of letting us work together. They were all disappointed to be caught so quickly. But Gary was downright outraged, spending all that time searching for us, looking high and low, only to learn that we had gone out of bounds, and now his turn to hide ending swiftly.

"This stinks! Who had the stupid idea to let them both find us?" Gary complained indignantly. No one took credit at this point. It seemed a brilliant idea at first, a just punishment for breaking the rules, but in the end it worked against them.

"Gary, Kenny, it's time to come home!" my mother yelled, her voice carrying a great distance in the evening air.

I could tell Gary was embarrassed. He hated when she did that.

We said goodbye to everyone and headed over to our house. When we passed the Horrigan's old apartment I saw a light on in the kitchen, and quickly realized I had forgotten all about the new boy, had forgotten to ask him if he wanted to come out and play with us, and I felt guilty. I promised myself the next time we did anything I would knock on his door and invite him.

My mom was waiting in the kitchen. "You two need to go upstairs and take your baths and put your pajamas on."

Gary looked at the time—seven o'clock. "We can watch TV after, right?" he said, half asking and half implying it was a right.

"As long as you're in bed by nine," she answered sharply, letting us know it was non-negotiable. We were showered, in our pajamas, and on the couch by eight o'clock, just in time for one of our favorite shows—the Six Million-Dollar Man. I crunched on a cookie as it began, first a fiery crash, then a voice saying, "Steve Austin, a man barely alive, we can rebuild him better, faster, stronger." He only had one bionic arm and when he moved it things went to slow motion and it made a grinding robotic sound. In this episode the villain was a robot who was completely bionic, not just one arm, and he was giving Steve Austin a good beating until the very end.

Then Steve threw a metal pipe right through him, like a stake in a vampire, and sparks were flying everywhere.

I looked over at Gary, "Man it would be great to have a bionic arm when the Paquettes come around, wouldn't it?"

He laughed, and then imitated the grinding sound as he pretended to be thrashing them.

My mom came and sat in the living room with us. She was quiet for a moment and then said, "Things are going to change around here a bit. I've been looking for a job and I finally found one. I'm tired of food stamps and stupid welfare."

"What about us?" Gary asked.

My mother shook her head. "I'm not going anywhere. I'll leave for work after you go to school and I'll be back around dinnertime."

I liked my mom being there when I got home and I didn't like this change.

"Where are you going to work?" I asked, sitting up.

"Downtown at a place called Goodwill."

"Goodwill!" Gary and I groaned at the same time. "Why Goodwill? Everyone will make fun of us."

"Because it's not easy finding a job and they offered me one. So I took it. There's nothing wrong with Goodwill. The two of you have too much pride. I start in a few weeks, now go upstairs and get to bed."

I couldn't believe it, not Goodwill, anyplace but Goodwill. It was a discount store that sold used clothes and other odds and ends that people didn't want anymore and donated for free. The place was the butt of many jokes in the project—if you didn't like someone's pants, you would say, "Hey, did you get those at Goodwill?" Didn't like their shoes, "Hey, did you get those at Goodwill?" And everyone would laugh. Now my mother was actually going to work there. When people found out she was working and asked, "Oh, where is your mom working?" I would have to answer, "Goodwill," and I knew they would crack up, and have a good old laugh at my expense.

I lay in bed thinking the situation over. After awhile I thought I had the perfect answer—I would just lie to people. When they asked where she worked I would shrug and say, "Downtown somewhere," and it wouldn't really be a lie because Goodwill was downtown.

3

The dismissal bell rang for the last time this school year and we all dashed out of the class. Our desks had been cleaned out and left open, the room cleaned and swept neatly by the brown-nose students, and Mrs. Jackson had given us her good-luck speech, complete with compliments on how good we really were. As we ran down the stairs there was a chorus of kids singing that same old song, "No more teachers, no more books, no more teacher's dirty looks. When the teacher rings the bell, drop your books and run like hell!" I sang along as loud as I could, my voice echoing in the stairwell, and then becoming reduced as I ran out the front door. Summer was here! The pool would be open tomorrow and there would be no responsibility for months. My new neighbor, Andy, fit well into the project and had made plenty of friends rather quickly. I got along well with him, played with him sometimes, but he had other friends in different parts of the project, so he wasn't always available when I went by his house.

I could barely sleep that night thinking about the pool the next day. When I woke up, I went straight over to Andy's house and knocked on the door, figuring I would invite him before someone else did. I could always go with Gary, but I was a little tired of hanging around with my brother every day, and he was a little tired of me tagging along everywhere he went. He was my best friend but sometimes he wanted to be with kids his age, and I wanted to be with kids my age, and Andy was pretty close. His mother answered the door and said she would go get him, and a minute later he came down the stairs and to the kitchen door where I was waiting patiently. He looked as though I woke him up.

"Hey, Andy, you know the pool opens today. Do you want to go with me?"

He turned and looked at his mother who was standing a few feet behind, looking for her reaction, and then asked, "Can I go?"

"I need you to watch your little sister for an hour first. Maybe until eleven or so," she said sternly.

"That's okay, it doesn't open until then anyways," I butted in, "so I'll come back around then."

He looked at his mother again, "Well, can I?"

"As long as you're done watching your sister. How much is it to get in?"

"A quarter," I butted in again.

"That's fine," his mother answered, turning to get something out of a cabinet.

"See you then," Andy said, smiling that he could go.

I ate a bowl of cereal quickly, went upstairs, got my swimsuit and towel ready, and read a Spiderman comic book while I waited, bursting with excitement as I counted down the minutes until the pool opened. Just before 11:00, I changed into my bathing suit and ran downstairs. My brothers were already gone, my mom at work, so I grabbed a quarter that she had left on the counter, slung the towel over my shoulder and went to Andy's house. He was already wearing his bathing suit and waiting for me by the kitchen door. Neither one of us had bothered to put on sneakers so we zigzagged up the sidewalk, avoiding pebbles and rocks that would sting our feet, doing the same as we made our way through the parking lot, and finally to the gate of the pool. The smell of chlorine filled the air and there was already a short line of kids waiting to get in. There was cheerful talking amongst the kids.

"Hey, Mikey, are you going to try the high-diving board this year?"

"No way!" was the answer.

And, of course, someone had to say, "He's a wimp," and there was good-natured laughter.

I turned to Andy, "Are you excited?"

"Yah!" he said with emphasis, grinning and looking around inside the gate.

"I'm gonna try the high-diving board this year. I haven't done it yet," I said, bravely.

"You never did it!" he said incredulously, like it was the simplest thing in the world.

"No, I climbed the ladder once and walked out on the diving board but chickened out. It looks easy at the bottom, but wait until you get up there."

"I bet you I won't chicken out." We paid our quarter at the front desk and ran around the corner to look at the pool.

There it was, a beautiful sky blue; the lifeguards already sitting up in their chairs with those orange shorts they wore, along with a dab of white stuff covering their noses, kids jumping in and pushing each other in, and the sound of the lifeguard's whistle when they got caught; the lifeguard screaming a warning—"Do that again and you're out for the day!"

"C'mon, Andy, let's start at the shallow end stairs," I said, placing my towel under a bench for safekeeping.

"Yah, right," he answered, running and jumping into the middle section of the pool with a big splash. I waited to see his reaction as his head came above water.

"Is it cold?"

"Nah, it's beautiful. Jump in." I didn't want to look like a sissy, especially in front of a new friend, so I took a running leap into the pool—s*plaasshh*. The water was icy cold all around me, shocking me for a few long seconds, and I burst to the top.

"Liar, this is freezing!" I screamed, my jaw shivering. He took one look at my anguished face and roared with laughter for a good minute, so hard he had trouble speaking.

"I did it, so you should, too." It was early in the summer and the water would not become comfortable until the heat of July. We were in the middle section, which was the longest and widest part of the pool. The majority of people were swimming here, and I wanted to see if I could make it all the way across, holding my breath under water. Even if I failed, all that swimming would warm me up.

"Andy, do you think that I can make it to the other side under water?"

He turned his head and looked at the distance, "No way, not even close!" I took an enormous breath and went under, kicking off the wall with all my strength, shooting forward with my cheeks puffed out, getting a good start. I thrust forward using my arms and legs. It was quiet under here. All the laughing and screaming above was muted and distorted, indecipherable words that carried to me below the surface, ghostly sounding laughs as I swam around the many legs in my way. My lungs were burning, but I continued forward fighting the pain. I could see the wall getting closer and closer, and then my hand finally touched it. I burst to the surface gasping for air and turned to see Andy's shocked face on the other side of the pool.

"Yah, I did it! Now you have to try!" I screamed, and he went to the wall and disappeared under the water.

He seemed to be under for a long time when he finally exploded out of the water next to me. "I did it, too!"

"That's cool," I said, but inside I was really disappointed that my accomplishment had been matched.

"C'mon, let's go to the diving boards" he said, climbing up the ladder out of the pool. I followed up the ladder and the warm sun felt good on my skin as we ran toward the diving boards, our wet feet making a smacking sound as they hit the concrete.

"Let's start on the small one," I blurted out, making sure he didn't go straight to the tall one that scared me. We waited impatiently in a long line. A chunky kid bounced up and down on the end of the diving board, then tried his best to do a dive, which turned into a loud smacking belly flop. He climbed out of the pool all red and grimacing. When my turn came I bounced a few times as high as I could and then did a cannonball, listening to the boom from under the water.

I came to the surface and yelled up to Andy who was now standing on the end of the diving board, "How big a splash did I make?"

"Pretty big!" he yelled back, then bounced off and did a mummy right next to me, sending a wave over my head.

We climbed out and he headed over to the line for the big diving board just as I feared he would do. I hesitantly got in line behind him, counting how many kids were in front of me and calculating how much time I had to back out of this. I saw a man bounce high into the air and slice into the water in a perfect dive, barely disturbing the surface as he broke through, then emerge right in front of the ladder to climb out. I wondered if I would be able to do that when I grew up. Then a kid about my age walked out to the end of the diving board, looked down nervously at the distance to the water, and turned right around and climbed back down the ladder. "Wimp!" someone yelled from the line and I felt bad for him, having done the same thing last summer.

When Andy's turn came he went up the ladder and walked to the end of the diving board, and stood there for a few long seconds. I knew what he was feeling. From the ground, the diving board looked big enough, but when you were actually up there it seemed like you were on top of a small building, being able to see way over the woods and down the path on the side of the hill. I hoped he would chicken out so that I wouldn't have to go through with this. But he bounced a few times and then went straight into the water feet first. I climbed the ladder with my heart thumping in my chest and my mouth going dry. When I walked out on the diving board, I looked over the pool and everyone looked small from up here, the breeze in the air making me feel unbalanced, my legs trembling, and I thought I might possibly die. There was no turning back now; not after Andy had done it and the other boy was ridiculed for chickening out. I figured the easiest thing was to just get it over with, and I bounced once and went straight down feet first. I was amazed at how your senses can slow things down when you are in a fearful state, and even though it was a mere second till I hit the water it seemed much longer. My feet slapped against the surface and I shot down deeper into the water than I ever had. I felt my ears pop and my nose burned inside as some water shot up into my nostrils. I came to the surface a very proud eight-year-old, beaming, having accomplished this milestone that had loomed over me for so long. I had gone off the big diving board!

I climbed up the side ladder feeling ten-foot tall and looked Andy straight in the eye, "Man, that was so cool!"

"Yah, it was! You want to do it again?" he said, laughing, seeing my fear as I had stood on the end of the diving board.

"Maybe later, the line is really long," I said, and laughed back.

"Hey, Kenny," I heard someone shout behind me and turned to see my brother, Gary, coming toward us with his towel around his waist.

"How long have you guys been here?" he asked, walking up and stopping in front of us.

"I don't know, maybe an hour. Why?"

"Because I didn't see you. I was looking for you. Mom gave me a dollar to give to you so you can get some lunch."

"Yes! I can go to the snack bar. It's only fifty cents for a piece of pizza!" I turned and gestured toward the diving boards. "I went off the big diving board," I said proudly.

"Yah, right, you're a liar," Gary mocked, with a disbelieving smirk on his face.

"He really did. I saw him," Andy said, sticking up for me.

"You really did?"

"Yes, I really did. Is Tommy here?" He pointed into the middle section of the pool and I saw Tommy bobbing up and down while squirting water out of his mouth and laughing to himself. I took my dollar and agreed to meet Andy at the snack bar after he went home and got some money for lunch.

I bought a slice of pizza and a hot dog, not wasting any money on a drink when there was a water fountain right on the corner of the building. Andy ordered the same and we complained to each other about the tiny slices of pizza—they weren't the triangular slices you got in a pizza shop, just little squares, but crunchy and mighty tasty. After we ate we saw everyone—PJ Timmons, Kevin Wilson, and most of the other kids in the project, including the troublemakers. We all swam together, taking turns going off the diving board and making fun of each other as we did, having contests who could hold their breath the longest, swim the fastest, and when we finally had our fill we got our towels and headed back across the street to the project.

I walked with Andy and Gary followed a little behind with Tommy as the sun finally started to relent a little and the heat began to slowly diminish. None of us had shoes on, and we frantically ran across the scorching hot pavement of the parking lot while avoiding pebbles that dug into our feet. Whenever one of us would step on a particularly hot spot, jump into the air, scream "*Oouucchh!*" and dance around, Tommy would find this incredibly funny and laugh from the belly up, until he stepped on a sizzling piece of tar.

"*Aaahhhhh!*" he yelped, and then he shot across the parking lot like a bullet, howling all the way.

Tommy went on ahead and was almost at the house when we saw three figures coming around the corner. When they saw Tommy heading for the house they walked faster, cut him off, and grabbed his arm. "Hey, look, it's Tommy Tinglebell," we heard one of the voices say. As we approached we could see it was Kevin Paquette, Hervey Bodwell, and his brother Billy; Timmy Paquette was not there and I felt a sense of relief because he was older and Gary was no match for him. The Bodwell brothers were actually cousins of the Paquettes who had moved here a few years ago. Hervey couldn't fight very well and if he weren't related to the Paquettes then he probably wouldn't start any trouble. Billy, on the other hand, was always looking for trouble. He was my age but weighed close to two hundred pounds, a sight of unhealthy obesity with a bad attitude. Although he couldn't fight very well, he used his size to intimidate people. He weighed three times what I did, but I had fought him to a standstill several times out of absolute terror that if I lost he would sit on me, which I had seen him do to several kids, their faces beet red and begging for mercy as they struggled to breathe. Both Bodwells had black greasy hair and Billy always smelled bad.

"Leave him alone!" Gary yelled as we came through the clothes-line section. Kevin turned to see who was coming, thinking Tommy was alone and still holding his arm tightly.

"Oh, look, it's Gary Tinglebell and little Tinglebell."

"I said let him go." Gary scowled, looking as tough as he could.

"What are you going to do about it pussy boy?" Kevin said, letting go of Tommy's arm and turning to stand face-to-face with Gary. The Bodwell brothers snickered when they heard this, and Andy stood there not knowing what to expect.

Then Kevin pushed Gary as hard as he could. "I said what are you going to do pussy?" Gary recoiled swiftly, bringing his right fist into Kevin's face with a sickening smacking sound. His head snapped back and he staggered backwards a few steps, stunned and off balance, his face swollen and red with watery eyes. He charged forward trying to tackle Gary, but wound up in a headlock and Gary wrestled him to the ground and they continued to struggle in the dirt, twisting, legs kicking violently. Suddenly out of the corner of my eye I saw Billy Bodwell lunging at me with his right fist coming straight at my face; there was no time to avoid the blow so I closed my eyes and my whole body tensed up waiting for the impact. But there was none. I opened my eyes slowly and saw Billy sitting on the ground. When he tried to sucker punch me Andy had leveled him with a hard punch to the face, sent him to the ground with a thud, and there he sat in disbelief with a red cheek, Andy standing over him daring him to get up. It was quite a task for Billy to get his large body up so he sat there defeated.

Hervey stepped forward like he was going to get involved, but Gary had beaten Kevin squarely and was back on his feet facing them. They stood there contemplating their next move, unsure what to do, finding themselves in a losing battle. Kevin's cheek was swollen and red and he stood there breathing heavily, Billy sitting on the ground beaten, and Hervey standing there afraid of being beaten like his tougher cousin.

"You're dead, Tinglebell. You just wait!" Kevin snarled, helping Billy slowly get to his feet. They turned away, walking back toward their house, yelling, "You're a dead man, you just wait!"

Tommy looked at Gary, grinned, and said, "Boy you kicked his ass." Gary looked more worried than happy, knowing there would be retaliation; when he least expected it the whole gang of them would show up for revenge.

I turned to Andy, "Well, you're one of us now," I said smiling.

"That tub of lard got what he deserved," he said chuckling, and we all laughed for a minute. But, I could sense Gary's was a nervous laughter—he was my brother and I knew him well.

Days passed and there was no immediate retaliation, no gang of Paquettes standing outside our door and screaming for Gary to come out for a rematch, which they would all make sure went Kevin's way. The Paquettes weren't always predictable. Maybe Kevin and Timmy were in the middle of a disagreement when it happened, maybe had been in a fight amongst themselves which they often did when there was no one else around, and when Mike and Timmy had seen his cheek laughed at him and said, "Ha, you got your ass kicked by Gary Tinglebell." There was no way of knowing, so you just had to be on guard for them all the time. But after that day Kevin Paquette never confronted Gary by himself again, only growing brave enough in the company of his older brothers, knowing they would jump in if he were losing. And Billy Bodwell had learned that Andy could take care of himself and kept his distance from him.

The days of summer were long and never ending, mostly spent cooling off at the pool during the day and playing hide and seek at night. Sometimes a large crowd of kids would venture down to the vast fields of the stadium to make the game more interesting. You could hide a dozen different places under the bleachers alone. Maybe under one of the cement ramps or up top on the side of the announcers' booth, or lay down behind one of the many benches, so many places that the games would sometimes last an hour apiece. But there was no rush in the long days and nights of the summer. Things were more relaxed, moms extending curfews, games going on much longer than usual, us roaming farther than we normally would.

Sometimes in the morning we would walk downtown to a store called, "Ye Old Book and Bottle Shop," which bought and sold used paperbacks and comic books. I never saw a bottle there so I guess the owner gave up on those. The owner was a guy named Bernie who was really odd and my mother always said he was strange. His store was in an old building and there were stacks and stacks of books everywhere, making it impossible sometimes to even get to some of the aisles, and the whole place had the musty smell of old paperbacks. Bernie was incredibly cheap and only kept one little light on in the center of the store. He wore the same clothes every-day—a pair of green Dickie janitor-type pants and the same color green Dickie shirt tucked in, black shoes, and often a long overcoat even when it was warm outside.

Bernie had a large pointy nose and one of his feet was perma-nently turned in, making him walk funny with a slight limp. My mom said he was "hen-toed," and I wondered if one foot was clawed and hen-like and the other normal. He didn't drive so every day at five his father would pick him up in a green station wagon, and they would drive around town looking through garbage cans and dump-sters for valuables. My mother couldn't believe that Bernie was in his forties and had never gotten his driver's license. Once, while she was at work, she went out back to dump the garbage and saw Bernie and his dad in the back alley digging through the dumpster.

Every so often he came across a rare comic book and that is why we went there, not caring about books. He actually had quite a col-lection of comics that he kept hidden behind the counter out of fear that kids would steal them. If you had one that he wanted to add to his collection, he would buy it. Taking out his wallet and going through his bizarre ritual—checking the serial numbers on the dol-lars, sometimes sniffing them, and mournfully handing them over to you pinched tightly between his fingers. And you would have to give a good pull to get it. One morning we walked in quickly and caught Bernie looking at a Playboy magazine. His face grew beet red and he chased us out of the store.

Other days we just looked for things to do. Sometimes taking a walk down to the dump, which really didn't have much garbage, was more like a giant field with tall grass and a few things scattered here and there; old car tires, useless gas cans, or a stack of old magazines.

One morning I picked up an old gas can and a black snake lunged out at me for moving his house. I sprang back barely avoiding his bite. I didn't pick up any cans after that. If you walked to the other side of the dump then you would come to the Shawsheen River, which went under a small highway bridge and became part of the massive Merrimac River. Sometimes we would put a stick or something else we found in the water and watch it drift slowly with the current into the mighty Merrimac, which flowed right through the city of Lawrence, dividing it into north and south. You had to cross large bridges to get from one side of the city to another. One was made of green metal and as cars drove across the grids it made a buzzing sound, and the other was built of concrete right next to an enormous waterfall where the Merrimac suddenly dropped down about sixty feet. There were large jagged rocks at the bottom, and I had heard the story of a man who was washed over the dam and fell to a gruesome death, splattered on the rocks as pedestrians looked over the side of the bridge in horror. There was a long system of canals in the north end of the city, and when they were drained down you could see large carp swimming at the bottom. I often had nightmares that I fell into the canal or the Shawsheen River and I floated face down, paralyzed and for some reason unable to swim, and I would wake up just before I drowned. I was always nervous when near either of them.

Sometimes we just hung around our rooms in the late afternoon heat and read comic books for hours at a time—my mother overjoyed at moments like this—or we played an adventure in one of our bedrooms. When the favorite TV shows like Six Million Dollar Man or Happy Days was on then the project would become instantly quiet as all the kids disappeared inside. Later on, while playing, there would always be an argument amongst kids. "I'm Steve Austin."

"No, I am. You were the last time we played."

"I'm the Fonze!"

"No, you're Richie Cunningham, ha ha ha." Then there was always the kid who saw Evil Knievel do something crazy and would build a ramp in front of his house. We would all stand around and watch him try to jump over a can or something, and they would usually wipe out in a painful failure, then run away crying while someone wheeled their bike back home for them.

One day we saw a flyer that was posted all over the place—a man was going to jump over the Shawsheen River on a bicycle. On the day announced, a bunch of kids from the project walked down through the dump to the river's edge. A long wooden ramp had been built down a steep slope, and a man appeared in a homemade costume that was purple with his underpants being worn on the outside. We watched as he sat on his bike at the top of the ramp, held our breath as he peddled down as fast as he could, and then he shot a little in the air. Splashing down handlebars first into the shallow water, he got stuck in the mud, and then climbed out to the booing and laughter of the small crowd. He left quickly in disgrace and we never heard of him again.

In the final weeks of summer there was a sense of urgency to have a little more fun, then a quiet acceptance that the carelessness was coming to an end and school was rapidly approaching. My mother had done my school shopping, to my horror, at Goodwill. There was a battle over her choices—checkered pants with bell-bottoms, long-sleeved turtleneck shirts, Hush Puppy shoes, or no-name cheap sneakers. To make matters worse the pants were way too tight, and I was always pulling at the crotch to try and loosen them up. My neighbor, Mike Conway, caught me several times pulling at myself and would yell, "Hey, quit pulling your pud!" He made sure other people were around to share the laugh.

My protests were in vain. My wardrobe was being furnished compliments of Goodwill and that was the end of it. At least there was one decent pair of Toughskin pants that were not checkered or bellbottoms, and I wore those and a simple T-shirt the first day of school.

I was sort of excited to be going to the third grade for several reasons. First of all, I was no longer one of the "little kids," being close to the fourth and final grade of the John Breen Elementary School. The second reason was that I had Mrs. Kalil for a teacher. She was a tall and pretty woman of a Middle Eastern background, strongly resembling the popular singer Cher, and all the boys thought she was beautiful. But I liked her because she was always kind and soft-spoken and treated all the kids nicely.

I was a lot less excited about Mrs. Kalil's class when I walked in and picked a desk to sit at, turned to see who was in my class, and there two rows away was big Billy Bodwell glaring back at me. He made a rude gesture with his finger and I returned the favor. Mrs. Kalil came in and assigned everyone a seat, so we all had to move anyway and fortunately, I was farther away from Billy. I turned to a friend that I hadn't seen in awhile, Kevin Tanguay, and asked, "How was your summer? Did you do anything cool?"

"No, not really. Just stayed around my neighborhood and stuff."

"I can't believe Billy Bodwell is in our class. This stinks."

"Better be careful he doesn't hear you or he might sit on you at recess," he said, looking over his shoulder and making sure he was out of hearing distance. A girl next to us heard everything and had to put her hand over her mouth to stop giggling.

I knew there would be trouble with Billy but I never expected it the very first day. Out at recess he saw me over by the fence. He walked up suddenly and pushed me without saying a word. Recess was almost over and the last thing I wanted was to fight, especially on the first day of school, and definitely not big Billy. But he pushed me again and I punched him as hard as I could in the stomach.

Then we were both swinging at each other as fast and hard as we could, some blows landing and some not, both of us crying and refusing to give up. The bell had rung and the schoolyard was completely empty except for the two of us beating each other senseless. A janitor must have seen us out the window because he suddenly grabbed us by the arms and marched us up to the office, still crying and blaming each other. We were scolded by the principal and sent back to Mrs. Kalil's class. She took us both out in the hallway and stood us against the wall, shook her head at us, and said, "I can't believe that you two got in a fight on the first day of school—"

"He pushed me!" I interrupted.

"No, I didn't! He pushed me!" Billy said, trying to convince her with a feigned sincerity.

"I don't care who started it. It better never happen again. Do you understand?" Mrs. Kalil said with a very stern voice that was unusual for her to use and we knew she meant business.

"Do you understand, Kenny?"

"Yes, I understand, Mrs. Kalil."

"Do you understand, Billy?"

"Yes, Mrs. Kalil, I understand."

"Good. Now go back to your seats and I better not hear a peep from you."

We did not fight again that school year, and I don't believe that I ever fought Billy again.

4

Autumn in New England creeps up on you gradually, in stages of subtle weather changes, where the air grows a little cool in the evening and the flowers slowly wilt away and then die in the morning frost. The leaves on the trees begin to change color a little here and a little there, the sun begins to set a little earlier, then suddenly it is dark by dinner time, and you realize that the long and lazy days of summer have surrendered for another year. The trees have continued their chameleon-like change below your very nose and one day you awaken to the feeling that you live in a painting. As you walk amongst the oaks and maples that were green a short time ago, now shooting up into the sky a burning red and yellow, and other trees a shade of purple mixed with green and orange, the smell of fall hovering in the air, you feel like heaven might look a little like this, and you're glad to be alive.

I often sat at my desk looking out the window at a leaf blowing by or a stray pigeon landing on the windowsill. I liked Mrs. Kalil a lot, but I was having more difficulty paying attention these days. She would be discussing a math lesson and I was thinking about what I would do when the bell rang, what I was doing a day ago, what I wanted to do a day from now. I know she liked me too, but could sense her becoming a little frustrated as I fell behind. I tried to pay attention, I really did, but I always felt a burst of energy and I could barely sit still in my seat. And when I needed to concentrate I had enormous difficulty. School became six hours of daily torture for me.

Before I knew it, Halloween was here. The decorations were strung all over the hallways and classrooms—black cats with their backs arched and a screeching mouth, smiling pumpkins, green faced witches with a big wart on their nose. In class on Halloween day there was a little party and everyone brought in some candy. When the bell rang I sprinted home to look for Gary and see what he was doing that night, where he was going, and who with. I found him upstairs in his room going through his drawers. "What are you looking for?" I asked, walking in and sitting on his bed.

"Something cool to wear with my mask. All I can find is these stupid checkered pants from Goodwill. How scary is this?" he said with disgust as he held up his monster mask and put the green-checkered bellbottom pants below it. "Look at this crap! I'm supposed to bang on someone's door looking like Danny Partridge!"

He was right. The mask was scary by itself—a big green head with a nail in the side, but when the person looked down and saw green-checkered bellbottom pants, they would more than likely laugh at this complete contradiction.

"I have an idea," I suggested.

"What?" he snapped, flinging the pants across the bedroom.

"All I have is a mask, but what I'm going to do is take a white sheet and cover my body so just the mask shows—like a ghost with a scary face."

"Hey, that's not a bad idea," his face lit up, "but Mom will get angry if she sees us taking her sheets."

"That's why we sneak them out. I can go with you, right?"

He paused for a second and then shook his head, "No, I'm not going in the project tonight. I'm going with a friend I met in school."

"Who? Why can't I go?"

"Because you don't know him and I'm sure he doesn't want my little brother tagging along. Besides, mom won't let you leave the project."

"She will if I'm with you," I pleaded.

"No! Go out with your own friends in the project. Now leave me alone."

"If I can't go with you then you can't use my idea for the sheet."

"I'll just use my own sheet," he said, laughing sarcastically.

"Then I'll tell Mom!"

"No, you won't. Because then you can't use your sheet either."

"I swear to God I'll tell her the minute she gets home from work."

"Fine! You're just a little baby, and you know that! Whenever you don't get what you want it's *Mom, Mom*. But you better not keep bugging me or my friend, or we'll take off on you, I swear. Got it?"

"Yah, I got it. I promise I won't bother you guys."

"Good, now get out of my room. I'm fed up with you."

After dark, we tucked our sheets into the old pillowcases that we would use to collect candy and walked past our mom as inconspicuously as possible, hiding the bulge under our arms as we walked out the door.

"Gary you keep an eye on your little brother and be home by eight-thirty!" my mom called out the door behind us as we made our way down the small hill in front of our house.

"Okay, I will," Gary hollered back, and as soon as we were out of her sight we took our sheets out, covered our bodies, and slipped our rubber masks on. "How do I look?" Gary asked, his voice muffled by his mask.

"Terrifying!" I answered sarcastically. We walked for about ten minutes to a twenty-four hour convenience store called, originally enough, the Store Twenty-Four, where Gary's friend John was already waiting.

"Hey, my little brother is tagging along," he said apologetically to his friend who was dressed in old clothes and had a creepy old man mask on. The two of them whispered something and laughed as we started to walk down South Union Street.

We weren't fifty feet down the road when a car with blasting music swerved to the side and teenagers hung out the windows and began hurling eggs at us. One, two, three, four, flew by barely missing our heads, and then one splattered on the ground at Gary's feet spraying his lower legs with yoke. "You son-of-a-bitch!" Gary screamed as the car sped off.

"Man, that sucks!" John said, watching the yoke drip from the bottom of Gary's sheet onto his shoes.

Gary muttered something to himself as we turned down a side street and banged on our first door. "Trick or treat" we called out, and a plump woman with rosy cheeks answered the door.

"Oh, my goodness, don't the three of you look scary," she said as she stuffed a candy bar in our pillowcases. A few houses later an old woman, to our irritation, gave each of us an apple. John stopped on the sidewalk a few houses down and mumbled, "Old bag, giving us an apple. What a cheapo."

"It's just one house. There's a hundred more," Gary said, impatiently, wanting to just keep going and fill his pillowcase.

"I'll show her." John said, turning and throwing his apple as hard as he could. It made a loud thud as it hit the side of the woman's house. The living room light flashed on and we ran laughing all the way to the end of that street and turned on to another, mixing in with a crowd of kids who were already at someone's door.

"I can't believe you did that," Gary whispered so this other crowd of kids wouldn't hear.

"Hey, give me an apple and that's what you get." They both laughed, but Gary's was kind of phony, like he was trying to fit in. I didn't know his new friend, but I didn't like him already. The old woman was sweet and didn't deserve that. I could see Gary was changing lately and I thought it was probably because of his new school and new friends. He was going to the Salem Street School now, which was fifth and sixth grade. He was often talking about different kids, unfamiliar names not associated with the project, how cool this one or that one was.

We made our way up and down several more streets and our pillowcases were bulging with candy and goody bags. Then someone made the mistake of giving us an apple again and John walked a few houses down and turned to throw it back at them. "You guys ready to bolt?" he asked, cocking his arm to throw.

"Don't! What if we get caught?" I said, hoping he would change his mind.

"Man, Gary, you didn't tell me your little brother was such a wimp!" Gary didn't say anything, just stood there waiting to see what would happen. Then John got into a stance like a pitcher in a baseball game, twisting forward with all his weight, hurling the apple like he was throwing a strike. The apple disappeared into the darkness for a second, and then we heard the sharp sound of glass shattering. The pieces fell to the ground noisily and echoed down the street.

The three of us stood there for a split second with our mouths hanging open in shock. Then, without anyone saying a word, we turned and sprinted back down the street and kept going until we were only a short distance to the project. We stopped on a corner under the glow of a streetlight. Most of the kids had finished trick-or-treating with only a few stragglers occasionally rambling by and disappearing into the darkness, a glowing skeleton costume the only visible thing in the shadows. "You better hope no one saw us," Gary said, catching his breath.

"Ha, you worry too much. I told you if someone gives me an apple then they pay for it," John boasted, proud of what he did.

"Gary, we need to get home. We promised Mom that we would be back by eight-thirty," I reminded him.

"You need to be home so your mommy won't get mad! Oh, Mommy, please don't be angry with me, ha, ha, ha," John teased us.

I could tell Gary was embarrassed and wanted to look cool in front of his new friend. He hesitated for a minute, "Nah, man, I'm out of here. I'm not getting caught for that window. I'll see you later."

"You're just worried about your mommy getting mad. I didn't know you were such a wimp!"

"Whatever," Gary answered over his shoulder as we walked away. A candy bar bounced past us on the street, and we turned to look back at John who was still standing under the streetlight.

"I'll see you in school tomorrow. Keep your mouth shut about the window," he said and grinned at Gary.

"Yah, I'll see you tomorrow." We turned the corner out of his sight.

When we walked in the house my mother and Tommy were in the kitchen where they had been giving out candy to the kids in the project. She saw us come in and head for the stairs, hoping to put the sheets back, but called to us from the kitchen when we were only half way up. "Not so fast you two. Come down here, I need to see you." We flung the sheets up to the top of the stairs and they slid a little way into the bathroom, then we turned and walked back down and into the kitchen. Gary and I looked at each other, both wondering how she knew about the window.

"Let me see the candy you collected," she said, holding her hand out.

"Why?" Gary asked innocently, assuming this was some kind of punishment.

"Because I heard on the news that some people were putting razorblades in candy and apples. Now dump your pillowcases on the table so I can go through it."

"It's fine. There's nothing in it, Mom."

"I said dump it on the table. If it even looks suspicious, it's going in the garbage."

"Oh, come on!" we both protested at the same time.

"Don't argue with me. How would you like to bite into a razor? Would you like that? Now dump it on the table and get upstairs and clean up for bed."

We reluctantly dumped our pillowcases into a giant pile of candy that scattered across the table and a few pieces bounced off onto the floor.

I picked one up, and asked, "Can I at least eat this?"

She studied it for a second, and said, "Go ahead. Now upstairs."

As I got ready and climbed into bed, I could hear the distant sound of ruffling candy wrappers and then the occasional sound of a piece landing in the trash. I wondered why someone would put a razorblade in some kid's candy. I tried to imagine what kind of person would do this, what they would look like, what kind of evil thoughts had brought them to this, but my mind was blank and I couldn't even imagine such a human being.

It wasn't long after Halloween when the first snowflake fell. I was in Mrs. Kalil's class, sitting at my desk and looking out the window, when I thought I was hallucinating. It didn't start as a storm with a canopy of white falling. First a small flake danced by and I squinted my eyes and wondered what it was, then a few more drifted slowly by piquing my curiosity. Suddenly the sky was filled with a million white flakes that accumulated quickly on the window ledge. Then everyone saw it.

"Look, it's snowing!" the girl behind me cried as she pointed out the window, and soon the whole class was out of their seats and standing at the windows looking out.

Mrs. Kalil smiled and walked over with us to see the first snow of the year.

She let us watch for a minute and then told us in that patient and motherly voice, "Okay kids, back to your seats. You can look at it all you want after school."

Gary had beaten me home, and as I walked up the sidewalk, a snowball came flying into my back. I fell to the ground in pain.

"I fricken hate you! I'm telling Mom," I screamed, trying not to cry from the stinging pain.

He held his hand out as if to help me to my feet, and I tried to kick his shin as he jumped back. "Okay, I'm sorry. Let's build a snowman," he said sincerely, and I let him pull me up out of the snow.

I grabbed a set of gloves in the house and joined him in rolling a snowball across the ground until it was enormous. This would be his lower body. We did the same thing, only made it a little smaller this time, and then the two of us picked it up together and placed it on top of the lower body, smoothing it out with our hands. We quickly rolled a head and carefully stuck it on the top.

"Hey, pretty good," I smiled. "Now all we need is a hat and scarf."

"What about a nose and eyes?" Gary inquired. I ran into the house and came back with an old hat and some marbles for eyes and a carrot for a nose. We put the hat on, stuck marbles in for the eyes and mouth, and then dug the carrot in while holding his head so it didn't fall off. We stood looking at our creation for a moment and then Gary said, "Wait, something is missing," and he ran around the corner out of sight. He reappeared a moment later with two skinny branches in his hand and stuck one in each side of the body. "It's perfect," he said, turning to me proudly.

We gave each other a slap on the hand, and I looked back at him. "This is the best snowman we ever made."

It was Friday night so we asked our mother to take us to Tower Hill in the morning, where the sledding was the best around. "How am I supposed to get the three of you across town with sleds?" she asked with exasperation, knowing there was a battle ahead with three determined kids.

"We can take a cab," Tommy suggested.

"A cab! Do you know how much that will cost? It's bad enough with four of us going all the way over there, but add in the sleds and I know I can't afford it."

"Maybe we can walk," Gary said out of desperation, sensing that my mom had the upper hand in this argument. Common sense was on her side.

"That's ridiculous. It would take half the day just to walk there. Do you think you can walk to the other side of the city carrying your sleds?" she said emphatically, knowing that even our stubborn little minds would have to give in to raw common sense.

"This stinks! We never get to do anything good. Everyone else gets to go to Tower Hill. Not us, we get to go down the stupid little hill in the dump!" I screamed at my mother and ran out of the room.

About an hour later my mother called us all into the living room and told us she phoned her friend Marie, that she would give us a ride there and then come back later and take us home.

"Don't you boys think you can make a habit of this," she cautioned. "I don't like asking Marie for anything. She will remind me of this for a long time. So make sure you dress warm and have plenty of fun tomorrow, because you won't be going there again anytime soon. Understand?"

We all gave our solemn oath that we would not bother her again with Tower Hill, or anywhere else, and went upstairs to get our warmest clothes ready.

In the morning we all scrambled to get ready as quick as possible, only to end up sitting around waiting, as Marie had called and said she was delayed an hour. Finally, we heard the sound of her horn blasting impatiently in the parking lot and we ran with our sleds to her car.

"Put those in the trunk," she commanded, not having much patience with kids.

My mom sat up front with her and the three of us boys crammed into the back of her blue Nova. The wheels spun a little in the slushy snow and the car swerved as we drove off. Marie made her way down the poorly plowed streets, complaining of lazy city workers and questioning where tax dollars went, my mom nodding in agreement just to keep her happy. Marie chose to stick with the main streets that were cleared the best due to heavy traffic. She followed South Union Street all the way across the green metal bridge that hummed below when crossed, the car swerving a little as the wheels slipped on the wet metal grids. She sighed with relief as she exited the bridge and turned left onto Essex Street. She followed it all the way through the downtown section and continued past the Essex Project and up a steep incline, turning right onto Ames Street and straight across to the Reservoir.

The Reservoir was undoubtedly the most beautiful part of Lawrence. It was set on the highest point of the city, with a large brick tower that is visible from many miles away. In the middle was an enormous stone basin that held millions of gallons of water and was surrounded by a black iron fence and a walking track. On three sides the terrain drops sharply from the edge of the track and down more than a hundred feet. Standing on top you can look over two large cemeteries and see most of the city's skyline, mill buildings with smokestacks reaching far into the sky, the clock tower in South Lawrence, Prospect Hill on the other side of North Lawrence, and even well into parts of neighboring towns.

We pulled our sleds from the trunk and headed past the water basin to the steepest hill. It was actually a double hill. The first hill went down about sixty feet, and then there was a flat area that was probably ten feet wide, and then it dropped off sharply into a second, smaller hill. If you went down with good speed then you would shoot across the flat surface and then become airborne as your sled failed to contact the top of the second hill. You stayed airborne about half the distance down until you landed carefully with a thud. Any loss of balance would result in a messy and painful wipeout.

There we stood looking down, wondering who would go first. We watched a kid sit on a large flattened cardboard box, the kind a refrigerator would come in, kick off with his feet and soar down the first hill. He skipped across the flat surface, then shot into the air a few feet and landed with a thump halfway down the second hill. He slid a good distance into the bottom field. "Did you see how fast he went?" I said to my brothers. Tommy was giggling to himself ever since the boy hit the ground with a bang. Those kinds of things really amused Tommy.

Gary and Tommy had those wooden sleds with iron tracks on the bottom and a wooden bar to steer them. You had to lay down frontward on them and they were not made for jumping. Landing on them could be very painful and possibly cost you a few teeth. My sled was one of those plastic discs that was a little curved and had handles on each side to steady yourself. Mine was good for jumping.

"Let me use your sled for a minute. I can do better than that kid," Gary said, taking my sled out of my hand.

He placed it at the edge of the hill and carefully sat down on it, steadying himself with the handles as he inched forward to start.

"You're only using it this one time," I assured him.

"Okay, if you say so," he halfheartedly agreed, then pushed off and started down the hill. He wasn't moving fast at first, but picked up a lot of speed as he approached the bottom of the first hill. He bounced across the flat piece, was airborne for a few seconds, and landed hard with a whiplash and an "*oopphhh.*" He managed to stay on the sled, sliding across the field to the cemetery fence. "Yahooo!" he screamed from a great distance and we could barely make out what he said.

"Give me back my sled!" I screamed from the top of the hill, the echo traveling all across the reservoir, so loud that people stopped sledding for a second and looked our way.

"Jeez, give me a second to make it back up the hill, will ya?" he screamed back with no echo. He was at the bottom of the hill and the acoustics were not the same down there.

My mom was standing on the track watching us. Gary made it to the top of the hill and reluctantly let go of my sled when I pulled it from his hand.

"Use your sled. You were bragging that you and Tommy had the good ones and mine was crappy," I said with a sense of satisfaction.

"Yah, on normal hills ours are better. But that jump is too dangerous for these wood ones. It kills when you land."

"That's too bad. I'm using mine!" I said stubbornly, making sure that I didn't wind up with his sled.

Gary was famous for that kind of last-minute scam. "Well, at least let Tommy go down on it once."

"No way! I'm afraid," Tommy said, stepping back from the edge.

"C'mon, it's a blast!" Gary reassured, and moved Tommy toward the sled with a push on the back.

"It will hurt when I land," Tommy pleaded.

"Let him make up his own mind," my mother said from behind.

"C'mon, you'll love it. I swear."

"Okay, okay, but don't push me!" Tommy warned, as he reluctantly sat on my sled and grabbed the side handles nervously. He was no sooner sitting when Gary gave a running push and the sled shot down the hill with Tommy screaming the whole way down. "*Gaaaarrrryyyy! Ahhhh!*" He made a sloppy landing halfway down the second hill and bounced off the sled and splattered snow with his tossed body. He jumped up, infuriated with snow dripping from his red face, and charged up the hill screaming, "You fricken jerk! I'm not sledding anymore!"

"Watch your mouth!" I heard my mom scream from behind. She went over to Gary and pinched his cold ear.

"*Ahhh,*" he screamed angrily.

"Serves you right. You can't go anywhere without starting trouble, can you? One more time and you're done. You can stand here and watch them."

I noticed the boy with the cardboard box was leaving and he wasn't taking it with him as he headed toward the road. I ran down the side of the hill, falling and tumbling on the steep part, and grabbed the box at the bottom. I yelled up to the boy. "Hey, can I use this?"

He turned and shrugged. "Go ahead. I don't care, I'm leaving," his voice echoed. I lugged the box awkwardly up the hill, digging my boots in sideways so I wouldn't slip, and stopped at the top where Gary and Tommy were standing.

"Hey, you have a good sled. Let us use the box. Me and Tommy can go down together," Gary said, disgruntled that he didn't see the box first.

"I'm not going down with you!" Tommy snapped, his face still red and snow still dripping from his hat.

"I promised I wouldn't do it again," Gary said, chuckling, and looked over his shoulder to make sure Mom wasn't about to pinch him again.

I put the large box down and sat in the middle. There was one problem; the box was so big that you couldn't use your feet to get going. "Gary, give me a little push. Just a little one. No, wait. Tommy you do it," I said, not trusting Gary. He put his hands on my shoulders and gave a little push. As I started to pick up speed I saw Gary running alongside of me, then he dove onto the box next to me. We soared down the slope sideways, skimmed across the flat piece, and laughed as we flew off the box and rolled down the hill. We lay in the snow laughing still. I looked up at the sky and the clouds drifted slowly by. "Hey, Gary, see that big cloud over there?"

"Which one?"

"The big one right there," I said, pointing above us a little to the right.

"Yah. I see it. What about it?"

"Doesn't it look like a dragon?"

"Yah, I guess it does," he said, studying it for a moment. He scanned the sky looking for another shape but gave up shortly when there was none to be found. So we just lay there for a minute watching the clouds slowly drift across the sky, looking at the little clouds created by our breath hitting the cold air.

Tommy came sliding up next to us on my sled and dug his boots in to stop when he reached us. "Hey, let me go down on the box with you guys," he said, jealously, afraid we were having more fun going down double.

"I thought you didn't want to do anything with me?" Gary said vindictively.

"I'm not. I'm going down with Kenny."

"Why don't you guys share the box and I can have my sled back," I offered, not really wanting to take turns going down.

"Okay, sounds good," Gary agreed, and he did something funny to make Tommy laugh and he was instantly forgiven.

We spent the rest of the morning there. Racing each other down, seeing who could jump the farthest with the sled, pushing each other down the hill sometimes, and getting a good pinch from Mom for doing it. Every so often Mom took the long walk around the track to warm up, warning us before she did, "I'll be right back. There better not be any funny business!" By the time the morning was over, we were wet, cold, and didn't put up a fight to stay when Marie honked her horn from the road. My mom was shivering and said, "Thank God" as we headed for her car, dragging our sleds behind. "Put the heat all the way up," she begged Marie as we climbed in, and she held her red hands in front of the vents as it blew out.

The first month of winter is always the honeymoon phase. When the snow first falls, there is that excitement of something new. A new world of fun that is unavailable during the summer and fall—snowmen and sledding, snowball fights that involve large groups of kids, the festivity of Christmas in the air. But, like all good things, the novelty wears off. Then you are stuck with the long and bitter winter. The walk home from school seems much longer with the howling and icy wind blowing in your frozen face. The frustrating search for things to do: play at a friend's house, hide and seek down in the basement, read, watch TV, and you long for spring as you walk down the slushy streets on a rare, sunny day.

In New England, winter loosens its grip reluctantly. Suddenly in March there is a warm week and the snow has all melted. You are happy that the misery is finally over, but then another snowstorm and you are right back into the same old rut. The weather in New England is always unpredictable.

Mother Nature was good to us that year and spring came early. February was milder than years past and all the splendor of spring began in March. The fresh smell in the air, things beginning to bud, people smiling more and spending time outside, no interruption from an untimely snowstorm to send us back inside. One of my favorite things of spring was that the high school track and field team would have their equipment out on the field of the stadium. There was a large, square cushion that was used to break the fall of pole-vaulters. If we got down there before the high school kids arrived to practice then we could jump up and down on the cushion, knocking each other over as we did, pushing each other off in a new version of king of the mountain. There were various other pieces of equipment scattered around on the field. Javelins, which we never touched because the groundskeeper would throw you out, smaller cushions that we used to beat each other up, and a few iron balls called "shot puts" that were for contests of strength, the object to see who could throw it the farthest.

One afternoon in early April, we rushed to the stadium after school in hopes of getting there before the high school kids did. We were successful. There was all the equipment laid out on the field and not a soul around but us kids from the project. There was Gary, Kevin Wilson, Andy Puglisi, PJ Timmons, me, and others.

We each grabbed a smaller cushion and began banging into each other. The battle moved onto the giant cushion, Gary pushing others off as they attempted to follow. Andy and PJ teamed up and pushed Gary backwards as they climbed on. I made my way up and was immediately knocked down with a blow from someone's cushion. I was laughing hysterically as I watched this brawl unfolding, people being pushed off the cushion and struggling violently to get back up, beating each other over the head with the cushions. I saw an opportunity and jumped on the cushion, crashing into PJ and he bounced on his back and rolled off onto the ground. I was now completely caught up in the melee. I was hitting anyone around me and being hit back, being knocked down over and over, only to bounce back up and knock someone else down. Then I took a serious blow to the back, and went flying off the cushion on my feet. I looked around and noticed that in the short time we were here the stadium had become more crowded. There were unfamiliar faces hanging around, older kids playing on the other side of the field, messing around with equipment we never touched.

I looked to the far end of the football field and thought I saw a friend down by the goal posts. I began to run toward him, and was about halfway down the field when everything went black and all I could hear was a loud ringing noise in my head. When I opened my eyes there was a crowd of people standing over me, looking down at me lying on the ground.

A stocky teenager with glasses and a white T-shirt kept saying, "I swear to God, I didn't see him. I swear to God!"

I put my right hand up to my head and felt a dent in my skull. Warm blood streamed through my fingers and down my arm.

"Oh, my God! Oh, my God!" I kept hearing. "Don't move, Kenny, you're gonna be okay," I heard one of the kids say as I went in and out of consciousness.

Suddenly two men in blue uniforms broke through the crowd and moved everyone back. They asked me a few questions and then carefully put me on a stretcher and wheeled me to an ambulance as the crowd of people followed behind with grave looks on their faces.

They drove across the city with the siren wailing, every so often asking how I was doing and checking my blood pressure. We pulled up to the emergency department of Lawrence General Hospital. A doctor gave me a shot and then there was blackness.

I woke the next day to the sound of a screaming baby who was lying in a crib a few feet from me, my head pounding like it would explode, the baby's screeching voice making it excruciating. I was in a fog and had no idea where I was. I put my right hand to the side of my head and it felt strange. There was no hair, just my bare scalp. As I ran my fingers along I felt something rough, like thread coming out of my head, like someone had sewn my scalp. I pulled on it lightly and it burned. A nurse came walking in the room and stopped at the foot of the bed. "Well, you're awake now," she said in a soft voice, smiling. "How are you feeling?"

"My head is pounding and that baby won't stop screaming. It makes it hurt more," I said with a rough, dry voice, like someone who had been sleeping for a long time. She looked over at the crib and called another nurse into the room.

They whispered amongst themselves for a second, and then one said, "I've seen some stupid things before, but this takes the cake."

Within a few minutes, they moved me to a different room with a boy who was my age and had his appendix taken out. He was really funny and I liked having him for a roommate, but my head hurt when he made me laugh, which he often did. He liked to keep track of how much he urinated. Whenever he went he would hold up his urinal proudly and then read the measurement on the side. "Look, 300cc's, look 500cc's, did you know I did 1500cc's yesterday?" he would say proudly, like he got a high grade on a math test. I had a good time talking to him, but he was discharged after a few days and I felt sad and alone in this hospital. My mother came every day after work, and asked every time if my father had come to see me. I told her he hadn't. The diagnosis was a fractured skull and the doctors told me I was lucky to be alive. I almost forgot that I was nine years old now. I had been hit in the head with the shot-put the day before my birthday, and they did the surgery to fix the injury on the day I turned nine. But, I didn't realize it until days later when my mom said, "Happy birthday," and gave me some toys from the hospital gift shop.

After about a week, the day before I was discharged home, my father came to see me with a stuffed animal in his hand. My father was a tall, thin man with dark hair and sharp features. My mom always said that when he got dressed up and walked down the street all the ladies heads would turn. He asked how I was doing and we talked for a little while, then he left. I wanted him to stay longer because I didn't see him very often. I didn't care if he left when I was one. I didn't care that my mother had only bad things to say about him. He was my father and I loved him. No, he never played catch with me. No, he never hugged me and said he loved me, never told me he was proud of me, but that natural mechanism inside said, *this is your father* and I loved him no matter what he did or didn't do. I felt special when he was around.

On the morning I was discharged I looked into the mirror and what a sight I was—the right side of my head was shaved bald with a 3-inch incision with sutures sticking out, the left side still had long blond hair. One of the nurses gave me some blue hospital-type caps to wear until my hair grew back and she wished me luck as I left. We took a taxi cab home, the driver's cigarette smoke making me nauseous. I couldn't wait to get to my house, back to my normal life. As we walked from the parking lot down to our apartment, some of the kids saw me and ran over. "Kenny, are you all right?" they asked, wide eyed and amazed that I was alive.

"Yah, I'm okay, I guess," I said uncomfortably, feeling like some kind of a freak show with all these kids standing around me.

"Do you have to wear that blue cap all the time?" they said inquisitively, and I knew they wanted to see underneath. "Can we see what happened?"

I gently slid the cap off and they were silent for a moment, then gasped, "Oh my God, are you going to be all right?"

"Yah, I'll be fine. My hair will grow back in a month or two and you won't even see it anymore. But the doctor said I can't play like I used to for awhile, until I get better."

I was tired of being stared at so I slipped my blue hat back on and turned to walk away. "Well, I need to get home now. Maybe I'll see you guys around."

"Yah, okay, we'll see you around," they answered, and I heard them whispering amongst themselves as I walked down the sidewalk. My mom helped me up to my room and I looked in the mirror at my shaved scalp and the sutures. How was I going to get through the next few months looking like this—half a head of hair and the other side looking like Frankenstein? I lay on my bed depressed and thought about it. I dreaded going back to school, knowing that everyone would stare at me and want to see under the blue cap. And they did.

When I walked into class the next morning every head turned and silently studied me, looking curiously at my blue hat, then looking me up and down, sizing me up like I was damaged goods. At recess, a crowd of kids encircled me and pleaded for me to remove the hat. I held out as long as I could, but eventually gave in to the pressure of a dozen kids egging me on. I removed the cap to a dozen curious eyes and a dozen voices saying, "Whoa, holy crap, look at that!" I quickly put it back on, having satisfied their need to see. Even my friends treated me differently, talked to me differently with a strange look on their faces, like they didn't know how to act around me anymore.

On Saturday morning, I asked my mom to take me to the barber shop. She looked at me funny, and said, "Why in the world do you want to go to a barber?"

"Because I want him to shave the other side so I don't look like a freak."

"But then you'll have no hair," she said, perplexed by the whole idea. So I removed my cap and pointed to my head for emphasis.

"Look, isn't this stupid? One side normal with hair and the other side bald. It's like I have two different heads."

She finally agreed and we walked to the local barber and sat down to wait. I flipped through a sports magazine and listened to the old men talking about things I couldn't care less about.

"Hey, Joe, doggone good weather lately, huh?"

"Sure is, Sam, sure is," a white-haired barber answered as he trimmed someone's mustache.

"Hey, Bill, how's the knee holding out?"

"Oh, you know, good days and bad days. Acts up when the weather is cold. You know how it is."

The barber nodded sympathetically, "Sure do. The old back gave me a hell of a time this winter."

When it was my turn, I climbed into the barber's chair and he pumped it up a few times to raise the height. He looked at my blue cap, "Son, you're gonna have to take that off." I removed the cap without making eye contact with him, knowing in advance what his expression would be. "What in the devil happened to you?" he asked, loud enough that the people waiting looked up from their magazines and stared my way.

"I got hit with a shot-put," I said meekly, so only he could hear.

"What's a shot-put?"

"It's a big metal ball that they throw in track and field."

"Oh, goodness, you got hit in the head with it?"

"Yah, the day before my ninth birthday. They operated the day I turned nine."

"Ah, what exactly do you want me to do?" he said awkwardly, looking at half a head of hair.

"Just shave the other half so it's all the same," I said impatiently, just wanting to get it done and leave.

"Okay, how about this—half price for half a head of hair," and he laughed at his own joke. I smiled politely but didn't think it was too funny.

I heard the buzzing of his clippers and it tickled as they dragged across my scalp, what was left of my blond hair falling across my shoulders and down to the floor. I ran my hand across my head and it felt so strange to be completely bald. My mom paid him, half price, and took advantage of his offer. At least now I looked less

freakish, felt less freakish, not having my head divided into sym-
metrical halves of normal and abnormal. This way my hair would
all grow back evenly at the same time.

There was only about six weeks of school left and I passed the
days with two goals to get me through. The first, waiting for my
hair to grow back and look normal again. The second, waiting for
the pool to open so I could have all those good times again. In a
short time, I was back playing with my friends again and after about
a month my hair was long enough to stop wearing the blue hat, the
scar only visible if you were looking for it. It was a hot spring and
this only made us long for the pool even more. In the early weeks of
June, they began to treat the water with chlorine and it went from
an uninviting, murky green, to a clear and tempting blue. Next, the
dividing ropes were put in place between the shallow, middle, and
deep ends, the pool ready for use, and we wondered why they made
us wait until school was out.

On the day the pool opened, it was blistering hot, and all the
kids walked over together and stood outside before the gate was
even unlocked. When the lifeguard came over and let us in, we paid
quickly and ran over to the water's edge. We were all there—Gary,
Tommy, Andy Puglisi, PJ Timmons, Kevin Wilson, and everyone
else from the project. Who would be the first one in the water this
year? The question was answered when Gary gave a good shove to
Tommy's back and he splashed into the middle section of the pool.
I thought a fight was brewing but Tommy bobbed above the water
with a smile and said, "The water's beautiful. Come on in."

Andy went first, jumping in close to us and attempting to make a
splash that would come out of the pool and soak us, but we jumped
back as the water just missed us. "Nice try." Kevin yelled. "Everyone
get him!" We all did cannonballs next to Andy in the water so the
waves went over his head, making him cough as he tried to laugh.
Summer was here!

5

Summer was back in all its splendor. No more being cooped up in the house, no more desperately searching for things to do, and no more lying around for hours in front of the TV. The entire project and everything that surrounded it was our playground again: the stadium, the Higgins Pool, the acres of woods across the road, and all the little grassy fields in between the apartment buildings. We had lost interest in these places during the freezing months of winter—the stadium icy and forbidding, the fields frozen and rock hard, the woods gloomy with leafless trees.

A new game became popular that summer. It was something created on the spur of the moment out of complete boredom. We were all standing on the grassy hill in front of my house with a Nerf football and unable to agree on two teams. Then someone tossed the football straight up and Andy caught it. Suddenly the entire crowd of us was chasing him, his eyes wide with fear, and a mob of us pummeled him to the ground. He lay in the grass laughing and groaning from the thrashing, and then he threw the football up and Gary grabbed it. He attempted to run to the other side of the field. The mob followed and brought him down violently to the ground, then he did the same as Andy and threw the ball straight up into the waiting arms of the next hopeful gladiator. We called this game "Muckle." The object was to get the ball and make it to the end of the field without being tackled. If brought down, then you had to throw the ball up so someone else got a chance. Those were the only rules. Only young boys could enjoy such a game. And even though I liked it, I avoided playing until well into July when my injury was completely healed and my hair was actually close to normal.

It was a carefree summer and I felt like the project would be my home forever. Yes, there were bullies and other trouble, but I knew who and what they were and how to avoid them. I walked home certain ways to avoid certain troublemakers. I knew when to come home; knew when trouble was brewing. I never went into the woods on my own. All the empty beer cans under a particular tree or little cubbyhole told me that older people were often present there. Although I never stumbled upon them, I didn't want to take the chance by myself. I knew the project well now and felt comfortable there—but only comfortable as I understood it. Never having experienced real security or comfort, never truly feeling at ease, unaware of what that actually felt like.

One afternoon in mid-August, my mother called us all into the living room and told us to take a seat. *Now what,* I thought, *one of us is in trouble.* I looked at the expression on Tommy and Gary's faces, looking for some sign of guilt to give them away. But they looked as puzzled as I did. My mom wasn't the type to sit us down for family meetings. "I'm going to Scotland for two weeks to see my family. I'm leaving this Saturday," she said apologetically, the look on her face told us we wouldn't be going. "I would take you kids, but I can't afford the airfare."

"What about us?" Gary said, his voice sounding stunned.

"You're going to your grandmother's house."

"Grandma's house!" the three of us said in a disbelieving chorus. We barely knew the woman, had seen her once every couple of years, and even then it was for an hour or so. All we knew was that she had a mean cat named Clancy, and if you tried to pet him he would scratch the heck out of your arm.

"Well, your father can take a few of you. They can figure it out," she continued, the sound of her voice knowing this was not going to be easy.

"I don't want to stay with our grandparents. They're old and boring," I added into the discussion.

"Ma, I can't believe you're doing this," Tommy said with disgust, then got up and went up the stairs, noisily stomping his feet.

"I'm sorry, but I haven't seen my sisters in years. Your damn father can watch you for a few weeks!" Then she got up and went into the kitchen, banging pots and pans as she put them away.

When we came down for breakfast on Saturday morning, there was a row of suitcases sitting neatly in the corner. There were three small ones on one side and two large ones a few feet away. We ate in silence, every so often glancing at the suitcases and then at each other. I had never been away from my mother for so long and I felt overwhelmed and anxious about the whole situation. Not only would I be without my mother, but I wouldn't even have my friends to hang around with. My mother looked at our gloomy faces and sat down at the table next to us.

"Boys, it's only for two weeks. It will pass before you know. Besides, you should spend some time with your father's side of the family."

"I don't want to go. I wish I could stay here by myself," Tommy said without looking up at her. Her face was sad and there was guilt in her voice. She was torn. It had been years since she saw her home and family, but she hated the idea of leaving us behind.

"I'm sorry boys, but I need to do this. When you're done, go upstairs and get ready. A cab is taking you to your grandmother's at ten o'clock."

Gary said nothing, didn't look at my mother once, just put his bowl in the sink and quietly went to get ready. I looked at my mom, "You're coming back, right?"

She laughed and gave me a kiss on the cheek "Of course I'm coming back you silly little beast."

We were dressed and ready, sitting by our suitcases, when the cab blew his horn and Mom walked us up into the parking lot where he was waiting. He pulled a clipboard down from the visor and asked, "Where to lady?" in a raspy smoker's voice.

"Seventy-five Packard Street," my mom told him, and he reluctantly got out to put the suitcases in the trunk, sighing heavily as he put them in. "Gary has Aunt Betty's phone number if you need me," she said looking at our three faces through the window. She smiled at us with watery eyes and waved to us as the cab drove out of the parking lot. I turned and looked out the back window and watched her waving until the cab turned the corner and she went out of sight. I missed her already, instantly, and wished she wasn't going. I didn't want my brothers to see me cry, so I put my face into my shoulder and looked out the window as we drove. Gary was silently looking out the other side, and Tommy in the middle with his own thoughts. The driver made his way across the south side of Lawrence, turned left and traveled along the Merrimac River for a few minutes, then turned right onto Packard Street.

He pulled into the driveway of my grandparent's small blue ranch and turned the engine off. He took our suitcases out of the trunk and Gary went to the door and rang the bell. My grandmother came to the door with an astonished look on her face and spoke with Gary for a second, but I couldn't make out the words from the driveway. She was a large woman and always wore dresses.

Then she threw her arms up and yelled, "Oh, for Christ's sake, what was your mother thinking? Tom, get over here!"

My grandfather appeared at the door and my grandmother told him what was happening, his face stern behind his glasses.

Then my grandmother yelled at the cab driver, "You just put them back in and take them back to their mother!"

"We can't go home; she's on her way to Scotland," Gary said, with a trace of desperation in his voice, knowing that the house was locked and empty.

The cab driver just stood there for a second, unsure of how to deal with this unique situation. People didn't usually reject their grandchildren in the middle of a driveway. "Listen, lady, I got nothing to do with this. I'm just a cab driver and I was paid to bring them here." Then he drove off with the three of us standing in the driveway with our suitcases at our feet.

"Come in here while I call your father!" my grandmother said, shaking her head and holding the door open. We walked shyly by her, like you would with a complete stranger, the smell of the cat litter greeting us upon entry, newspapers scattered on the table. "Tom! Can you believe this!" she said frantically dialing my father's number.

My grandfather never said much. He was from the South originally and still had an accent. When he said my name it wasn't Kenny, it sounded like "Kinney." "Kinney, put your suitcase down over there son," he instructed, pointing to the corner. In his younger days, he was quite a drinker and would get so drunk that he couldn't find his car for days.

My grandmother got a busy signal and slammed the phone down, "You boys just sit still until I reach your father."

We were sitting nervously at the table, fidgeting with the newspapers, when Tommy saw Clancy the cat around the corner and went into the living room to pet him. We could hear growling, then hissing, and Tommy ran back into the kitchen screaming and holding his arm. "Damned cat," he said angrily, and showed us three bleeding scratches from his wrist halfway up to his elbow. Gary and I started chuckling and this made Tommy angrier. "That cat needs a kick in the ass!" he said loudly.

"Don't you touch my Clancy!" my grandmother snapped at Tommy while she dialed the phone again.

"Tom," she said, finally getting through. My father's name was Tom also. My grandfather, my father, and my brother were all named Tom, but had different middle names. "Tom, you need to get over here. Frances has gone off to Scotland and sent the three boys here in a cab." She paused for a moment to let him speak, and continued, "I don't know what she was thinking. You need to get over here. We're too old to watch these kids." I felt like a complete idiot sitting there, like a hot potato that no one wanted to catch. She hung up the phone. "Your father will be here in a little while. Go outside to play until he does."

There was a giant rock in their backyard and we went out and took turns climbing on it and then jumping off, careful to avoid small pieces of crap from the neighbor's dog. "Do you think Dad will let us stay with him?" Tommy asked, climbing on the rock.

"I don't know. Maybe Mary Jane won't like it," Gary said, matter-of-factly. Mary Jane was his second wife; we also had a half brother, Scott, and a half sister, Katie, who we never saw and barely knew. My father's car pulled into the driveway and I was a little nervous that he was going to be really mad, start yelling at us like it was our fault or something.

He was actually pretty calm as he strolled across the grass of the back yard and casually said, "You boys having fun?" as he tousled Gary's hair.

"I guess so," I said, grinning shyly, always a little self-conscious around my father.

"You better watch out for all the dog poop," Tommy said and burst into that crazy laughter of his. Dad just looked at Tommy for a second and grinned an understanding smile. Tommy was Tommy. "You kids have fun. I'm going inside to discuss this with your grandmother."

He gave me a pat on the shoulder and walked back across the lawn and into the house, my grandmother's voice audible from the distance. "Tom, thank God you're here," and he closed the door behind him. That was all I heard.

We continued to play on the rock for what seemed like a long time, when my grandmother came to the door and told us to come in for lunch. She had made hot dogs and beans. "You boys take a seat," she said, putting out plates on the table with the food already on them, bottles of relish and ketchup placed in the middle.

"After lunch you kids are coming with me," my father said, biting off a piece of hot dog, talking as he chewed. I wondered what it would be like actually living with my father for two weeks. Maybe he would throw a baseball around with me or something, play a game of football on the grass, and I felt a little excited. I could get to know my half brother and sister better.

"You boys grab your suitcases so we can be on our way," he said, putting his dish in the sink and we followed along, putting our dishes away and getting our bags. We put our suitcases in the trunk and he drove off toward the north end of the city, crossing the stone bridge by the waterfall and heading up Broadway until he turned left on Haverhill Street. "Your mother still going to that church?" he turned to ask Gary who was sitting next to him up front.

"Yah, we still go on Sundays."

"Repent, repent!" my father said, mockingly, pointing a finger at us and laughing as he said it. I was confused by this, being taught that it was a sin to mock God, something only evil people did.

I saw the sign that said we were entering the next town, Methuen, and wondered why we were going this way. My father lived in the other direction in a town called Haverhill. We slowed down and turned at a sign that said "St. Ann's Home," and drove slowly up the long driveway. We passed a slope on the right that tapered down to a field where kids were playing kickball, and pulled up to a large brick building. My father turned the engine off and turned around to look at Tommy and me in the back seat, "You boys know I live in a small house. I can only take Gary. You two are staying here until your mother gets back."

"What is this place?" I asked, disappointed and sad that I wasn't going with him.

Now I would be without my mother, my friends, and even without Gary who I was never separated from. "It's like an orphanage, well, I guess it is an orphanage, same thing anyways. But there are kids your age here so at least you can have fun for the next two weeks."

"I don't want to stay in this stinky place. I'm not staying here!" Tommy said with determination, feeling like he was tricked into being here. I couldn't believe he was dumping us off at some orphanage. I would have slept on the floor of his house, anywhere, I didn't care, and I was sure Tommy wouldn't care either.

I was angry inside. Why didn't he care anything about me. He took care of my half brother and sister every day; wasn't I worth two lousy weeks? I never asked him for anything, and he never gave me anything either. No clothes, no money, no anything, and the one time I needed him he dumped me off in an orphanage. I stepped out of the car in a mild state of shock, something inside of me turning off at that instant, changing me a little forever. I walked up the large stone stairs and insisted on carrying my own suitcase inside. Tommy stood at the top of the stairs still arguing with my father, "I don't want to stay here. Why do I have to?"

"I told you I only have room for Gary. It's only for two weeks, now go inside."

Tommy reluctantly walked through the double doors with me, and we stood against the wall as my father talked to some people at a desk. He signed some papers and said, "See you boys soon." He walked down the hall and exited the door. We looked at each other with a sense of disbelief as we waited there in the lobby with our suitcases at our feet. We didn't say anything; at significant moments like this you already know how the other person feels. There is an unspoken understanding that goes beyond words. We knew we wouldn't see our father again anytime soon.

We waited there in the lobby for some time when a short, chubby man in khaki pants and a button-down shirt came walking down the hall, waddling side to side as he approached. "You boys follow me, I'll take you up to your ward," he said, directing us to an elevator around the corner. We stopped on the fourth floor and walked down the hall a short distance, going through a door into what looked like a really big apartment. There was a living room area with couches and chairs, a TV against the wall, bedrooms along the back wall, and a kitchen across the corridor.

"What are your names?" the man asked.

"I'm Tommy and he's Kenny," my brother answered for both of us.

"Well, Kenny, you stay here a moment while I bring your brother to his room and then I'll be back for you."

I sat on the couch and wondered where all the kids were, but then I remembered seeing them outside playing kickball. The man was back a few minutes later as he promised. "Okay, Kenny, give me your suitcase and follow me." I handed it to him and followed to the bedrooms in the back. "How old are you, son?"

"Nine."

"Oh, you know what? I'm not going to put you in this room. This boy is a teenager and I don't think someone your age should be with teenagers." He stood for a moment, deep in thought, then his face lit up like he had a great idea, "This boy is staying overnight at his aunt's house. You'll have the room to yourself tonight. We'll figure the rest out tomorrow," he said as he put my suitcase down next to an empty bed. The other bed was made with a quilt and there were posters of girls and rock stars on that side of the room.

"You boys can go outside and play for awhile if you like. Or, you can stay here and watch TV."

"I think I'll go outside," I said turning to Tommy, who had come back into the living room. "Want to come with me, Tommy?"

"No, I'm going to stay here and watch the boob tube," he answered, looking straight ahead, his mind a million miles away.

"C'mon Tommy, let's go outside. The heck with TV," I said with an emphasis on TV, with contempt for the word, as though watching it on an August afternoon was a terrible thing.

"No, I don't want to. You go," he said with a hint of irritation in his voice, and I knew he wanted to be alone. That was the way Tommy dealt with everything—alone. Tommy could be in a crowded room, yet he was still alone.

I took the elevator down and walked out into the afternoon sun. I stood at the top of the slope that led to the playing fields and watched a group of kids in the midst of a kickball game. In the background, I saw a long green building that looked like a row of garages, and beyond that, a man was throwing a baseball back and forth with several kids, every so often stopping to demonstrate proper technique. What if I got stuck here forever? What if all these kids I saw had been dropped off the same way; the mom or dad saying it was for a few weeks. Then someone told them it was going to be a few more weeks, then a few more, and suddenly they had been here years.

I started to worry that my mother was never coming back—that this would be Tommy's and my new home forever. The games began to break up and most of the kids headed inside, a few stragglers kicking the ball across the field and racing after it. I mingled in with the crowd and headed inside back up to the fourth floor. When the elevator door opened, I thought I was in the wrong place, the ward no longer quiet and orderly as the boys had returned and there was noise everywhere. But I saw Tommy talking to someone in the living room and knew this was where we were staying.

The boys were all older than me, mostly closer to Tommy's age, and I felt out of place as I took a seat on the couch. One of them came over to me, "Hey, you want to hear an awesome song? You need to hear this drum solo."

"All right," I said politely, the way you do when you first meet someone. I had no idea what a "drum solo" was, but acted interested anyway. He showed me his room and put a record album on. The needle skipped a few times and made a loud screechy sound. Then the song began, "Na na na there must be fifty ways to leave your lover, just jump on a bus Gus, you don't need to be coy Roy, just listen to me," and then the drums beat, like a military cadence, and I felt like I should be marching. He studied my face, looking for a reaction, like I was supposed to explode with joy.

"Did you hear that? Wasn't that awesome!" he said excitedly, his eyes wide and glaring.

"Yah, that was really cool!" I answered, afraid that if I said I didn't like it he would burst into some kind of rage.

It didn't take long to realize that these boys were here for a reason. When you talked to them, you could tell they were a little different. Some seemed normal at first, but after a few minutes, some strange behavior would emerge—a sudden screaming spell that required the counselors to intervene, or a compulsion to kick the bathroom stall open when someone was on the toilet, which I learned the hard way. Or an obsession with some detail or fact that most people wouldn't think twice about.

One of the older boys, Johnny Swicker, called me into the kitchen after supper. "Hey, it's snack time. Here's a glass of milk for you," he said, handing a glass to me and another boy. We all took a sip and my throat burned, my stomach heaved a little like I wanted to vomit, and they both started laughing. He held up a bottle of dish washing liquid and I realized that was the awful taste in my mouth. "Got you, ha, ha, ha."

"Don't feel bad. He gets everyone with that," the other boy said, and I felt a little less stupid knowing that others fell for the same trick. Besides, he was a lot bigger than me and there wasn't much I could do about it anyway.

I went to bed in that empty room, glad the other kid was away overnight, not sure of what to expect from him or anyone else in this place. I lay there for a long time, my mind full of questions and unable to fall asleep. I looked at his poster of Linda Ronstadt; she looked so beautiful to me and I wondered if I would ever have a girlfriend like that. I wondered what Gary was doing right now. Was he up watching TV with Dad, maybe sharing a little popcorn and having a good laugh or two? Eventually, my eyelids grew heavy and I hoped I would soon be asleep. I had been through enough this day and I was glad to see the end of it.

In the morning, I was awakened by the sound of kids moving around and the television blaring. I ate a bowl of cereal, feeling uncomfortable with all these older kids looking at me like a stranger. As soon as I was finished the chubby man who had brought us to the ward came looking for me, wearing the same khaki pants and button-down shirt, the same waddling walk as he came into the kitchen. "Kenny, you need to take a shower and get ready."

"What for?" I asked, still a little groggy.

"Because you're going to be staying with a family in Methuen. It's a better place for you."

"Why can't I stay here with Tommy?"

"This ward is really for teenagers. It's not appropriate for a nine-year-old. Your brother is a teenager and will be staying."

I was tired of all this rapid change, this complete uncertainty, and became frustrated and angry. "I don't want to stay with some family I don't know. I want to stay with my brother."

"I know the last few days have been tough, but you'll like the Dunns. They're nice people," he said sympathetically. I went into the bathroom and took a shower, and when I glanced up, I was completely startled by some kid looking over the stall at my naked body.

"Get out of here!" I yelled, trying to look tough and hoping someone would come to see what the commotion was. He chuckled and his head disappeared.

I found Tommy in his room and sat down on his bed. "Tommy, they're taking me to some family's house. I guess I'll see you in a couple of weeks."

"What, why can't you stay here?"

"I guess you have to be a teenager" I shrugged. His face was blank. When my father dropped us off here, something in Tommy must have shut off, too. He just sat on the other bed and looked blankly at the floor. I patted him on the shoulder, "I'll see you at home," I said, and I walked out to the ward and found the chubby man in the living room waiting for me.

"Ready to go?" he asked, handing me my suitcase. I nodded, and we took the elevator down, my eyes squinting as we stepped out into the morning sun. I followed him to his sedan and he slid my suitcase into his back seat. "The Dunns really are nice people. You're going to like them," he said as he unlocked the passenger side for me. I didn't care if they were the nicest people in the world. They weren't my family. I just wanted my family back.

He drove through the back roads of Methuen, taking a long and winding road that passed through large open pastures, and I studied the long green stalks of a cornfield as we passed, having never seen a real one before. He turned onto a quiet street lined with nice little houses and flower gardens, then stopped in the driveway of a white house with a welcome sign out front. I didn't want to get out of the car. I felt embarrassed to walk into someone's house with a suitcase and just move in. I sat there as long as I could, the man removing my suitcase and standing outside my door waiting. I reluctantly got out and walked up to the front door with him, looking down at the ground as I walked. My heart started to pound as he rang the doorbell.

An older woman with black hair came to the door. "Come in, come in. You must be Kenny. They didn't tell me you were so cute," she said, petting my shoulder. I glanced up, blushing, and then looked back down again at the floor. "I'm Mrs. Dunn and my husband is Bill. He's not home right now. He's at work, he's a mailman." She paused for a minute to see my reaction, thinking I might say, "A mailman! Cool!" like you would to a firefighter or policeman, but I was completely embarrassed and just looked at the floor. "Our teenage granddaughter lives with us too," she said, hoping this would get some kind of response.

She spoke with the man from St. Ann's for a moment and then he left, patting me on the back and wishing me luck as he went out the door. I had no idea what I was going to do in this house for the next two weeks. It was so quiet here, nothing like the project. She showed me around the house, putting my suitcase in a small bedroom that was to be mine, showed me a girl's bike that I was free to use, and then took me through the cellar where a really cool motorcycle was parked. "Whose motorcycle is this?" I asked; my first words since arriving.

"This belongs to our son. He keeps it here for safe storage."

"Wow, it's really cool," I said with great interest.

"If he comes by, maybe he could give you a ride on it. Would you like that?"

"Yah! I hope he comes by!" She looked pleased at my excitement, happy to have found something I liked.

Later that afternoon I met the granddaughter. She had black frizzy hair, always wore jean pants and a jean jacket, and seemed completely disinterested in my presence—like I was just another nuisance, another kid passing through. Most of the time she was out with her friend, and when she was there she basically ignored me. The Dunns were in fact very nice people. Mrs. Dunn was always offering a snack or something. Mr. Dunn would get home from work in the early afternoon and sit in his recliner, watching TV for hours. Finding something to do was the most difficult part of staying there.

And even though I had sworn I wouldn't be caught dead riding a girl's bike, every afternoon I took her bike and rode in circles in the street out front, careful not to venture far enough for the local kids to see me. Cautious as I was, a neighborhood boy walked by one day as I went round and round. He stopped walking and looked at me funny for a second, then got up the nerve to say, "Hey, that's a girl's bike you know."

"No, duh," I said very sarcastically, suddenly becoming quite defensive as I sat on a pink girl's bike. He continued to look at me funny as he walked down the street to his house. I regretted being so sarcastic. There was one kid my age in this incredibly boring neighborhood, and not only had he seen me riding a girl's bike, but I had been rude about it. Any chance of hanging around with him was pretty much gone.

One afternoon Mrs. Dunn stepped out for a few odds and ends, instructing me before she left, "You listen to Lisa. She's in charge until I get back. I shouldn't be gone that long."

Her granddaughter waited a few minutes until she was sure that Mrs. Dunn was far away, then turned to me and said, "You want to do something fun?" in a mischievous tone.

"Sure," I gladly agreed, willing to do anything to break up this dull routine, and also glad she was showing me a little attention.

"Come on," she said, opening the cellar door and waiting for me to follow. She went down and walked to the back of the dark and musty room, stopping in front of the motorcycle. She grabbed the cap on the gas tank and used all her might to unscrew it. She looked at me and grinned, "I love the smell of gas. Have you ever smelled it?"

"Yah, at a gas station. I guess."

"No, I mean like this," she said, bending over and holding her nose above the open gas tank for a minute. Then she lifted her head and took a few unsteady steps backwards. "Whoa, I'm so dizzy right now. This is really cool, you need to try it."

"Are we going to get in trouble for touching the motorcycle," I asked, still feeling somewhat like an imposing stranger here.

"How is anyone going to know? I do this all the time. Don't worry about it." I stepped in front of the motorcycle, put my nose directly over the open gas cap, and breathed in the strong fumes for a minute. Then I lifted my head, and everything around me was spinning. My ears were ringing.

"Pretty cool, huh," she said, laughing, then went back over and sniffed it again for a minute.

Then it was my turn again. After keeping my nose there for a minute, and reaching a new level of dizziness, we heard a car door slamming in the driveway. "Oh no, my grandmother's back!" and she ran up the stairs, leaving me standing down there completely dizzy and clueless about what to do next. I instinctively made my way up the stairs, staggering a little and putting my hand against the wall for support, hoping to make it into the kitchen before Mrs. Dunn did, but as I came out the door, she was putting things on the kitchen table.

"What were you doing down there?" she asked, a little startled by me coming out the door in front of her.

"I don't know," I answered, slurring a little and looking around for their granddaughter, who was nowhere to be seen. She had made a clean escape and was no doubt getting herself together at this moment.

She walked over and studied my eyes for a second. "You reek of gasoline. What is this brown stuff above your lip?" Apparently, I had put my nose a little too close to the gas tank and got some kind of gassy residue on my face. "I asked you what you were doing?" she said, impatient and waiting for some kind of confession. I just shrugged, not wanting to talk and have the words come out funny again.

"Oh, for God's sake, you were sniffing gasoline, weren't you?"

I maintained my silence, far too humiliated to admit this stupid act. They were nice enough to let me stay at their house, and the minute she steps out, I'm sniffing gas in the basement. "Go take a bath. Clean up and you'll feel better," she said, dumbfounded by the whole situation. "And where is Lisa? Lisa! Lisa! You get out here right now!" I saw her coming out of her room as I walked down the hall and turned into the bathroom. I turned the water on and could vaguely hear Mrs. Dunn questioning her granddaughter in the kitchen, "Did you have anything to do with this?"

"With what?" she answered innocently, like she couldn't possibly know what was going on.

"Don't play stupid with me," Mrs. Dunn snapped at her, the tone of their voices suddenly lowering, and with the sound of the running water, all I could make out were hushed mumblings.

When the bathtub was full, I turned the water off and lay there for awhile. My senses started to go back to normal, the world no longer spinning, the low-key ringing in my ears gone. I was glad Mr. Dunn wasn't home for the whole fiasco. He was a nice old guy, he didn't say much, but his look of disapproval would have made me feel really bad. The look on Mrs. Dunn's face had made me feel bad enough as it was and I wasn't looking forward to walking out of the bathroom and facing her. I was happy that I only had a few more days here, then my mom would be back and we would all be together again. Back to our life in the project, swapping stories of what we did for the last two weeks. Back with our friends; our life completely back to normal.

As I stepped out of the tub, I heard Mr. Dunn come home and thought for sure he was going to scold me something fierce. But he never said a word. I knew Mrs. Dunn told him. I could tell by the way he glanced at me during supper—a perplexed sort of look on his face, his expression saying, "What the hell is going on with this kid?" I was extremely tempted to tell them that their wonderful granddaughter had thought the whole thing up, but I kept my mouth shut.

After dinner, I went to the living room to eat my dessert while watching TV. Mr. Dunn turned the TV on and got in his recliner, leaning way back until his feet were parallel with his body. The nightly news came on and I considered leaving the room. I had no idea why anyone would want to sit and listen to someone yap about gas prices, the long lines at gas stations, and other depressing stuff.

I wasn't really paying attention when the reporter's words suddenly snapped me out of my careless oblivion and had my undivided attention: "We're joining you live from Lawrence, where the search for Andy Puglisi continues, missing from the Higgins Memorial Pool."

There were images of the project and pool, of policemen combing the woods with dogs, and people I knew being interviewed. "Oh my God!" I jumped to my feet screaming, "That's my friend! That's my friend Andy!"

Mr. Dunn brought the recliner down quickly, with a bang. Mrs. Dunn ran into the room and looked at my panicking face. "I have to help look for him! I think I know where he is!" They rushed me to the car and drove as fast as they could to Lawrence, Mr. Dunn tapping his fingers nervously on the steering wheel at every red light.

When we got to the project there were people everywhere, crowds looking everywhere: the woods, behind the Higgins Pool, walking through the dump, yelling his name, a helicopter buzzing overhead and going back and forth to scan the area. Mr. Dunn told the police that I was a friend of Andy's and that I thought I knew where he was. A large man with a German shepherd walked up and said, "Come with me." We walked through the project, crossing all the way to the other side of the stadium, people hurrying along with us, hoping that I was right.

I took them through a hole in the chain link fence that was directly across from the bowling alley, the officer ducking down as he went through. I went to an enormous sign that towered fifty feet or so into the air, visible from the highway. At the bottom of the steel-supporting pole, there was a large gray electrical box with a broken lock and nothing inside. It was the perfect size for a kid to hide in, and we often did during hide-and-seek. I was sure Andy was there.

As the officer opened the box, a reporter rushed up and stuck a camera right behind us, filming the entire thing. The box was empty. I fully expected to see Andy, for him to say, "Ah, you found me," and to step out grinning. My heart dropped as I walked slowly back to the project, the magnitude of what was really happening eluding me. All these frantic people hurrying around me seemed unreal. It wasn't really happening; none of it. When my mother got back from Scotland everything would be the way it was. We would all be together: my family, my friends, and Andy would be running around the project with us.

My mother returned a few days later, as promised, and I hugged her for a long time. I was never so happy to see her. She was beyond outraged with my father and my grandparents, completely and utterly shocked that they sent us to an orphanage. The only thing that diminished her anger was her greater shock and sadness about Andy. I still refused to believe it was happening. I had it all figured out—Andy had gotten angry about something and decided to run away, would come back when he was good and ready.

Our house was not the same after my mom came back; the conversation was always about Andy. *Had anyone heard anything, have any ideas, what was the rumor of the day, of the moment?* In fact, the entire project was living the same way—in a sort of quiet shock. We would stand in the parking lot across from the pool, a group of us boys, throwing pebbles in the hot August sun, watching them bounce across the pavement as we talked about Andy. He became almost a mythical figure. Each day the stories and rumors becoming a little more far-fetched—Andy was actually too mature for his age, a teenager's mind in a ten-year-old's body, Andy had "known" girls, and on and on it went.

I kept expecting him to suddenly walk out of the woods, see us standing there in the parking lot, and say, "Man, I fooled you guys good." Convinced that he would be back soon, he would tell his mother, "I'm sorry, I don't know why I ran away."

He never came out of the woods, never popped up from behind a bush, never came strolling back into the project, or anywhere else. One August morning, an innocent ten-year-old boy named Andy Puglisi said goodbye to his mother and walked across the street to the Higgins Memorial Pool. He was never seen again.

During the aftermath of all this, my mother called me and my brothers into the living room.

"Boys, I need to talk with you," she said, sitting on the couch.

We took a seat and listened, wondering if she had news about Andy.

"I've been speaking a lot lately with the people from St. Ann's. While Tommy was there they had time to do a complete evaluation of him."

"What's an evaluation?" I asked curiously, this word sounding awfully scientific to me.

"It's when you figure out what is best for someone. And what is best for Tommy is to live at St. Ann's."

"For how long?" Gary inquired.

"Permanently. It will be his new home," she answered, her voice cracking a little.

I looked at Tommy. "You want to go back there?" I asked incredulously.

"Mom thinks it's best. The people at St. Ann's think I should stay." His voice was emotionless, like he had already resigned himself to this inevitable fact, had already had this conversation before Gary and I were told.

"When do you leave?" I asked him, looking for some sign of reluctance. I thought maybe he would suddenly refuse to leave his family.

"They're picking me up this morning. I have to get my stuff ready."

He got up from the chair and went upstairs, and we heard the sound of bureau drawers opening and closing, the sound of his odds and ends clattering together as he packed them.

He came back down shortly, carrying the same suitcase that he had just unpacked not so long ago. "Wait one minute," Gary said, and disappeared up the stairs, coming back down with a small stack of comic books. "I never let you read these. I know they're your favorites. You can have them."

"Gee, thanks. Are you sure?"

"Yah, I'm sure." I could tell Gary was keeping his feelings hidden. I was doing my best to keep mine hidden too. We weren't the kind of family that was always hugging and saying, "I love you."

We just took it for granted that everyone knew. "Don't forget your Statue of Liberty doll," I reminded, knowing he would never forget it, but I was searching for something to say.

"Come on, Tommy. We're going to wait outside," my mom said, and I knew she wanted to say goodbye to him alone.

As he walked toward the kitchen door Gary called out to him, "Hey, take care of yourself."

"Okay, I will." Tommy smiled, and we both gave him an awkward hug. Gary and I watched from the kitchen window as he and Mom walked slowly up the path, her rubbing his back as they went, and they stopped to wait in the parking lot. I didn't want to see him get in the car. That was too final, so I went up to my room and lay face down on the bed. And I felt something deep down inside of me shutoff. Gary had quietly gone into his room and closed the door behind him, saying nothing, a confused look on his face.

The days that followed were doubly unreal now. Not only was the search for Andy still going, but now there was no Tommy. I missed seeing him run across the fields, or sitting somewhere laughing to himself. I felt so guilty about every little argument or fight I ever had with him. It was much quieter in our house now. Not only quieter because of Tommy's absence, but because Gary and I had become quieter, often deep in thought about all that was happening around us.

I don't know if my mother had been planning it, or if the shock of Andy brought it on, but one day shortly after Tommy left she informed us we were moving out of the project. Not only moving from the project, but all the way to North Lawrence. Gary and I fought bitterly against this. We had just begun school, back with all the people we had known for years. Now, we were heading somewhere completely unknown, almost like moving to a new town, with entirely different schools and kids we had never seen. All I had ever known was the insulated world of the project.

We decided that the best way to deal with this was to just flat-out refuse to go. Gary argued with my mother daily, screaming he wouldn't leave. As I watched my mother pack a few things each day,

I began to feel hopeless. I lost interest in almost everything. After this last month of summer, I forgot what it was like to be happy and carefree, and I wished I could go back to the end of June, redo the entire summer over. But there would be no St. Ann's and Andy would still be here. Somehow I would will those things into never happening.

On the morning we were to leave, I told my mother I wasn't going and I walked out the front door and sat under an oak tree in front of the next building. I could see the movers taking the last of our things out. I sat there barefoot in the morning sun and thought about maybe running away. My mother waited a good long time for me to come back, but ran out of patience and found me under the oak tree. "Come on. Get your shoes and get in the truck," she said angrily, in a hurry as the movers were ready to leave.

"I'm not going!" I said, not budging from under the tree.

"We've already been through this. Now get up!" I still didn't budge. She became infuriated, "The movers are ready to go!" Still I didn't budge; didn't even look at her. She grabbed my T-shirt and slapped me hard across the face, catching me off guard, my face burning and my ear ringing. "Damn it, get up or I'll give you another one!" The last month caught up with me and I sobbed uncontrollably, could taste the tears as they ran down over my lips. I got to my feet and looked my mother in the eyes.

"I hate you. I hate your freakin' guts!" She slapped me again, harder this time and at that moment, I hated her more than anything. I walked toward the moving truck with her, looking all around the project as I went, saying goodbye in my mind, nine years of memories rushing by. The world as I knew it was crumbling all around me.

6

I knew my world was changing, but at the time I had no idea just how much. In the next four years, I would experience this same upheaval five times. Just when I would start to feel a little settled it was time to leave again, and I always felt a little off balance. Always felt like a stranger in a new neighborhood. Always the new kid in school, dreading that introduction when the teacher would say, "Why don't you tell the class your name."

"Kenny Tingle," I would answer, halfheartedly. Then the students would burst into laughter, thinking I had made this name up or something. I hated my last name more than anything—had been in a dozen fights because of it. Gary hated it too, getting the same response whenever he introduced himself.

My mother chose an apartment on a corner of Basswood Street, right behind a Haffener's gas station and a stone's throw from a busy road. It was in one of the toughest neighborhoods in Lawrence; surrounded by row after row of three tenements, street-wise kids and strange people constantly walking by. The strangest of them all was our landlord, Joe Borin, who owned just about the whole block. He would drive his car like a maniac up and down the street, and if he saw you sitting on the stairs by the road he would turn his car right at you and come to a screeching stop inches from your legs, then stick his head out the window and say, "Your mother around? Tell her I need the rent."

He lived in one of the three tenements himself, liking to keep a watchful eye on all his properties. My mother had once sent Gary and I to pay him, and he invited us inside his apartment. On the wall there was a picture of him as a younger man, wearing shorts and boxing gloves, posing with his hands up in a fighter's stance. It hung in the hall as soon as you walked in so you couldn't miss it. Most of the kids in the neighborhood thought he was crazy and were deathly afraid of him. I often wondered if he put on an act to keep everyone in check, until years later at a high school graduation ceremony. The podium was set up in the middle of the football field, the commencement speaker giving his address, when suddenly Joe Borin jogs right through the middle of the field and starts doing pushups on the visitor's bleachers. The police took him by the arm and escorted him off the field. Then I knew it was no act.

I started fourth grade at the local school, the Tarbox, and longed for the familiarity of the Breen School. Not only was I a stranger here, but a lot of the students were from a completely different world then me. In South Lawrence, there were very few Hispanics, and I had almost no exposure to them or their culture. But North Lawrence was quickly becoming more and more mixed. They seemed so foreign to me. They way they dressed was different, often wearing Dickie pants and canvas Converse sneakers, some of them with Afros, and when they talked it seemed like they went so fast. I sat between several of them in class and they would talk to each other in their native language, and my lack of understanding made me feel like I was the one from a different country.

It was a tough school and I was always on my guard. I felt completely alone there, not always able to rely on Gary who wanted to hang around with kids his age. Finally, one day I met a friend—in an odd sort of way. I was walking through the slushy streets near my house on a sunny winter day, when a snowball splattered at my feet, and I looked up to see a boy around my age on top of a garage roof. He had blond hair and buckteeth. He reached down into the snow on the roof, made another snowball, then hurled it at me and it barely grazed my back as I turned away.

"Hey, you want a punch in the face," I yelled up at him. He grinned and I saw his big buckteeth, making me even angrier. "Throw another snowball and I'm gonna punch you in the face!" I stood there facing him, trying to look tough.

"Na, na, na," he mocked, then threw another one that just missed my head. I grabbed a handful of snow and whipped one back at him, and it struck the roof a few inches below his head, the rest of his body hidden behind the peak. He threw another one. I hurled a barrage of snowballs at him, bending quickly for more snow, hurling them before he had a chance to react, and his head disappeared behind the roof.

I saw him climbing down in the back, first jumping down to a shed and then to the ground. As he landed, he lost his balance and slipped on his rear end. I ran up quickly with a snowball, and stood over him with my arm cocked to throw. "You're not so funny now, huh?"

"Go ahead, I dare you," he said defiantly, like he would beat me up if I did. I gestured like I was going to throw, and he covered his face with his arm. "Okay! Okay! You win! Don't throw it, I'm on the ground."

I accepted his surrender, knowing that if I hit him at close range there would definitely be a fight, and I wasn't in the mood to roll around in the snow with him. I lowered my arm and he looked up at me for a second, studied me, and then said, "You wanna throw snowballs at cars with me?"

"Who are you?" I asked suspiciously, wondering if this was some kind of a trick. Maybe he wanted me to help him up and then he would throw some snow in my face and try to jump me.

"Kevin Boutin," he said, looking at my face to see if I recognized the name. I didn't. I thought his name was pretty weird, pronounced *Boot-in*, and thought about making fun of it, but knew mine was worse so I kept my mouth shut.

"Who are you," he asked, when it became obvious that I wasn't going to introduce myself.

"Kenny."

"Kenny who?"

"None of your business, that's who."

He got up from the ground and brushed the snow off his butt. "You wanna hit cars with snowballs or what?"

"Yah, I guess so," I said shrugging, trying not to look too enthusiastic in case it was in fact a trick. I didn't have any friends and I wasn't in the position to turn any new ones away. I was just happy to hang around with someone close to my age, and I didn't care what we did.

"Come on," he said with a grin; those big buckteeth protruding and he gestured with his arm for me to follow. We walked through a short alley between two buildings and came out on Lawrence Street. We waited for all the cars to pass and crossed over by a twenty-four-hour store called Cumberland Farms, which was located on a corner, and we went around the back of the store. "This is the best place. You can make an easy get away," he said, picking up a handful of snow and packing it tightly between his gloves.

"What? Right here? There's nowhere to run to," I questioned, thinking this kid wasn't too bright.

"Sure there is—my house." And he pointed at a small house that was diagonally across from the front of the store. "You're going to hit a car and then run right to your house? Duh, they'll see you and go to your door."

"No, we run through my neighbor's yard and hop the fence to my house. Geez, quit worrying, I've done this a bunch of times."

He waited as several cars passed in front of us, looking for the right opportunity, then threw as hard as he could at a small truck. The snowball splattered unnoticed in the slush well behind its intended target. "Man, you stink!" I said, shaking my head in disappointment.

"Why don't you try if you're so good?"

"I will. Let me show you how it's done." I packed a snowball and picked a car that was driving slower than usual, and I threw a line drive right into the passenger's side, making a loud metallic thud and the driver hit the brakes.

"Oh, crap! Run!" he said, taking off, and I followed behind him as he headed for his neighbor's yard. There was the sound of tires spinning in the slush as the car turned around to look for us. We ran up the shoveled path of his neighbor's, into the back yard, and scrambled over the fence, ducking down out of sight. I could hear a car passing slowly in the street out front, and then the voice of a man.

"You better hope I don't get my hands on you, you little son-of-a-bitch."

"Let's hide in your house," I whispered, crouching behind him.

"If we get up and walk he'll see us," he whispered back. So we stayed there while the car went up and down the street a few times, the man determined to catch us, but eventually getting frustrated and driving off for good.

When we were sure it was safe to come out, we walked out of his yard and back out to the street, stopping in front of the store. We stood there for a moment trying to decide our next move. We came awfully close to getting caught, and neither one of us wanted a beating. "Why don't we think of something else? That was pretty close," I suggested.

"Yah, okay," he reluctantly agreed. Then he stopped talking and stared off in the distance for a moment, like he saw something familiar but wasn't quite sure, his eyes squinting as he tried to focus far away. "No way! Is that who I think it is?" In the distance, I saw someone peddling toward us on a bike, staying on the sidewalk and avoiding the snow.

"Hah, it is! It's mental Porter!" he said, chuckling.

"Who's mental Porter?" I asked, wondering how someone could get such a nickname.

"You don't know mental Porter?" he said incredulously, like everyone on planet earth knew who this guy was.

"No, never heard of him." As he approached, I could see he was a bizarre character. He had ghostly pale skin, a mop of uncombed red hair, wore blue mechanic-type pants with a matching blue shirt, and big clunky work boots. He was a young man, but rode a boy's bike, which made him look large and even odder. There was a shoe-shine box attached to the front handlebars; he made his living riding around and shining shoes wherever he could find a customer.

When he was passing us, Kevin yelled to him, "Hey, mental Porter!" and his bike came to a slow stop about twenty feet in front.

He turned to us, the look in his eye said he did not like this nickname. "Wh—wh—what did you call me?" he stuttered.

"I said, hey mental Porter," Kevin repeated, laughing so his big buckteeth showed.

"You b—b—better cut it out!"

"Na, na, na, mental Porter. Na, na, na, mental Porter!" he continued, encouraged by Porter's anger. He began to peddle his bike, turning toward us. Kevin made a snowball and missed him with a clumsy throw, then started to run toward his house, not wanting to actually face the larger and older Porter. He stopped his bike and picked up a piece of ice from the ground, and made a surprisingly good throw for his appearance. But it flew by Kevin's head and hit a porch window dead center, the sound of shattering glass filling the neighborhood.

"You're in big trouble now, mental Porter. You just broke my window."

"I—I—I didn't mean it. You threw one first." Kevin's mother came out and walked hurriedly to the front.

She looked at the broken window, then down at the pieces of glass sitting in the snow. "What the hell happened? Who did this?" She was furious, looking back and forth at our three faces, not recognizing mine and assuming me a suspect.

Kevin pointed at Porter, "He threw a chunk of ice at me."

"He—he threw one first," Porter said, sounding almost like a small child would when he knew he was in trouble.

"You did this Eddie. You know you're going to pay for this," she said, using his first name with a tone of familiarity, like she had known him for a long time.

He stood for a moment, not knowing what to do, then said apologetically, "I d—don't have any money."

"Well, you can tell that to the police. I called them before I came out. You don't think I'm paying do you? You should have thought about it before you threw something."

"I—I—don't have any money," he repeated, sounding a little fearful knowing the police were coming.

"You just stay right here until they arrive." Then she turned to Kevin, "It's always something with you! You are a pest! Not happy unless you're starting something!"

A moment later, a police cruiser came around the corner with the dispatcher's voice squawking over the radio, and pulled to a stop in front of the house. Two police officers stepped out and questioned Kevin and Porter. There was no need to ask me because Porter did not deny what he did. He just looked at the ground and agreed to a payment plan worked out by the officers, saying it would take time because most of his shoeshine money went to his mother. As he stood there, making a deal with money he didn't have, I felt bad for him, the same sadness I felt for my brother Tommy. I got so angry when people made fun of him. I should have stuck up for Porter, told Kevin to shut his mouth, and maybe none of this would have happened. But I stood there and did nothing, more interested in keeping a new friend than doing what was right. When the police left, Kevin's mother grounded him to the house, which did not last long, and I went on my way.

No, I didn't stick up for Porter that day or any other. On the rare occasions I saw him, usually riding his bike, someone would always scream, "Hey, look it's mental Porter!" There was almost a celebrity air about him, all eyes turning to look as he passed. Sometimes it was people I didn't know, other times it was my friends standing right next to me. And I always remembered Tommy, the way I felt when people ridiculed him. But I kept it inside, worrying that if I spoke up then they would just turn on me. So I quietly sympathized with a tormented man named Eddie Porter.

Gary and I never liked this neighborhood. We didn't like the school, didn't like the people who lived around here, and really hadn't made any good friends. So when mom said we were moving again, we gave no resistance whatsoever. We never even bothered to inquire why. Was it the bad atmosphere? Had Joe Borin drove her crazy? We didn't know and didn't care. We knew we were heading back to South Lawrence and that was it. We were excited to return to everything we knew.

For a little while, things were looking up. The apartment we moved to on Bailey Street was our nicest yet, with some decent furniture, and a cute Polish girl living on the third floor. We were both ten years old, and sometimes she would glance at me out of the corner of her eye as she passed, and I would do the same. There was a dirt alley behind the apartments that ran the entire length of Bailey and Abbot Streets, passing directly between the two roads, and you could look into everyone's back yard while walking down it. But some people had put up tall fences for privacy and you couldn't see anything. There were three garages to the side of our tenement, one belonging to each apartment, and my mother had put a padlock on ours and was secretive about what was inside. Any inquiries about it were quickly brushed off.

Then one day my mother informed us that she had been taking driving lessons, and opened the door to show us a used Dodge Coronet. "What do you think?" she asked, showing off her car proudly.

"Wow, it looks really fast," Gary said, happy and somewhat excited that we actually had a car. It was a sporty looking thing, but was obviously well used. The paint was a faded vomit green color with several small dents and some rust along the bottom.

"Well, I saved up and now I finally have a car. It took me to age forty, but I did it," she said laughing. It wasn't much to look at, but to my mother, on that day, it was an expensive import. She got in and turned the key and the engine roared, my mother's face beaming as she drove up and down the alley. She was still working on her license and didn't dare go far.

We returned to our same schools: Gary to the Salem Street School and me to the John Breen, although both of us would be moving up to the next school at the end of the year. Gary would move on to seventh grade at the Kane School, and I would start the fifth grade at the Salem Street School. Gary had been hanging around with two boys who were completely different, but both bizarre characters in their own way. The first was a kid named Bob Ordway who had the skinniest legs I ever saw. He always wore skin-tight corduroy pants, giving the appearance that two pencils supported his body with hush puppy shoes at the ends. His hair was so blond it was almost white, and he spent enormous amounts of time blow drying it and parting it in the middle. He considered himself to be some kind of a lady's man, but had never actually dated a girl. He was thirteen years old, lived entirely off of junk food like Twinkies and grape soda, and smoked a lot of menthol cigarettes. He would lose his breath with the shortest run; the most un-athletic kid I ever saw.

The other kid, John Perry, was a natural athlete with muscular legs and capable of great bursts of speed. He could walk on his hands a good distance, and was always doing flips and climbing things. He had a habit of making his voice like a girl and screaming as he ran down the street, thinking this to be extremely funny. He liked to imitate famous rock stars, singing their songs and making up some kind of dance that always resulted in him shaking his butt. The only things he had in common with Bobby Ordway was that he also smoked and that they were both extremely sneaky. And when they were together without Gary, they were even sneakier.

Gary's bedroom window was right along the back alley and one day he came home to find that somebody had come in and stolen a bunch of his old comic books. They had decent value, and after awhile he found out that it was Ordway and Perry who had broken in and taken them. They never actually admitted it, but had sold them to Bernie at the used bookstore and he gave a good description of them. Ordway's unique appearance was the dead giveaway. Even though Gary remained friends with them, he never trusted them again. He kept a close eye on them.

It wasn't long before Gary was skipping school with them, smoking like them, and staying out a lot later than he was allowed. He was changing a lot. He didn't like me tagging along with him and his friends, and we often got in fights with each other when my mother wasn't home from work. Yelling at each other, fist fights, throwing things around the apartment, and there were complaints to the landlord. I was constantly calling my mother at work, "Gary hit me ... Gary won't let me hang around with his friends ... Gary threw a rock at me ... Gary gave me a black eye."

And my mother's frustrated voice on the other end, "I'm going to lose my job if you keep calling me like this. The neighbors are complaining. We're going to get evicted." I didn't understand that word, "evicted," until one day we were moving again, and then I finally got it.

We moved a few blocks away on South Union Street. It was a complete nightmare. We had an apartment above a Chinese restaurant and a smoky old barroom. I was never so embarrassed in my life. The front was on a busy road and I absolutely never used that door out of fear someone would see me entering this dilapidated building, instead using the dark stairway at the back of the building. The door was right next to the back entrance of the Chinese restaurant, and sometimes I saw them dumping their garbage out back or taking a smoke break, telling a joke in Chinese and having a laugh. Directly below us was the smoky old barroom filled with old, depressed men. There was a small hole in the floor of Gary's closet, and if you peeped through you could see the top of someone's head seated at the bar.

One night, Gary and I heated a small pot of water on the stove, and when it was fairly warm we poured it down the hole. There was yelling and screaming in the bar below and then pounding fists on our back door, "Open up, you little shits!" We turned the lights out and were as quiet as possible until they went away. To make matters worse, Gary's bedroom window was directly above the side entrance of the bar, and he would stick his head out at closing time and mock the old drunks as they staggered down the sidewalk. "Hey Wino," he would yell, then back in quickly as they looked up to see where this annoying voice came from. They would shake their heads, like maybe they were hearing things, and dismiss it as good liquor as they went along their way.

Diagonally across the street, there was a sub shop on the corner, the Busy Bee. We would sneak down the back stairway and hit their large windows with eggs, then listen as they came out front yelling and swearing in Greek. It didn't take them long to figure out it was the two awful kids above the barroom, and there were complaints to the landlord. We probably would have been evicted again, but this place was such a dump that the landlord was happy to have it rented. My mother began to look weary, and she basically withdrew. She would come home from her job and usually just go to her room and close the door. We made our own dinner most of the time, opening a can of Franco American macaroni and cheese, or some ravioli or something. Gary's room became a cluttered mess of junk thrown everywhere, with a bare mattress on the floor and a blanket he used to cover. My room was a little better; my bed having an actual frame.

We were spending more time with Bobby Ordway and John Perry, skipping school and roaming the streets of Lawrence. This old mill city was filled with things to amuse street kids like us. Old, abandoned mills everywhere that were easy to sneak inside, miles of railroad tracks, with passing trains that we sometimes hopped for a short ride, or the banks of the Merrimac River.

We got into everything. We had climbed up into the clock tower, where you could see over the entire city, were experts on sneaking into the movie theater, had climbed a conveyor belt into an abandoned cement factory, and once inside turned the power on and started up all the machinery. The belts were all turning on their tracks, and from the control room we made the large steel garage doors go up and down. We left just in time, could see the police arriving as we ran down the railroad tracks, completely unaware of things like consequences and punishment. We were young. There was no time except the present moment and we were certain we would live forever. There was nothing in life except the pursuit of immediate adventure, because it was easy to forget your problems when you were having fun.

One night Bobby Ordway actually invited me along with him and Gary. I was surprised because I couldn't stand him, and to him I was nothing more than a nuisance who always wanted to tag along.

"You wanna go or what?" he mumbled, his menthol cigarette hanging from his lip.

"Yah, where are you guys going?" I asked suspiciously, knowing that Ordway was the type to pull something on you at the last second. Make an ass of you in front of other people. He lived for those kinds of moments. But only to younger kids; he rarely picked on anyone his own age.

"Why the heck do you want him to come?" Gary interrupted, irritated by my constant presence, wanting to be with kids his age and only kids his age.

"Lighten up, Gary. It's cool," he said as he blew a puff of smoke from his mouth, and he turned to me. "You want a cigarette?"

"You know I don't smoke. What, you put a firecracker in one? Like you did to Perry."

He laughed a deep and satisfied laugh, like I mentioned his crowning achievement. "I got his ass good, didn't I?" His laugh turned into a cough, the way it usually happens to heavy smokers. "No, I didn't put anything in it. You're just a little pussy and you can't handle a cigarette."

"What's so hard about smoking a cigarette? It doesn't make you cool." The dare was on. He had called me a pussy and the only way out was for me to prove I could smoke one. He handed me a cigarette and I put it in my mouth.

"How old are you again?" he asked, holding up a lit match in front of me.

"I'm eleven."

"Yah, that's about when I started." Then he put the match to the end of my cigarette, and I breathed in deeply as I had seen them do a hundred times.

My lungs burned and my face turned beet red as I coughed uncontrollably. Ordway got a deep sense of satisfaction at this. "See, he's just a little pussy. Ah hah hah hah." This made me more determined to finish the cigarette, so I took shallow puffs. I finished it, but was nauseous for awhile after as we walked along South Union Street.

"Where are we going anyways?" I asked again.

"Yah, where are we going?" Gary joined in.

"We're gonna do a B and E."

"What the hell is a B and E," I said, trying to make my voice sound tough.

Gary stopped walking and turned to Ordway, "You didn't say anything about no B and E."

"Don't worry, I got it under control. It's easy," Ordway said, with fake laughter at the end, the way people do when they want to appear more relaxed than they really are.

"What the hell is a B and E?" I asked again, impatiently and louder this time.

"It's what the cops use for *breaking and entering*. Like when you break into a store and steal stuff," Gary finally answered. He turned to Ordway again, "You serious? You're not just kidding around are you?"

"Dead serious. Why? You gonna pussy out?" he said, flicking a cigarette into the street.

Gary stopped walking again, "Where are you going to do it?"

Ordway stopped and faced Gary. "I'm gonna do it at the Zayre store on Jackson Street. Someone told me the alarm doesn't work."

"I'm not going in," I said, just in case Ordway had some bright idea of sending me in to do his dirty work.

"I didn't think you would. I know you're a little pussy. You can be the lookout."

"You better stop calling me a pussy," I said angrily as I pushed Ordway hard from the back.

"Gary, you better tell your little brother to watch it or I'll kick his ass."

"Go ahead," he answered, knowing that Ordway was too lazy to actually do it.

We walked for a long time in the cool air of the night, crossing the bridge into North Lawrence and traveling up Union Street, then crossing over to Jackson Street, and walking all the way to the Methuen line. We came to a large parking lot. On one side there was a big grocery store, directly across was a department store called Zayre's, and in the corner, there was a bank with drive-through service. I didn't really expect Ordway to go through with this; he often boasted about things he would do, only to back out at the last minute. I thought this was just another one of those times.

He searched the ground for a moment and picked up a few big rocks, stuck them in his pocket and told us to follow him as he walked behind the bank and stood next to a tall wooden fence. He looked around for a minute and made sure no one was around. The businesses in the area were all closed, and there weren't any houses in the immediate area.

"Gary, c'mon let's go. You stay here and keep lookout. If you see the cops whistle loud."

"I can't whistle," I said, somewhat embarrassed.

"Jeez! Then just yell I guess."

"You're really gonna do this?" Gary asked again, still having doubts that he would go through with it.

"How many fricken times you gonna ask me that? We're here, right? Let's go!"

I watched as the two of them crossed the parking lot, walking along the edge to stay in the shadows, and they stopped behind a dumpster, which gave them cover from the street. When it had been quiet for a moment, Ordway crept out from behind the dumpster and threw a rock as hard as he could at the center of an enormous window. It made a loud smacking sound as it bounced off, and he retreated back behind the dumpster. I could see him looking on the ground for something bigger. When at last he found what he was looking for, he walked back out and hurled it at the same window. Whatever he used that time did the trick, as large sheets of glass fell out and shattered noisily on the sidewalk in front, echoing through the large parking lot. They stayed hidden behind the dumpster for a few minutes, seeing if someone would come to investigate the noise.

When no one did, they slowly crept to the broken window and Ordway disappeared inside. Gary looked back and forth for a second, and then he climbed through the window, avoiding any jagged glass as he went through. The air had grown cooler and I was shivering. I wondered what we were doing there. I was worried about Gary and I just wanted to be home in my warm bed. At that moment, I wished I had a normal family, with a father who would never let us out at this time of night, wished we lived in a decent house that I didn't have to sneak into out of embarrassment, and wished I had some nice clothes that weren't from Goodwill.

I saw Gary come back out the window and he ran along the side of the parking lot until he reached me by the fence. "I can't believe you went in," I said, my teeth chattering as I shivered.

"Ordway is fricken nuts! I went in a little way and got scared. He's running all over the place, grabbing all kinds of stuff like he's shopping. He's filling a huge bag. I didn't take anything, I was too afraid." Gary's eyes were open wide, his adrenaline pumping as he told me what it was like in there. "I turned a corner and a mannequin scared the hell out of me. I thought it was a night watchman or something."

Just then, we saw Ordway climbing out of the window, maneuvering two big shopping bags past the jagged edges of the glass as he stepped out, and moved quickly through the shadows toward us. He hadn't made it far when we heard screeching tires and saw a police cruiser turning the corner into the parking lot. The lights flashed and the siren went on, screeching loudly, and disrupting the quiet of the night. A large spotlight shined from the side of the car and found Ordway trying to duck in the shadows. "Stay right where you are," a voice over an intercom echoed throughout the parking lot, and he looked like a cornered animal standing there in the bright light. An officer jumped out and threw him against the side of the cruiser, then put his hands behind his back, the handcuffs glistening in the spotlight as he put them on.

"Let's get the hell out of here," Gary whispered into my ear with urgency, and we sprinted along the fence and turned onto the street. We ran as fast as we could without looking back once. We had made it a good way down Jackson Street when the cruiser pulled up quickly alongside of us. We saw Ordway sitting in the back with a grin on his face, and without a word, the officers climbed out and handcuffed us, pushing us forcefully into the back seat. I couldn't believe this was happening. Only an hour ago I was walking in my neighborhood and now I was handcuffed in the back of a cruiser. We didn't say anything to each other, but Gary gave a look to Ordway that said, "I know you ratted us out."

They pulled into the police station and turned the flashing lights out, then walked us in through the front door, and the dispatcher buzzed the door unlocked. There were a dozen officers roaming around and they all stared at me. "How old are you?" one of them asked, looking me up and down.

"Eleven," I said, looking at the worn tiles of the floor.

"Jesus Christ! Eleven years old and you're breaking into stores! You should be home in bed," he said, looking at the other officers and shaking his head. They booked us and we were allowed our one phone call, which we used to call our mother. Then they led us into a jail cell and slammed the door shut. Gary was accusing Ordway of finking on us, but I wasn't paying attention to their conversation. I began to panic, felt claustrophobic in the tiny cell, and wondered how long we would be there. I lay on the hard iron bench and curled up into a ball to try and warm up. It wasn't much warmer in there than outside.

After an hour or so, an officer unlocked the cell. "Your mother's here," he said and brought us back upstairs to the booking area. My mother was at the desk, telling the officers, "I should have left them here all night. They're out of control. Skipping school, staying out to all hours of the night. I don't know what to do anymore."

"Well, I'll tell you what we're gonna do. We're gonna make a referral to the Division of Youth Services," the officer said, handing my mom the papers for our court date. She looked at us as they unlocked the door and let us out into the lobby where she was standing. "I'm disgusted with the two of you. I hope you're proud of yourselves." We didn't answer; there was no good answer at this moment.

I went to court a few weeks later and the judge screamed at me and placed me on probation for two years. He pointed his finger at me, and threatened, "If you miss probation one time, if you're out of school again, if I see you again, I'll have you locked up in the Division of Youth Services. Don't think because you're young I won't. Do you understand me?"

"Yes, your honor," I said as respectfully as I could. I had no intention of being here again.

It was about this time in my life when I began to feel like I was less than other kids. I became acutely aware of my circumstances. I became ashamed of who I was. I looked at my clothes from Goodwill, my house in a slum, my brother Tommy in a group home, a mother who had just given up, and a father whom I never saw. Why couldn't my life be like other kids? Most of my school friends had a mother and father, lived in decent places, and wore nice clothes. I was bitter and angry. I felt cheated by life.

A friend of mine lived a short walk from my house and came to visit me one day. I noted the look on his face as he surveyed our apartment. When he saw Gary's room, the single mattress on the floor and things just scattered everywhere, I felt like I needed to say something. "Oh, we're going to be buying a house," I said, red faced and trying to get attention away from the clutter.

"Uh, you really think you guys can afford it?' he said with a tone of disbelief. Like the idea of us owning a house was incomprehensible, absurd at best. I didn't show it, but his words cut through me like a knife. I felt like a nothing, and now his words confirmed it. At that moment, I believed I would never be anything. My life would never be anything more than it was. I would always be a scruffy street kid, would always live in dumps, would always wear clothes from Goodwill, and would always feel a sense of shame for who I was.

I listened to the judge for awhile, attending school regularly and not staying out too late, avoiding Ordway and Perry who brought mischief with them whenever they were around. They were magnets for trouble, incapable of walking down the street without finding something to get into. But when your life is chaos, old habits pull you back in without warning. In your longing to escape reality, to be accepted by someone, you disregard consequences and live for the moment. I wanted to just be a normal eleven-year-old. Do the things an eleven-year-old boy would do. Maybe play on a baseball team and go for an ice cream after. Go to a first school dance and maybe dance with a cute girl, or be able to bring friends to my house without being embarrassed. But that life belonged to other kids, so I slipped back into my old ways. Sometimes I would get some food stamps from my mother, skip school, and go to Home-Aid subs and buy a sandwich and candy. They were the only ones who would let you buy a sandwich with food stamps.

I checked in regularly with my Probation Officer, Dick Kelly, who was a stern but decent guy. His office was in the courthouse and I would make the long walk downtown to see him. As I walked up the steps there were always other kids sitting there, smoking, and waiting for their appointments. Gary was assigned to a guy named Mr. Pettoruto, who was a tall man with a black mustache and a permanent scowl on his face. He was mean and intimidating, and I was glad I didn't have to report to him.

On my walk home one day, I took a different route and walked across the bridge by the waterfall and down South Broadway. I didn't have anything to do so I just strolled down the road deep in thought. I stopped in front of a sporting goods store and looked at the display in the window: basketballs, baseball gloves, hockey shirts, and on a small stand, a pair of work boots caught my eye. They were made of nice leather and kids from well-to-do families wore shoes like them. I wanted them badly. If I had nice things like this then maybe I would fit in; would be as cool as everyone else.

As I walked home, I entertained the idea of breaking the window and taking them. There was no point in asking for them. My mother could never afford it. I waited as a train thundered past and crossed the railroad tracks, playing out the scenario in my mind. It wouldn't be so tough; I could do just as Ordway had done—find a big rock and throw it through the window, then grab the shoes and leave. The storeowner was probably rich and it wouldn't be a big deal to him. You can justify anything when you're feeling sorry for yourself.

That night I snuck out of the house shortly after eleven, walked up Abbot Street until I came to the end, and crossed the dark railroad tracks, continuing until I reached South Broadway. During the day, this was one of the busiest streets in the city, but it was quiet and desolate now. Any small noise was magnified in the still of the night. Any car coming could be heard from a good distance. I sat on the curb across from the sporting goods store and looked at the surroundings. On one side of the street a Chinese restaurant, a bicycle shop, and an imported goods store—all closed. On the other side a big Catholic church with a towering steeple, and, about forty feet away, the sporting goods store. The night air was cold and I took out a cigarette that I borrowed from Gary and warmed my hands with the match I used to light it. I walked along the curb until I found a good-sized rock and stuck it in my pocket. I stood there under the streetlight and stared across the road at the shoes in the window.

I crossed over and took a better look at them. It would be so easy: just throw the rock, break the window, and run home to my house. Everything would be better if I just had these shoes. But each time I thought I was ready to do it, I would remove the rock from my pocket, cock my arm to throw, then ... back in my pocket it would go. This continued for several minutes, until I saw the headlights of an approaching car and I ducked around the corner out of sight. When they were well past I came back out and stood on the curb out front again. One more look around, I thought, nothing could be more embarrassing than being arrested for a pair of shoes. I glanced down at my dirty, raggedy sneakers and cursed my cowardice. Then, suddenly furious with having less in life than other kids, I sprang forward and hurled the stone with all my heart. It hit the window dead center and the glass just seemed to disintegrate. A loud, pulsating alarm shrieked and echoed urgently through the streets. The church bell clanged and I knew it must be midnight. I grabbed the shoes from beneath a pile of broken glass and started down the sidewalk. But, strangely enough, I didn't run. I just tucked the boots into my jacket and turned the corner casually toward the railroad tracks, and walked all the way home as though nothing had happened.

I skipped school the next day and when my mother asked about my new shoes, I just told her that I sold some comics. The school must have reported my continued truancy, as I took a day off whenever I felt like it. Not to mention the fact that whenever something bad happened in our neighborhood, we were the immediate suspects. We were once accused of breaking into an antique store down the street, for no other reason except that we lived in the area. We had nothing to do with it, but it reeked of something Ordway and Perry would have done. Then, one afternoon, there was a knock on the door and I heard Gary's probation officer barging in. "Where's your mother?" he shouted angrily.

"She's not back from work yet," Gary answered meekly.

"Where's that little brother of yours? He skipped school for the last time!"

"I don't know." I was around the corner in the kitchen. I knew Gary would cover for me, so I slipped under my bed.

"You don't know. That's a bunch of shit! You never know anything. Just like you didn't know anything about the antique store. Well I'm just gonna take a look around for myself."

"I swear, I don't know where he is," Gary repeated, trying to sound sincere. I could hear Mr. Pettoruto walking around the apartment, opening closet doors, checking behind things, and when he got to Gary's room, I heard him mumbling, "Jesus Christ." His heels sounded loudly against the linoleum of my bedroom floor as he entered. My heart began to pound as his shiny shoes passed closely by my face, and I was certain that he would bend down and catch me. But he never did, just rummaged through my closet and left the room. Before he left, I could hear him in the living room. "Tell your little brother to get his things ready. He's headed for foster homes." I couldn't hear Gary's answer, just the sound of the door closing.

I slid out from under the bed and found Gary grinning in the kitchen. "Man, when he went in your room I thought for sure you were busted."

"So did I! His feet were like one foot from my face! What was he talking about when he left?"

"Oh, he always makes threats. He keeps threatening me with foster homes and he said you're going to one," Gary said, his tone dismissing it as just nonsense. And I felt reassured, figuring that Gary knew him a lot better than I did. If Gary said it was nonsense, then it was.

Not long after my mother was home from work, there was a knock on the door. A woman came in and said she was from the Department of Social Services, and she spoke with my mother in the living room for awhile. Gary and I were in the kitchen, only catching bits and pieces of the conversation. "Who the heck is that?" he asked me curiously.

"I don't know. I never saw her before," I said shrugging.

"What does she want?" he asked rhetorically, knowing that I had no answers.

I noticed what a young and pretty woman she was as she came walking into the kitchen and stood before me, looking at me for a moment before she spoke. "Kenny, you need to get your things together. You're coming with me," she said in a stern voice that didn't fit her soft face and easy manner.

"Going where?" I asked, completely forgetting about Mr. Pettoruto's visit.

"You're going to spend some time in foster care." She studied my face for a reaction, wondering if I would bolt out the door. But I just stood there. It was as though I became a spectator in my own life. It wasn't really happening to me. I gave no resistance, no struggle whatsoever. There was no fight in me at that moment, just a quiet surrender.

Gary watched silently, shocked as I packed my clothes into a green garbage bag. I had no suitcase and there was nothing else worth taking. When she walked back into the living room Gary grabbed my arm, "What are you doing?" I turned to him and we stood face-to-face. "You're not really going with her, are you?"

I shrugged passively, and he saw there was no fight in me. His eyes were watery and a tear started down his face. I hadn't seen him cry since we were little boys and it made the situation even more unreal. I just stood there blankly, and I felt a complete numbness inside, like a deeper part of me was shutting off. Tears came from both his eyes now, and his voice was pleading, "C'mon, you don't have to go with her. We can run away. We can run far away."

When he realized I truly had no fight in me, he turned and ran down the back stairway. I walked into the living room and looked at my mother's face. She had a sad, but weary and defeated look, like she knew this day would come. For a second I remembered sitting on her lap as a little boy, her smiling face looking down at me, both of us counting apples and giggling. The social worker stood silently, then slowly walked toward the door, and motioned for me to follow. "Goodbye, Mom," was all I said, and I closed the door behind me.

7

We drove on into the dark of the night, the social worker making small talk from time to time. "My name's Patty, by the way." I didn't answer her, just kept my head turned to look out my window. She looked like a *Patty*; the name suited her. As far as I was concerned, she was my enemy, took me from my home and was taking me far away into the dark. I knew not where. Only that it was someplace I didn't belong. "Do you like sports?" she asked after awhile, searching for something to catch my interest.

"I guess so," I mumbled into my shoulder, my head resting there and looking at the moonlit landscape as we drove.

She eventually gave up on the small talk and got down to business. "I'm taking you to a temporary placement until we find something more permanent. This all came about kind of sudden. We didn't really have a chance to find the right place. It will probably be a few days until we do."

"When can I go home?"

"That depends on a lot of things. But for now you need to adjust and do the best you can."

"Where are we going?"

"To a home in Lynnfield. They're good people."

After an hour or so, she turned into the driveway of a neatly kept white house, the porch light shining down onto the path as though they expected someone. I tensed up as she turned the engine off. I had been through this before—the uncomfortable feeling of being at the mercy of strangers—feeling out of place. Not wanting to go into the refrigerator for a drink when they were watching you, afraid to take too long in the bathroom, sleeping in a strange bed. The social worker rang the bell and both Mrs. and Mr. Pritchard came to the door. They were an older couple. He had white hair and she looked a lot older than my mother. "Come in, come in," Mrs. Pritchard said, smiling at me.

Mr. Pritchard shook my hand and introduced himself, "Mr. Pritchard, what's your name?"

"Kenny Tingle," I answered, and waited for the usual response.

"Oh, that's a funny name. What kind of name is that?"

"I guess it's English."

"What a cute little name," Mrs. Pritchard said, lightly pinching my cheek.

They talked with the social worker for a few minutes and I sat in the living room and looked around. It was a clean and well-kept house. When she left they showed me around a little, where I would sleep, and then the finished basement with a nice weight set and posters of rock stars all over the wall—guitarists with intense looks on their faces and veins popping out of their arms as they played. "We have a teenage son," Mrs. Pritchard explained, as though I might think this was her room. I watched TV for awhile to pass the time, Mrs. Pritchard offering me a snack and asking if I needed anything, and waited for bedtime so I could escape the world for the night.

At around nine o'clock, I heard a commotion outside the door and Mr. Pritchard was walking their son in. He had a dazed look on his face and some blood was coming from his lip. "What happened? What happened?" Mrs. Pritchard kept asking frantically.

"I don't know. I guess he punched me in the mouth," he said, sluggishly and slightly confused.

Mr. Pritchard kept shaking his head. "This is your friend? What the hell kind of friend does something like this?" He was well built from the weights and looked to me about eighteen or nineteen. Apparently, according to their son, his friend pulled into their driveway and then just punched him in the mouth for no particular reason. Just drove off and left him lying there. And that was the only explanation given.

I never really fell asleep that night. I tossed and turned, over and over, made multiple trips to the bathroom, and lay there thinking about my family. I missed my mother. I missed Gary. I even missed Tommy, although he didn't live with us and I only saw him once in awhile. I wondered if I would ever see them again. And when dawn came, I was still partially awake. I had been half asleep at best for most of the night.

I was only with the Pritchard family for a couple of days when the social worker called and said they had found a more permanent placement. I could tell they were relieved, had grown tired of trying to entertain an eleven-year-old, and their son didn't like me in the basement touching his weights and whatever else I could find to keep myself busy. I was relieved too. I was bored out of my mind after two days of just hanging around in limbo. This was one move I was looking forward to. There was another change also; I was assigned a permanent social worker that would follow my case.

He came shortly before lunch and I was a little startled by his appearance. He was a big man, big in every sense of the word, tall and morbidly obese, with a fluffy brown beard. He held out his large hand for me to shake, and my hand disappeared into his. "Jim Gallagher," he said smiling, "and you must be Kenny?"

I nodded. "Yah, that's me."

"Let me fix you something for lunch before you go," Mrs. Pritchard offered.

"Oh, thanks for offering, but we're gonna stop on the way and pick something up. I figured Kenny and I would stop at McDonalds and grab a bite. You do like McDonalds?" he asked, looking down at me.

"I love it," I said, and he patted me on the back and laughed.

"What kid doesn't like McDonalds?" He glanced at his watch and then at me, "Got your stuff? Ready to go?"

I held my bag up. "I've been ready for awhile." Mrs. Pritchard gave me a kiss on the cheek and we walked out the door.

When we got to the driveway I thought it strange that a man as big as him would have such a small car. He drove a Dodge Dart, and when he got in the driver's seat, the whole car tilted over to that side. I actually looked down at him from the passenger seat. I felt a little awkward going down the road in this slanted car, hoping that people didn't mistake us as father and son. "Is the new house around here?" I asked, looking at Jim and noticing that the bottom of the steering wheel dug a little into his stomach. He could let go of the wheel sometimes and the car would continue straight.

"No, actually it's in a small southern New Hampshire town called Hampstead. Ever been there?"

"No I haven't." The New Hampshire border wasn't far from Lawrence, but to me it was a faraway place, like Wyoming or something. With the exception of a week in Scotland with my mother when I was three, I hadn't really been out of Massachusetts.

"Ooh, look, there's a McDonalds," he said, and he put his directional on and pulled in. I found a seat and Jim went to the counter and ordered for both of us, returning a moment later with a tray full of food. He couldn't squeeze into the small two person table I picked.

"You would think they could make these a little bigger," he complained, a little red faced as he slid uncomfortably into a booth. I worked on my hamburger and fries, Jim finishing a few Big Macs and washing it down with a shake before I was half done. He glanced a few times at my food, then would turn around and look at the surroundings.

When I finished we got back in the car, the Dodge Dart tilting over again, and started down the highway. "You're going to be staying with the Gregori's," he began. "They're a well-to-do family. They own a real estate business; have a nice house and a whole bunch of land. They have four kids of their own . . . all girls."

"What!" I gasped, and he laughed heartily.

"Ah, c'mon, it won't be that bad. You'll be the only boy; the center of attention."

"Oh, great," I said, rolling my eyes. I knew nothing about girls, only that I was uncomfortable around them.

"Well, if it makes you feel any better, they're mostly older than you," he said laughing. Jim almost always laughed after he said something—a jovial and likable guy.

The Gregori family lived in a small town named Hampstead, and when we pulled into the driveway, I couldn't help but notice behind the house. It was a large, wide-open, grassy field that rolled softly until way in the distance where it met the woods. They owned thirty-five acres of land that extended well beyond the grassy field and deep into the woods. I got out of the car with that same apprehension of walking into a strange house, my heart speeding up. Both husband and wife greeted us at the door of their big, blue home and invited us into the kitchen. They both had dark hair, although he had lost most of his, and appeared a little older than my mother. We sat at a large, fancy wood table and I felt more shy than usual. I leaned forward and put my arms on the table, then buried my face in them—the way you would take a nap on your school desk. I didn't want to make any eye contact. There was an uncomfortable pause for a moment, and then Jim broke the ice and talked with them a little. I didn't pay attention to what they were saying, and when they spoke to me directly, I answered with a "Yup" or "Nope" without lifting my head. Mrs. Gregori tried to get my attention a few times, but I continued to look down. I just didn't want to be in a stranger's house anymore.

"Oh, we were hoping to take him to Florida with us," she said to Jim, and I sat up straight.

"Florida! I'm staying." They all laughed heavily for a moment, breathing a sigh of relief that I had not gone into some kind of withdrawal.

I could hear the girls giggling in the next room, every so often taking a quick peek around the corner to look at me. Their oldest daughter was eighteen, and she was always out with her boyfriend or something. The two middle daughters were fourteen and fifteen. The fifteen-year-old, Elizabeth, had long, shiny blonde hair, blue eyes and was very pretty. The fourteen-year-old, Sally, had short, dark hair, with a pretty face and a case of acne that she was extremely sensitive about. The youngest, Joanie, was only nine but her hormones were a little active for her age. She was always trying to cuddle up to me, wanting to play some kind of boyfriend-girlfriend type of game. I could tell this made the mother a little nervous, and that made me a little nervous, so I tried to avoid Joanie if I could. She even tried to trick me into kissing her, in one of her little games, but there was no way my first kiss would be with a nine-year-old. She had dark hair like Sally and was very cute, though.

The Gregori's were really nice people and always treated me well. I had my own nice bedroom, went to a fancy hair stylist, and they bought me nice clothes that made me look like a little preppy. I didn't mind at all. It was a good feeling to have confidence in the way I looked. Mr. Gregori taught me how to shoot a gun in the backfields, and we once shot an owl in his barn. The rifle banged and echoed loudly, the owl fell from the air, making loops as he did, and then thumped on the wooden floor. That was the only hunting I ever did, if you could call it that. Their home was surrounded by nature, and sometimes deer would come close to the house to taste the salt lick that Mr. Gregori had put out. I saw beavers, and large birds like heron would land in the field and drink water from puddles. I never saw these kinds of things in Lawrence.

I behaved well there, fit in well, and with the exception of a fight in school, there were no problems. Some spoiled kid who had never been in a fight decided to antagonize me, not knowing I grew up in a city where you had to defend yourself often. He didn't even know how to block a punch, and I hit him so many times that a crowd of kids stopped me out of sympathy. He had bruises all over his face and I felt sorry for him. But he never bothered me again. I made a few friends, and instead of Florida, the Gregori's took me with them to North Carolina to see some family. They decided to drive down. They rented a van, and it seemed like it took forever to get there—stuck in the back with Joanie and all her little games. She leaned on me one time to change position, and put her hand in a place where she shouldn't have, then moved it away quickly. I lay there a little shocked and not knowing what to do; her hand gone before I had a chance to react. Sally saw this and said, "Mom, Joanie just put her hand on Kenny's private and he didn't do anything about it."

"Joanie, did you do that!" Mrs. Gregori yelled from the front of the van.

"It was an accident. I'm sick of Sally. I hate her!" she yelled back. Then it was quiet for awhile and I lay there red faced and humiliated.

I mostly got along with the sisters, only an occasional fight. Sometimes, when I was trying to mind my business, they would pick on me about something stupid, and then make it look like it was completely my fault. They were experts at this. And if I tried to retreat away, they would follow and continue to irritate me. Once I actually went out to the field and just lay there in the cold until the parents came home, just to get away from them. Another time, in a moment of anger, I called Sally a pizza face. She wouldn't leave me alone and I knew how sensitive she was about her acne. This was a scandal in the house. When Sally told her mother, with no mention of the nasty things she had said to me, Mrs. Gregori yelled angrily at me. "You need a good slap in the mouth!"

I noticed a tension growing between Mr. and Mrs. Gregori, and I sensed it was because of me. I saw them one time sitting in their car in the driveway, the engine off and the two of them talking for a long time. I couldn't hear what they were saying, but Mrs. Gregori was crying and he was arguing with her. I didn't find out until years later that they wanted to adopt me, had decided to move to North Carolina, and wanted to take me with them. Of all people, my father objected. It did not come as a shock when I learned I would be moving on again. Since that day I saw them in the driveway, I sensed a change was coming.

I lay on my bed and listened to the little radio they put in my room for me, and thought about everything: my family, wondering where they were and what they were doing, about Lawrence and the things I used to do there, and thought about my old friends. A sad song came on, "I'm not in love, so don't forget it, it's just a silly phase I'm going through," and then a soft voice singing over angelic music, "be quiet, big boys don't cry, big boys don't cry." I didn't let myself cry.

They wanted to make sure this new foster home was a good fit, so I spent a weekend there to see how it would work out. It was in Salem, Massachusetts, which was a lot more like Lawrence than Hampstead. Like Lawrence, Salem was an old city and there were a lot of similarities. There were streets of three tenements in both, plenty of street-wise kids in both, although many more in Lawrence. And there were a few small mill buildings in Salem, but nothing compared to the colossal mills of my city. Lawrence was bigger, and definitely meaner, but Salem had its neighborhoods. I stayed in the home of two women who lived together, Louise and Claire, although Louise was always referred to as Lou. They lived on the bottom floor of a two-family home. Lou's mother owned the house, and her sister June lived upstairs with her family. She married a guy named Jack Reynolds and had three kids. Marie, the oldest at seventeen, who drank Pepsi all day and smoked like a chimney, watching her soap operas religiously. Johnny, the middle kid, sixteen and muscular from weight lifting, and Joey who was one year older than me and swore constantly.

It was a good fit. They took to me right away. They had only one foster kid in the past and he was a great guitarist, but got into drugs and was stealing from them. After he left, he even broke into their house and robbed them. He was older when he got there, and they liked the idea that I was young enough to have some influence on. Besides that, everyone said I looked a lot like Lou—could pass for her son. Lou was a stocky woman with short hair and glasses. Claire had longer hair, was pretty, but always had dark bags under her eyes from lack of sleep. She was quiet most of the time, letting Lou do the talking and making most of the decisions. However, she could get moody and Lou would back off and give her space.

They really wanted me to stay there, and when they found out my birthday was coming they said they would buy me a bike if I came. I really wanted to stay there too; not because of the bike, but because this place reminded me of my home. Not to mention I hit it off with the boy upstairs, Joey, who was close to my age. We had a lot in common: we both swore, would smoke cigarettes whenever we could get our hands on some, and were generally little punks.

It was settled; this would be my new home.

On the morning I was leaving the Gregori's, I found a green garbage bag and stuffed all my clothes inside. Mrs. Gregori saw me and found a small suitcase and put it on the table. "What are you doing with that trash bag? Use this suitcase."

"It's not mine. I'm just going to use this bag," I said, tucking a magazine in between the clothes.

"You can keep it. It's all right."

"I don't want anything that isn't mine," I said, looking down at the floor. She began to cry heavily; breathing heavily.

"You're not leaving here with a garbage bag. You put your clothes in here right now!" She slammed the suitcase on the table. I looked up at her, the tears steadily flowing down her face.

"I came here with a garbage bag and that's how I'm going to leave."

"You just want them to feel sorry for you. So they buy you a bike," she said sobbing.

"I didn't ask for a bike. They said they wanted to buy me one."

She put her hands in her face for a moment, and then left the room without saying anything further. I said goodbye to Mr. Gregori and the four daughters. I would miss them, as much as I was capable of missing anyone anymore.

Jim picked me up, and when we were a short distance from the house, he turned to me and said, "You know what I like about you Kenny?"

"No, what?" I answered.

"You have the ability to change just like that," he said, snapping his fingers for emphasis. "Most people can't adjust like you do. You can just change right away."

I didn't really understand what he meant, but deep down I felt this was his way of trying to make me strong. Like he was worried about me, and thought a word of encouragement was necessary.

I was quiet for the entire drive, looking out the window at all the people around me just going about their business. It didn't seem fair that someone was just happily shopping and I was headed to another foster home. I felt like rolling the window down and shouting, "Hey! I hope you're having a good time. Do you want to know where I'm going? Do you give a crap?" Jim fidgeted with the radio knob, looking for a good song as he headed up route 114. He would try one, but then static would cut in and he would change again, finally settling on one clear station. A familiar song by Bob Segar came on, "We've got tonight, who needs tomorrow, we've got tonight, babe, why don't you stay? ... Turn out the light, come take my hand now," At that moment, I resented Bob Segar. He was with some beautiful woman, turning the lights out, and I was driving with a social worker, everything I owned in a green garbage bag on my lap.

When we got to the house, we walked into the kitchen and I saw a banner hanging on the wall with the words, "*Welcome Back Kenny We Love You.*" There was a shiny new bike parked underneath, Lou and Claire standing there with a smile, waiting for my reaction. I burst into a smile, overwhelmed by this welcome. I didn't know what to say. After one weekend, they said they loved me. The room was full of people: Jim, Lou, Claire, Joey, and Johnny from upstairs, and their mother, June. "Wow," was all that I could come up with. They all laughed for a minute and I thanked them for the bike.

"Thanks a lot. I thought I had to wait for my birthday?" I said shyly, all eyes on me.

"We wanted you to have it now," Claire said smiling, and we all had cake and ice cream.

That afternoon I rode my bike all over the neighborhood. "Hey, I'll show you around," Joey said, hopping on his bike. "Follow me." We went around the block, and I studied all the different kids I saw playing in the street. Joey would tell me a little about each one as we passed. "See her, that's Heidi. She's easy," he said, pointing at a thin girl with dark hair and glasses. "See him, that's Danny. He thinks he's tough. He's a pussy," he told me as we passed an athletic-looking kid with a sneer on his face. I did my share of swearing, but Joey couldn't complete a sentence without a few strong adjectives. The neighborhood could easily have fit into Lawrence. They lived on Beaver Street—a long row of mostly two-family homes—a narrow one way road that people were constantly getting confused on, making awkward U-turns in the middle.

Lou had registered me at the local school, the Bowditch, and I would start the next morning. I already had decent clothes from the Gregori's, but they went out and got me a few more things anyway. Everyone wanted to dress me up. For my first day of school, they laid out some clothes, and picked a blue baseball-type of shirt for me. It had sleeves that went three quarters of the way down my arm, and one big word in white letters on the front—*Jock*. That was it; that one big gaudy word. No one wore such a tacky shirt. Even if you were a jock, you didn't advertise it for the world to see. It seemed to me that this was a shirt for someone who wasn't a jock but wanted everyone to think they were. I didn't want to wear it, but they had been so nice to me and I was afraid they would be offended if I didn't.

I tried to make my way around that first day of school as inconspicuously as possible, hindered by this bright blue shirt that advertised athletic prowess, clumsily trying to find my classes each time the bell rang. The curious looks of other students telling me I stuck out like a sore thumb. I ate my lunch in a corner of the cafeteria, leaning forward in an attempt to hide the front of my shirt. A small group of boys stood in the doorway, looked at me, and then the biggest one yelled across the room, "Hey, Jock, you wanna play kickball with us?"

I looked them over for a second. They looked like a pretty good bunch of guys. "Yah, sure," I said nodding, finishing a bite of food. I followed them outside to the schoolyard.

They used whatever they could for bases: a paper plate for first, a can for second, the cover of a magazine for third, and a circle of chalk for home. The boy who had invited me to play was Bruce Moody, a tall and stocky blond kid. He always wore big and expensive work boots. He picked me for his team, trusting my shirt to be true. When he was up he blasted the ball with the steel toe of his boot and it bounced out of the hands of a kid in the outfield. He made it safely to second base. Then it was my turn. I walked up to the plate nervously, knowing great things were expected of someone who advertised they were a jock. The pitcher rolled the ball at me and I kicked as hard as I could, the ball shooting off toward third, and I sprinted to first. The first baseman was standing a little in the way and we collided slightly. "Hey, watch it," he said, staring me down. Then he pushed me.

"Ooohh," went a chorus of boys' voices, and I knew all eyes were on us. This was a moment of truth. If I didn't defend myself, I would be shamed. I pushed him back even harder.

"You watch it. You were in the way!" He grabbed my shirt with both hands trying to push me back. My fists pounded his stomach, like two pistons going back and forth rapidly.

He doubled over breathless, and I threw him to the ground. "Ooohh," the chorus of voices went again. "Hogan got his ass kicked! Jock kicked Hogan's ass!" I didn't want to fight. I didn't want to be a tough guy. I just wanted friends and a little respect, and by standing up at that moment, I had respect as long as I went to the Bowditch. They all became my close friends, even Hogan. There was Bruce Moody, the biggest of all and the leader. Tommy Doran, who reminded me of Popeye; he had long skinny legs, exaggerated by the cowboy boots he wore, a skinny body, and big muscular arms that looked out of place. Randy Benjamin, a brown-haired, totally average looking kid. And Peter Brookings, black haired and a slight sneer at all times. Hogan was sort of the black sheep of the crowd—picked on often.

They brought me into their little gang, showing me the alley behind the school where we all met every morning to sneak a cigarette, listen to Led Zeppelin, Pink Floyd, The Who, and whoever else was "cool" at the time. There was a set of graffiti-covered stairs that led into the back of the gym, and that was where we sat. Talking about music, girls, and the teachers we couldn't stand, boasting of reprimands and detentions. You never knew who would show up there, cruising up after school on their ten-speed bike. Dubious characters coming through at times, and marijuana soon found its way to the alley. One by one, everyone had broken down and tried it. I held out, giving excuses why I couldn't smoke it—my foster parents would smell it, I would get sick, or maybe the police were around the corner.

In the seventh grade, the dances at the local YMCA became wildly popular. One day after school, Bruce found me outside and asked me if I wanted to go with them. "Hey, Ken, we're all heading to the dance tonight. If you want to go, then meet us in the alley at seven. Maybe Cindy Rybicki will be there, woooo!"

"Let me ask my foster parents," I said, laughing. Everyone had been teasing me about this girl. She was one of the prettiest girls in the school and I had been told several times she liked me. I didn't know what to do. I never had a girlfriend before, and I was always shy and uncomfortable around them.

Lou and Claire said I could go, so after dinner I took a shower and picked my best clothes. I blow-dried my hair and looked in the mirror for a long time, checking for a rogue pimple or any other imperfection I could hide. "Jeez, how long you gonna take? You look beautiful, okay," Joey Reynolds said walking past the bathroom. The Reynolds came downstairs whenever they wanted. There was no distinct boundary between upstairs and downstairs, as relatives sometimes do when they live in a duplex.

"You're just jealous," I shot back, and he laughed from the kitchen. "Are you going?" I asked.

"No! Those dances are for wimps. Wimps!" he said, scornfully. But I knew better than that. Joey never took care of his teeth, and at thirteen, he already had some visible rot in the front. He was insecure about this, and this was the real reason he didn't want to go. Joey was actually a sensitive kid who hid behind this mask of swearing and sarcastic toughness, but would lie on his bed listening to love songs when he thought no one was around.

I met Bruce and the gang in the alley at seven as agreed on. They were all there already, sitting on the steps, joking and smoking cigarettes. "Kennneyyy," Bruce said with an appreciative exaggeration of my name, like he didn't think I could make it. "You're just in time. We're heading for the packy." Packy was short for Package store, the place where you could buy liquor.

We left the alley and took the short walk down the street, standing on the corner to the side of the liquor store. It was on a busy road and we took great care to look out for the police. They weren't stupid. If they drove by and saw a bunch of kids hanging out right there then they would know what we were up to. The game was simple: wait until you saw someone heading in and ask them to buy for you. Sometimes you only had to ask one or two people; other times it took forever to get someone to finally agree.

"Hey, here comes someone," Peter said, and we watched an old man get out of the car.

"Forget it. That guy would never," I said. I imitated an old man's voice, "*You little whipper snappers should be home in bed. I'm gonna call the police on you!*" and we all laughed for a minute.

"Hey, who's gonna ask anyway?" Bruce inquired.

"I'm not. No way, my father might see me," Tommy Doran said.

"How about you, Benj? You're the only one with balls," Bruce said to Randy. Benj was a short nickname for Benjamin.

"Yah, I'll do it." Bruce's patronizing comment about "balls" worked as intended.

A younger guy pulled up out front and Randy rushed over and waited as he climbed out of the car. "Hey, you think you could get us something if we—"

"Forget it. I'm not getting arrested for you," the man quickly cut in, and walked into the store shaking his head. We waited until he was long gone, and spotted a hippy-looking guy coming down the street toward us.

"Hey, if we give you the money would you pick us up something inside?" Randy asked as he passed us. The man stopped and looked at us, twisting his handlebar mustache with his fingers as he pondered our request.

"What's in it for me?" he asked, matter-of-factly. We looked back and forth at each other, and figured out how much money we had.

"What do you want?" Bruce asked.

"Buy me a six of Budweiser and you got a deal." We put our money together, told him what we wanted, and agreed to meet him around the corner out of sight. He met us as promised, handing a large brown bag to Bruce, the bottles clanking as he did.

"You guys keep it low. Don't go getting busted," he said, and went along his way with the six-pack he earned.

We went back to the alley and Bruce handed out the booze, "Whose Bacardi?"

"That's me and Tommy's!" Pete quickly answered, afraid some-one else might claim it. "Who's Mad Dog 20/20?"

"Mine," I said grinning. It was a cheap, but very strong wine. I had no tolerance for hard liquor. I would vomit if I drank very much of it. Bruce and Randy were splitting a bottle of Peppermint Schnapps. We sat around for awhile trying to finish what we bought: me sipping the Mad Dog, Bruce and Randy passing the bottle back and forth between them, making sour faces each time they took a sip, Pete and Tommy drinking that powerful Bacardi. Carrying it around with us was out of the question. The more we finished, the sillier we became. Things not usually considered funny suddenly becoming very funny. Our voices getting louder, cigarettes being lit, an easy euphoria coming over the bunch of us.

"Whoa, what time is it?" Tommy suddenly interrupted, disrupt-ing an argument about who was the best guitarist.

"Almost 8:30," Randy said, glancing at his watch. "Oh man, we better get to the YMCA!" The dances started at 7:30 and ended around 10:30 or 11:00. We had already missed the first hour so we ran down Essex Street, laughing and pushing each other around as we did, knocking over a trashcan or two. We were out of breath as we arrived outside. Randy gave us all a piece of gum to cover up the alcohol smell. The loud music could be heard as we walked up the stairs, paying our two dollars to a man as we went in.

The dance was held in a dimly lit gymnasium. A disk jockey stood on a platform, bending down to take requests from time to time. Most of the kids were just standing against the wall, and out in the middle a small group of girls danced together, giggling and looking around to see who was watching them. As we entered the disk jockey played someone's request, "We don't need no education. Hey! Teacher, leave those kids alone!" As it came on a crowd of girls screamed and ran to the dance floor, and suddenly it was full of people, a strobe light flashing off beat. "You guys can stand around if you want, but I'm finding a chick to dance with," Bruce said, and he disappeared into the crowd.

I stood against the wall, talking to friends and trying to look cool, like I really didn't want to be there. Then across the room, I saw Cindy Rybicki. She was a tall blonde girl with blue eyes, always wore Levi corduroys, and clogs that made her stand a few inches above me. I had never danced with a girl before. Tommy Doran caught me looking across at her and nudged my arm. "Go ahead. I heard she likes you."

"No way! What if she says no?" I said defiantly.

"So what. No big deal. Girls tell me no all the time. You want me to ask her for you?"

"Yah, sure," I agreed. At least if she rejected me it wouldn't be to my face. I could claim Doran was full of crap and I had never really wanted to dance with her.

He made his way in and out of the crowd, disappearing for a second, and then I saw him talking to her. She glanced over at me and I turned the other way as though I had no idea what was going on. He returned a moment later and grinned.

"She said yes." At that moment, I felt proud and nervous. Now I actually had to dance with her, stand face-to-face, and carry on a conversation. The disc jockey played a slow song, "Hello girl it's been awhile, you'll be glad to know I've learned how to laugh and smile ... I go crazy, when I look in your eyes I still go crazy." I made my way across the floor awkwardly, her turning to look at me as I walked up.

"Would you like to dance?"

"Okay," she said, smiling and blushing.

I put my hands on her hips, the way I saw other people doing, and she put her hands on my shoulders. I felt warm inside when she touched me, and I could smell her perfume, could smell the shampoo in her hair. Her hips felt so soft. We looked at each other's faces as we slowly turned in circles, hypnotized by the moment and the soft music. "Do you come to these dances a lot?" I asked her, struggling for the right thing to say.

"No, not really," she said shyly. She put her head on my shoulder and her long blonde hair brushed my nose, my senses filling with her. I wanted this song to last forever; to live in this moment forever.

Another slow song came on, "Do you want to dance again?" I asked hopefully.

"Okay," she said, smiling. At least it would last a little longer.

I left the dance that night on top of the world, elated. My mind filled with the thoughts of a pretty girl. She became my girlfriend not long after that. We never went on dates or anything. Her strict parents never really let her out and we were barely able to even talk on the phone. I wanted to know what it would be like to kiss her. I had never kissed a girl and hoped the first time would be with her, but we were never alone and no opportunity ever came up. I tried to never let myself get too attached to anyone, but I definitely had a case of puppy love. I was surprised how much it really hurt when we broke up.

There was a place on Boston Street called the AOH—the Ancient Order of Hibernians. It was an Irish club with a bar downstairs and a large empty room upstairs, sometimes used for functions, other times converted into a makeshift gymnasium. I started to take boxing lessons there; figured it would help if I had to defend myself. The trainers worked me hard, telling me, "Tingle, now that's a name people will remember." For the first time I wasn't embarrassed by my name. The man said it was one worth remembering. There were hours of pounding the heavy bag, jumping rope, push-ups, and I would leave sweaty and exhausted. After awhile I was sparring with other fighters in my weight class: the wiry Chris Post, who had some moves but in the end I usually knocked down, and the Italian kid, Ernie, who I went toe-to-toe with, slugging and trading blows to the head. He was a much more experienced fighter than I was, and I was happy to fight him to a draw. The trainers signed me up for the Silver Mittens competition, but for whatever reason we never actually went.

Lou and Claire always took good care of me. They took dinner seriously in that house, always home-cooked chicken, steak, and large salads. I gained some weight there. I sat around watching these new and amazing things: MTV—music videos all day long—or HBO. I was comfortable there, had friends and security, but deep down I always longed for my mother and my city. Jim Gallagher had mentioned that my mother had found a new job and moved to a better part of Lawrence; that she wanted me to come back home. They were going to hold a meeting at the Department of Social Services soon, and as the day came closer I could tell Lou and Claire were anxious. I knew they wanted me to stay.

I didn't quite know what to do. If I stayed, my mother would be hurt. If I left, Lou and Claire would be hurt.

"Why would you even want to go back to Lawrence?" Lou asked one morning over breakfast.

"I don't know," I said, not really able to put together a good answer. One that wouldn't hurt feelings.

"That place is nothing but trouble. Just tell them there's nothing there for you." Claire was sitting on the other side of the table, and she nodded sadly in agreement with Lou. They knew I was going for the meeting the next day, and that was all they ever said about it. Making things even harder was the fact that they had been extra nice to me for the last few days, making my favorite foods and not getting angry with me about anything.

The next day Jim came and we took the long drive down 114 all the way to Lawrence. I quietly looked over the familiar landscape as we went along. As we entered the city I saw the stadium and beyond that the project; memories of Gary and me running wild came rushing back. As we traveled down South Union Street, I saw our old apartment above the Chinese restaurant and laughed at the memory of pouring water into the bar. We crossed the green metal bridge, the tires humming familiarly on the grids below, and turned onto Essex Street. The meeting was downtown in the Bay State building. We took the elevator up a few floors into the Department of Social Services, a woman meeting Jim and me in the hallway. "The meeting is in the conference room," she said, motioning for us to follow. I had never seen this woman, and I was a little disappointed. I had hoped it would be the social worker Patty who had taken me to that first foster home.

She opened the door to a large room with a big wooden table that could seat a dozen people. My mother was sitting there with another woman. Her face lit up when she saw me. "Kenny!" she said happily.

"Hi, Mom." I grinned back shyly as I sat down.

"Okay, why don't we get started," Jim said, squeezing into the biggest chair he could find. "As you know we're here to decide what's best for you Kenny. To see if you're ready to come home." I nodded in acknowledgment. "Your mother's situation has changed," he continued. "She feels that she is ready for you to come back. She has moved to a better place and feels financially stable enough to make things work. A lot of this depends on you, Kenny. Do you feel ready to come home?" I glanced around the table as all eyes focused on me, and saw my mother's hopeful face. She smiled at me. There was a long pause.

"There's nothing here for me," I said, the words just falling out, almost involuntarily. My mother's face just sort of dropped, her smile disappearing and her eyes becoming watery. The years had toughened my mother and she rarely ever cried, but I could tell she was fighting back the tears.

"What do you mean? Don't you want to come home?" she asked softly, looking at the expression on my face.

"I guess there's nothing here for me," I said, again, looking away, not able to bear the expression on my mother's face.

It was quiet for a moment, then Jim said, "Well, we can try this again in a few months," trying to lessen the blow to my mother.

The whole drive back I felt horrible. I was never a sensitive kid, never really considered other people's feelings. But I knew I had hurt my mother deeply, and the expression on her face haunted me for days. When I got back, Lou and Claire asked what happened. "I told them there was nothing in Lawrence for me," I explained, and their faces broke into a relieved smile. I went to my room without saying anything further and lay on the bed for a long while—feeling

I had done the wrong thing. Deep down I knew it wasn't right to hurt my mother like that.

I continued my life as usual, meeting my friends for a game of Nerf football on Saturday mornings, hanging around Gallows Hill weekend nights and drinking beer when we could get it, going to YMCA dances, but in the back of my mind knowing I wanted to return to my home. Lawrence was a part of me. Had become a part of my very soul. Had worked its way into my bones. No matter where I lived the rest of my life, I would always be Kenny Tingle from Lawrence. It was as much a part of me as the color of my hair. I felt an almost spiritual connection to it, like I was born there for a reason. Like all the immigrants who moved there in the 1800s to work in the colossal mills that lined the banks of the Merrimac River; coming from Italy, France, Canada and other corners of the earth. The same hand of destiny that brought them there had put me there also.

One afternoon Claire asked me to bring out the garbage. She was in a very bad mood to begin with, and I told her no. I wasn't wearing a shirt and she angrily slapped me across the back, so hard it could be heard across the apartment. "Go to your room! I don't even want to see your face!" she said, shaking with anger. I had caught her at a very bad moment. I went to my room, my back stinging as though I had been whipped. Lou heard the commotion and came to my room, looked at the red handprint on my back, and went into the kitchen without saying anything to me.

I could hear her whispering to Claire, "You can't do that. Did you see his back?"

"I didn't mean it. I was just so angry. I didn't want to put up with his mouth," Claire whispered back.

I could tell she felt bad almost instantly. Nothing like this had happened before. When they asked me to do something I always did, and they had never hit me like this. I sat in my room, seething with anger. I began to formulate a plan: I would get my things together, and get ready for school as usual. But instead of school, I would hitchhike back to Lawrence. About a year ago, in a moment of anger and confusion, I had tried to run away unsuccessfully. I had put everything I owned in a green garbage bag and hopped on my bike. I intended on riding all twenty miles there, but somehow wound up on route 128 heading into Beverly. As I rode along the highway with the garbage bag dangling over the handlebars, a police car pulled over and the officer put my bike in the trunk and brought me to the police station. I asked how he knew I was running away. "C'mon, a twelve-year-old riding his bike down the side of a highway with a big bag. Someone called and reported it," he said laughing, like it was common sense.

I would not make the same mistake again. I would stick to route 114 all the way—no shortcuts, no chance of getting lost. Before I went to bed that night I went through my clothes, deciding which I liked best, and quietly put them into a large duffel bag I had found in the basement. I gently opened the window to my room, and dropped the bag softly to the ground. This way everything was ready for the morning. I didn't have to worry about sneaking my stuff out. I could just go around the side of the house and be on my way.

I woke up with a lot of doubt going through my mind. What if I got caught? It was a long way to Lawrence. Could I really make it? What if no one gave me a ride? Even if I made it, would they just come and take me back? I thought it over while I showered and dried my hair. Lou and Claire had already left for work, every morning leaving the house by six for their job in a can factory. I glanced nervously at June Reynolds while eating my cereal. She would come down from upstairs every morning to see me off to school, sitting in a rocking chair by the window and smoking Winston cigarettes. I looked at the expression on her face, looking for any hint of suspicion. *She couldn't possibly know*, I thought. "I'm on my way to school," I said to her, putting my coat on and walking to the door.

"Stay out of trouble," she said, rocking in the chair and taking a deep drag of her cigarette.

When I walked out front, I made sure I was out of her sight.

Instead of turning left on Beaver Street toward my school, I turned right and hopped the fence in front of the house. I was relieved to see my duffel bag sitting there in the grass untouched. I grabbed it, hopped back over the fence, and made my way to Boston Street. I started down toward the next town, Peabody, and looked nervously at the passing cars as I went, hoping someone I knew wouldn't drive by and see me heading in the wrong direction with a big duffel bag on my shoulder. It didn't take long to get to the town line. I felt relieved as I walked on, knowing that I wouldn't be recognized there. It seemed to take forever to get through Peabody, and when I did, it was already nine o'clock. I marched on, getting a little tired now, considering the possibility of sticking my thumb out for a ride. But I knew that would draw attention to me. It was during school hours, and people would question a young boy with a duffel bag hitchhiking at this time. If I kept walking then maybe they would just think I was late for school or something.

I trudged on, my feet getting a little sore, and by eleven I was passing a big mall in Danvers. I needed to rest awhile. I went in and sat on a bench as long as I could, but I noticed mall security looking at me and my duffel bag suspiciously, so I left by the back door. It had started to rain lightly, and I was still a little tired. I saw a large cardboard box sitting in a remote corner out of sight, so I placed it sideways and climbed in out of the rain. I put my head on my duffel bag and tried to take a short nap, the sound of the raindrops hitting the box echoing softly inside. But I was too nervous to actually fall asleep—worrying that some mall worker would find me and think I was a bum.

The rain had stopped so I climbed out and headed on my way again, but by the time I reached Middleton I was exhausted. I stopped at a sub shop and ordered a sandwich and Coke, taking my time, resting my feet and enjoying the warmth. This time of spring was usually nice, but today was an overcast and chilly day, my jean jacket not really enough.

I wanted to sit there longer, but the man behind the counter looked curiously at my duffel bag from time to time, and I knew it was time to leave. On I went. It seemed like such an easy trip when you were in a car, but walking was an entirely different story. It felt like you were walking to another state. I had walked well over ten miles and could feel blisters starting on my feet. Middleton went on and on, and by the time I reached North Andover school would be getting dismissed. Lawrence was only one town away now, but North Andover was huge. And even when I did reach Lawrence, I would have to go all the way across the city, because my mother had moved to Prospect Hill.

I started to wonder if I could make it. When I was halfway through North Andover, I decided that it was time to hitchhike. My whole body was tired now, and I figured since school was out I would look a lot less suspicious. I turned and walked backwards, my arm extended with my thumb stuck out. Cars whizzed by unsympathetically, drivers turning to look at me and my duffel bag for a second, and then turning their heads back to the road. I walked on and on in that manner, becoming frustrated and just wanting to sit down. When I was close to the Lawrence line, I sat on a guardrail for awhile and watched as the sky was growing dark. I stuck my thumb out while sitting there, hoping someone would finally stop. Then a car pulled to the side of the road and I anxiously ran over to the passenger side. A man rolled down the window and I felt the warmth of the car flow out on my face. "Where are you going?" he asked.

"Lawrence," I answered hopefully.

"Where abouts?"

"Prospect Hill."

"I'll tell you what. I can drop you off at the bottom, at the edge of the highway. Is that good enough?"

"Yes! I really appreciate it!" I said gratefully.

I hopped in the front seat and felt the warmth surround me. He looked at my duffel bag and I thought he was going to ask a bunch of questions, but he didn't ask any. We went a short way and turned onto route 495 toward North Lawrence. It would only be a short drive, but if he hadn't stopped, I would have walked a few more painful hours.

He took the Marston Street exit and pulled into the parking lot of an ambulance place that was strategically located at the edge of the highway. "Hope this helps," he said, pulling to a stop.

"This is perfect. My mother lives right up the street. I really appreciate this," I said sincerely. He gave me a firm handshake, and I watched him turn back onto the highway and disappear down the ramp. It was completely dark now. I stood under a streetlight and looked up the slope of Woodland Street. I could see my mother's apartment from there. What was I going to tell her? There was no way around the truth. The duffel bag was a dead giveaway. Besides, why would I just be showing up at her doorstep in the dark?

I put my bag over my shoulder and started up the incline of Woodland Street, and stopped in the driveway of her apartment complex. I thought for a minute about which one she lived in, having only been there once for a visit. There was a three tenement and a six tenement across from each other, and a four unit apartment building in the front. I remembered her apartment was on the third floor of the building to my right. I looked up and saw a light on in the kitchen. I was happy that she was home. There was no light in the hallway so I made my way up the stairs like a blind man. A dog barked in the second floor apartment as I passed. I stood outside of my mother's door for a minute. I hadn't seen her in awhile and I was a little nervous. I knocked softly a few times. "Just a minute," came the familiar voice of my mother. She opened the door and was stunned for a minute. "Kenny," she paused for a second, "what are you doing here? Lou and Claire called, asked if I had seen you."

"I ran away. I wanted to come back home," I said sheepishly, hungry and exhausted. I stepped inside.

"The social workers are going to know you came here. You may be in trouble."

"Can I have something to eat?"

"Oh, sit down. I just made some Hamburger Helper." She fixed me a big plate, seeming happy to do it. As I wolfed down my food, she called Lou and Claire and told them I was safe and sound with her; that everything could be worked out with the Department of Social Services in the morning. They had already given me the choice of coming home and I thought there was a really good chance I could stay. My mother didn't yell at me for running away, for walking twenty miles by myself. Instead, she seemed pleased I was home.

"Can I lie on the couch for a little while?" I asked.

"Of course. Let me get you a blanket."

I lay on the soft couch. My eyes were heavy already. My mother covered me with a big warm blanket and stood there smiling for a moment as I drifted off. Right as I was falling asleep, I felt her kiss me on the forehead. Everything was going to be all right—I was home now.

8

The social workers and the Department of Social Services weren't sure what to do. They had given me the option of returning home some time ago, but if they just let me stay then they felt like they were rewarding me for running away. My mother said she would ask my father if I could stay with him until they reached a decision. He came by our house one afternoon wearing his tennis outfit. He had a game scheduled that night at his health club. He sat on the couch across the room from my mother and crossed his legs comfortably. My mother began the conversation, "Tom, you know Kenny has been in foster homes awhile now. Well, he ran away recently and came back home. I want him to stay, but the Department of Social Services wants a few weeks to decide what to do. Instead of him going to another foster home we thought maybe he could stay with you for a short time."

He looked at my mother and me for a moment and tapped his fingers on his knee. "Well, Frances, you know things didn't work out with Mary Jane and the divorce is final. I've been seeing a woman for awhile now named Nancy. I wouldn't ask it of her." I looked at the strands of gray that were mixing in with his black hair, and he looked so smug to me. I sat there silently seething with anger and feeling humiliated at the same time. He wouldn't even take me for a few weeks—this woman "Nancy" more important than his own son.

I wanted to scream out, "What's wrong with you? I'm your son. Don't you give one shit about me? You're my father; for once can you help me?" But I sat there silently listening to the two of them.

My mother was outraged, her face growing red with anger. "What kind of man are you?" she snapped. "You're more concerned about this woman you're seeing than your own son!"

"Listen, Frances, I don't need this!" He got up from the couch and stormed out of the house. My mother looked at me, at a loss for words, and went quietly into her room, shutting the door behind her.

The next day I was taken to a foster home in Chelsea, a city just outside of Boston that was every bit as tough as Lawrence. It was a two-story house on a street full of similar-looking homes, run by a gruff old woman named Evelyn. She chain smoked all day and looked as though she lost all interest in her appearance long ago. Her hair was dyed red with streaks of white breaking through, her clothes were old and worn, and her face wrinkled and without makeup. She took foster kids in on a temporary basis. The years of kids coming and going hardened her. She didn't smile often and was very direct when she spoke to you. There were five of us at that particular time—me, a fourteen-year-old named Tony, who had long, straight blond hair and reminded me of the comic book character "Thor;" a skinny kid who everyone called "Bogart" because he always had a cigarette hanging from his lip, and actually looked like Humphrey Bogart; a quiet fifteen-year-old named Dave, who had short brown hair and kept to himself; and a seventeen-year-old, Steve, who had long, curly blond hair like a rock star.

We were all awaiting something—a permanent foster home, a court date, or returning to our family. Tony had been there longer than anyone, two months, and you could tell Evelyn had grown fond of him, talked a little differently to him. Since we were there for a short time, none of us were enrolled in school, so we just milled about the house all day or went for a walk in the neighborhood. Sometimes when we were all just sitting there watching television Evelyn would look at us, shake her head, and say, "Look at the bunch of you. Just sitting around like cattle waiting for the state to get off their asses and do something. Like a herd of damn cattle."

Other days I walked down to the variety store on the corner and looked at magazines for awhile, or I walked up the hill behind her house to a large open area. There was a water tower that had "Soldiers Home" painted across the top in large letters, and below it a building amongst a park-like setting. There were old men sitting on benches, and alongside them were women in white nurse's uniforms speaking softly with their hand on their shoulder, or joking with them. I assumed this was the kind of place old war veterans wound up in their final years. It was so peaceful there, and I liked walking around the sidewalk by the bushes and shrubs, looking down over the landscape like I did in Lawrence.

I lay awake in my bed at night long after the lights went out, thinking about my family and what had become of us. Tommy was out of St. Ann's now and in some kind of group home, and I hadn't seen him in a few years. My mother and Gary never could get along very well and she had thrown him out of the house when he was sixteen. He was staying with some guy named Chuck. Chuck sat up late every night drinking Scotch and watching the Tonight Show with Johnny Carson, demanding complete silence during the monologue and laughing hysterically, asking, "Did ya hear that? Ah ha ha ha." Chuck looked like a distinguished businessman with his hair neatly combed and his mustache neatly trimmed. He didn't work at all and basically let Gary do whatever he wanted. Gary dropped out of school in the tenth grade and I saw him once or twice a year, sometimes less.

I wondered if my family was cursed or something. I felt like someone had torn us to pieces; shred any resemblance to a normal family. Why us? Why so many bad things for one family? It was bad enough that we had no father and had to live in the project, but also a brother who was mentally ill and a horrible last name like "Tingle." I wondered if the name itself brought bad luck. It wasn't self-pity that I felt; it was anger and frustration. I wished my family was normal and together, my mother and father still married, maybe a decent little house somewhere. But that was for other kids and I felt cheated by life, as though something that was rightfully mine had been cruelly ripped away. But as messed up as my family was I loved them and just wanted us to be together.

One afternoon we were playing football in the street in front of Evelyn's when a blue van with two men inside pulled up. They looked at the bunch of us for a moment, and as soon as I saw them, a bad feeling came over me. The driver was a big stocky man with tattoos on his arms; the passenger had a thin face with his hair cropped close in a crew cut. Their eyes were hollow, vacant of any conscience. They looked about thirty years old. "Tony, is Evelyn home?" the passenger asked, expressionless.

"No, she went to the store for a little while."

"Tell her I came by," he said, and the van pulled away slowly, the men looking us over as they rode off.

"Who were they?" I asked Tony.

"The passenger, Rob, used to be a foster kid here a long time ago. He visits Evelyn sometimes. The other guy is his friend, Paul. He's kind of scary. I guess they live out of the van, have no house or anything," he said, throwing the football to me.

When Evelyn returned from the store, she made us dinner and said she was going out with some girlfriends to play bingo. "The bunch of ya better behave," she said slinging her pocketbook over her shoulder and walking out the front door. We sat around the kitchen for a little while smoking cigarettes and trying to figure out something to do. The sky grew dark and a crack of thunder sounded in the distance, and suddenly rain was falling in sheets, splashing loudly against the pavement outside.

"Shit," Steve said, looking out the window, "well I guess we're not going outside."

"Hey, Bogart, slide over," Tony said, sitting on the couch next to him.

"What's this crap you're watching?" he teased, leaning forward and turning the channel to some wrestling show.

"This is a bunch of phony bullshit," Bogart complained.

"It's better than that nature-boy stuff you were watching," Tony shot back, and we all laughed for a minute. After wrestling we watched some cop show, taking turns making each other laugh by mocking the characters and complaining how unrealistic the fight scenes were. Every so often, a flash of lightning would light up the living room and we would scream, "Whoa!" as the thunder followed.

Around nine that night there was a knock on the door. "Who the hell is this in the pouring rain?" Steve asked rhetorically. Bogart crossed the living room and opened the door. It was the two guys in the van, Rob and Paul, standing on the doorstep drenched from the rain.

"Evelyn here?" the skinny-faced one asked, and they both stepped in uninvited.

"No, she's at bingo. Won't be back until late," Tony answered from across the living room. They stood there with blank expressions on their faces, showing no intention of leaving. I felt myself tense up a little. They just looked at us for a minute, seated in our chairs, then they walked into the living room and stood in front of the television. They were big men, each well over two hundred pounds, and as I glanced around the room I knew everyone had the same bad feeling about these guys. Paul was stocky with a big hairy chest, tattoos on both arms and a menacing look about him. The other, Rob, was taller and not as heavily built, his crew cut making his thin face panther like.

"Where you from?" Paul suddenly asked Steve.

"Lowell," he answered uneasily.

They turned their attention to me, "Where you from?"

"Lawrence," I said, trying not to make too much eye contact. It was uncomfortably quiet for a moment, and then they turned to Dave.

"Where you from?"

"Over by Worcester," Dave answered. I looked at their eyes, hollow and blank, and knew something wasn't right with them.

"Think you're tough?" Paul suddenly snapped at Dave. He looked nervous sitting there with all eyes on him.

"No," he answered in a surprised tone.

"Stand up!" Paul said loudly, walking closer to him. Dave stood up in front of him awkwardly, wondering what this was all about. With no warning or provocation, Paul swung his fist into Dave's face, making a loud and fleshy smacking sound. He stumbled back and fell over the arm of the recliner to the floor. We sat there stunned at the senselessness of the situation. Dave had done nothing to them. Didn't even know them. He was just a skinny fifteen-year-old who was half their age and size.

He slowly got to his feet and the side of his face was swollen, blood coming out the corner of his mouth. "What was that for?" he asked, his voice trembling. Paul slammed his fist into his face again with that same sickening smacking sound and he flew backwards against the wall. He slid down onto his hands and knees, dazed and bleeding.

"What the hell is going on?" Steve said standing up. Rob's crew-cut head turned to him.

"What did you say?" he said, scowling at Steve.

"He didn't do anything. Leave him alone," he said in a reasoning tone.

The two men exchanged a grin. "You think you can kick my ass?" Rob said walking toward him, then lunged at him with a punch.

Steve was a good-sized seventeen-year-old and he stepped out of the way, grabbed Rob from behind and wrestled him down to the floor. Rob struggled violently to break free, but couldn't. Paul stood over them watching, waiting to see if his buddy would get beaten.

Steve must have sensed that Paul was ready to jump in and let Rob break free. He flipped Steve over and sat on his chest, using his knees to pin his arms down. Then he punched him in the face over and over, welts popping up on his face and he looked like he lost consciousness. His head fell to the side and drool ran from the side of his mouth. Rob got up and turned to Paul, "He had me. The little son-of-a-bitch had me."

"No he didn't," Paul said, trying to make him feel better. Steve just lay there and my heart was pounding so hard in my chest that I thought I was going to pass out. Then Paul turned to me and brought his big fist crashing into my face. My ears rang and I couldn't hear anything as I fell to the floor. I lay there with my head throbbing and the side of my face feeling numb. He pulled me up and brought his fist into my face again, slamming me back down against the floor with the taste of blood in my mouth.

They crossed the room and started throwing Bogart around, and I got to my feet and snuck up the stairs. I could hear the sound of skin smacking as they punched Tony, his voice pleading, "I didn't do anything!"

There was no lock on the bedroom door so I went into the bathroom, closed the door behind me and closed the latch tightly. After a few minutes of crashing sounds downstairs, I heard their heavy steps as they climbed the staircase. They looked around the bedrooms, realized no one was there and pounded on the bathroom door. "Open up you little shit!" I thought about ignoring them, but knew they could easily break the door down. I felt my heart pounding again as I slowly opened it.

They walked in and stared at me for a moment. Paul put his big arm around me. "You know, be cool and I'll take you under my wing."

Rob looked at my face, and with a legitimately concerned tone said, "Oh, man, look at your face." Without warning, he punched me in the mouth and my head snapped back.

I heard the screen door slamming downstairs and they turned to look at each other. Without a word, they ran quickly down the stairs. "Get back here you little bastard!" I heard them yelling out the door, their voices muffled by the heavy rain. They said a few things to the other guys downstairs and I heard them leaving. I slowly went downstairs, afraid of what I would see, and looked at everyone—black eyes, swollen lips, bloody noses, torn clothes, and a look of battered shock on their faces.

"What happened to Dave?" I asked.

"He ran out with no shirt, no shoes, no socks, or nothing, screaming as he went down the street. That's the only reason they left. He probably saved our lives," Tony said, his whole body shaking.

I looked out the window at the heavy rain, knew it was cold outside and hoped Dave got away without freezing to death. Bogart was sitting in a corner, crying quietly to himself with his head down on his knees. Steve had gotten up and was sitting in a chair with his head down and his face in his hands. He stood up and locked the door, latching the little chain for extra protection. "Nobody open the door if those bastards come back! Grab a knife in the kitchen if they do!" he said angrily.

I went upstairs and looked into the bathroom mirror; both my eyes were swollen and black, my face looking puffy and disfigured. I felt like I was looking at some grotesque creature from a horror movie. I laid on the bed and put the covers over me to block out the chilly night air, and heard Evelyn coming through the door downstairs. Her bewildered voice screamed, "What the hell happened here?" as though she thought we had a fight amongst ourselves. I heard Steve telling the story and then it grew quiet, Evelyn talking softly to them in a sympathetic voice.

There was a loud knock on the front door, and I heard voices shouting, "Chelsea Police! Open up!" I felt relieved, thinking Dave had gotten away. They talked to Evelyn downstairs for awhile, talked to the other guys, and then I heard their footsteps coming up the stairs. I could see the black leather jackets and shiny badges the officers were wearing and I closed my eyes as they entered the room like I was asleep. I didn't feel like talking about it; just wanted to be left alone. Through my closed eyelids I could still see the glare of their flashlights scanning over my face in the dark. "Christ," one of the officers mumbled under his breath, and then the clomping of their shoes as they went back downstairs.

Everything was kept pretty quiet. The police were supposedly looking for those guys, but Tony said they drove by the next night looking for Dave, wanting to make him pay for escaping and telling the police. I was afraid to go outside out of fear that they would drive up and pull me into their van and I would never be seen again. The social workers and the Department of Social Services never talked to me about what happened. They acted like they didn't even know, but all of a sudden they decided I could stay at home.

But there was one condition—I had to attend something called Key Program. It was in a big, old Victorian style house on the corner of Franklin and Cross Streets. There was nothing distinguishing about it, no sign or any other marking to let you know it was for troubled youths. The meetings were held downstairs in the living room, and the upstairs was for kids who had to live there under constant supervision. To me the meetings were a big waste of time—a group of teenage boys sitting in a circle, the counselor trying to get us talking about our problems—and I resented going there. But at least I was back in Lawrence, and it was there that I met Ron June. He was a quiet boy, but for some reason took to me right from the start. He told me all about his life, and even though I had it tough, I soon realized he had it even tougher. That is one thing I learned from our friendship: when you think that life gave you a bad deal, there are others suffering a lot more.

Ron had spent his entire life bouncing in and out of foster homes, the social workers telling him that his parents were dead. For some reason he never believed that. Without any help, or any clues, he ran away from a foster home and found his real father in a small town about fifty miles northwest of Boston. Unfortunately, it was not the happy ending to a sad story. Ron stayed with his father for awhile, who was a small-town sheriff, but told me he was an alcoholic who beat him up sometimes. He came home drunk one night and threw a refrigerator that broke Ron's arm, so back to foster homes he went. But, even after the way his father treated him, Ron never said one hateful thing about the guy. He still loved his father. That's the kind of kid Ron was. After everything he had been through there was no chip on his shoulder, no bitterness, no anger against the world. Most of the kids at Key Program thought they had to swear a lot and look tough, but not Ron. He was comfortable just being himself, always a sincere smile on his face when he happily greeted you. He liked to wear old jeans, flannel shirts or a tank top when it was hot, work boots, and had his straight blond hair cut like a Dutch boy.

I always hung out with Ron when I attended Key Program or any of their outings—softball games, the beach, group sessions. It was always Ron and me. For the short time we had as friends, we learned a lot about each other and became pretty close. He surprised me one day by just showing up at my house unannounced. It was early in the afternoon on a scorching hot summer day when I heard a knock on the door—and there was Ron standing with a grin. I had never told him where I lived. Had no idea how he found it.

I invited him in and we sat around my living room, sluggish from the heat and humidity. He had some pot with him and asked me if I wanted to smoke some. "Want to get high?" he asked, taking out a small plastic bag and holding it up.

"Nah, not really," I told him, feeling a little bad about turning him down. I was no angel, had tried it in Salem, but always under peer pressure. I just didn't like it; the smell, the taste, the dry mouth it gave you, and the spaced-out feeling that lingered for the rest of the day.

"Do you care if I smoke a joint?" he asked.

"No, go ahead." He took out a rolling paper, placed a pinch of dark green marijuana in the middle, and twisted it between his fingers until it resembled a thin cigarette. He put a match to the end and took a deep drag, the end glowing bright red as he inhaled. He held it in as long as he could, and then blew out a huge cloud of smoke that filled the living room. Soon the entire apartment was filled with the distinct odor of marijuana, and I hoped it would all drift out the windows before my mother came home.

Ron's eyes were very glossy and he stared at the television for a long time. "Ron, how's that new foster home you're in?" I asked, breaking up a long period of silence.

"It sucks. She has this super long list of rules, and if you break any, she locks you up in your room. She keeps a padlock on the refrigerator so you can't sneak a snack."

"What! She has a padlock on the refrigerator!" I said, incredulously, then couldn't help but burst into a fit of laughter.

"I'm serious. She really does," he blurted out, and began laughing with me until his face turned a bright red. "She locked me in my room one time and I got so pissed I climbed out the window. And it's on the second floor so I had to climb down the house."

"What, you—" I couldn't even finish a sentence I was laughing so hard. I wasn't laughing at Ron, but I pictured this ogre-type woman locking the refrigerator and it got the best of me.

"Man, you didn't even smoke any of that joint. I think you're high from the fumes."

"No, I'm all right," I said, getting myself back together.

I took the short walk up to Storrow Park with him and stood at the edge of the slope. From there Prospect Hill began to taper down until it met the highway a few hundred feet below. There was an incredible view of the city. You could see over the roof of Lawrence General Hospital, beyond the mills and tall buildings of downtown, all the way across the city to Tower Hill. Looking south, you could see across the Merrimac River into parts of South Lawrence, even the big water tower in the Mount Vernon section. A slight breeze came by, and we stood quietly looking over the city. Ron had never been there before, and I could tell he appreciated it by the look on his face. He absorbed the panoramic view ahead.

"I'm gonna take off. I was supposed to be back awhile ago," Ron suddenly realized, and he started down the long flight of cement stairs that led down to the road below.

"Hey, I'll see you next Tuesday at Key," I yelled down to him.

He turned to look back at me, smiled, and waved. "See you there."

That was the last time I saw him. I had a new social worker, Don Silva, and he also supervised Ron. When I didn't see him anymore on Tuesdays at Key, I asked Don where he was, and he said things didn't work out at the foster home so Ron was transferred over by Worcester. I really wished I had a chance to say good-bye.

I wasn't crazy about the new neighborhood my mother picked. The inside of the apartment was actually nice, but the outside just looked like a run-down three tenement and I wished for once we could live in something else. It was just a tall rectangular building with no decoration whatsoever, and during storms where the wind blew strong, I could actually feel it sway a little. There was a gray four unit apartment building to the front, and in the back a dilapidated garage with holes in the roof. On each side of the garage rested a short row of garbage cans.

This place was full of unique characters. Below us lived Leo Desjardins, a white-haired veteran of World War Two. He sat at the kitchen table most of the day, chain smoking and peering out the window over the complex, aware of everything anyone did. He had actually put his television at the end of his kitchen table, so he could watch it without missing anything going on in the neighborhood. As I walked up the driveway after dark there was always the flicker of his television illuminating the night air, and his shadow in the window. I could hear him coughing constantly, going into long and terrible fits. He had a dog that stayed in the apartment all day, and the years of heavy smoke had taken its toll on her too. He considered her to be somewhat of an attack dog, but she got winded just going up the stairs and couldn't really protect anyone. Leo generally liked me, but at times considered me a wise ass. He was still a big man, and sometimes he would grab me by the shirt and hold up his fist. "You know what we did to the Germans back in World War Two?"

Then he would wait until I said, "No, what?"

"We'd march them until they couldn't take it anymore. And if they complained—Wham-O, I'd gives um one!" he would say, waving his fist around. "One time this big German tried to give me the business, wouldn't dig a hole. So I straightened out the son-of-a-bitch—Wham-O, I gives um one," he said, stepping forward and throwing a mock punch, reliving the moment. And whenever I did anything to irritate him, he would start toward me, knowing I would run, not really intending on catching me. "You better run, you son-of-a-bitch," he would mumble, grinning, glad he didn't have to actually get me. To him "son-of-a-bitch" was actually a playful tease, as he used it constantly. Leo knew everyone's business.

Across from us, on the first floor of the six-family, were the Johnsons. The parents were older, and had kids from ten years old up to their thirties, all but one still living at home. The grandmother lived in the apartment above. She must have watched the garbage cans all day, because anytime I tried to throw something away on their side her window would shoot open and her shrieking voice would shoot down, "You get the hell out of here! Throw it in your trash cans!" Even though they lived in the city, they considered themselves to be some kind of country and western people. They wore cowboy boots, Stetson type hats, and big belt buckles. The father was a thin man who always had white stubble on his face. He never talked, spent all his time working on cars; all day bent over under the hood, and at night he ran a long extension cord and hung a light above him. The mother rarely came out, once in a great while strolling to the trash cans in her nightgown to throw something away. Their oldest son, Chuck, must have been close to thirty. He was chunky with a full brown beard, and was always tucking a little bit of chewing tobacco in his lower lip. He left high school, earned his GED, and was constantly lecturing about the great waste of time high school really was. When I asked him the difference between the two, he said, "One takes four years and the other takes four hours," with the air of an expert.

Chuck's lifelong dream was to be a police officer but he couldn't get on the force. Instead of just accepting that fact, he took a strange path: He worked as a security guard, with a blue uniform that could almost pass for a police officer, and then he converted his car into a make-shift police cruiser. It was an old two-door sedan. First, he sanded it down and covered it in a rust-colored primer. Then he bolted a long, thin board across the roof and attached a light on each end, like the kind you would see on a police car. He wired them to the battery so that they would turn flashing at the push of a button. His intention was clear—he would wear his blue uniform and then get into this car and people would believe he was some sort of law enforcement, some extension of the long arm of the law. It was a failure. As he rode down the street people were perplexed, scratching their heads and asking, "What the hell was that? Has the police department gone bankrupt?"

In the bottom of the four-unit was a neurotic drunk named Mark. He talked really fast and was always working on an old, broken-down Porsche propped up on cinder blocks. It sat there for years, never in running condition. One night I heard Mark yelling in the street out front and then a loud gunshot, followed by the sound of screeching tires and a car speeding off. Chuck Johnson came out and asked him what happened, and from my window, I heard his rapid and neurotic voice, "Some pricks were chasing me all the way home, so I got my shotgun and fired a round at their car." The police showed up and confiscated the gun and Mark could never get it back.

When I ran away from Salem and they decided I could stay, I finished what was left of the eighth grade at the Oliver School. As soon as that was done, they got me a job for the summer in a program called CETA. I had no idea what it stood for, only that I was working for the city and getting paid minimum wage. Sometimes we worked for the Housing Department doing next to nothing, other times breaking our back for the Street Department.

It was a scorching summer day, and they had us shoveling dirt and garbage from the curbside and throwing it into the back of a city truck. I had my shirt off and was already deeply tanned, sweat coming from every pore. They gave us a ten-minute break and I lit a cigarette. I noticed this kid looking at me for a minute, and then he finally asked, "Got an extra smoke?"

"Ya, sure," I answered, tossing one to him.

He finished it and then said, "Hey, my name's Mike."

"Ken," I said, shaking his hand. I started to talk to him at work sometimes and he invited me over to his house on a Friday night, said his uncle would buy beer if you gave him the money. He lived a few blocks behind the Essex Projects on Butler Street, in a three tenement like me. I showed up at seven thirty like I promised, and he brought me inside and introduced me to his family. They were Portuguese and French Canadian. There was his mother, dark haired and pretty, his chubby younger sister who wanted to tag along, and the uncle who came down from Canada and only spoke French. He was supposedly a boxer but was thin and unhealthy looking.

Mike got some money from me and the mother told him in French to get us a few quarts of beer; the catch, of course, was that we had to buy some for him. But I really didn't care. I was happy that his mother was letting us drink in the house with no worries. He returned shortly with a brown paper bag and handed out beer to everyone, Mike and I each getting two quarts of Budweiser. I had never drank in front of someone's mother before, felt uncomfortable sitting across the table from her, and even more uncomfortable with the uncle glaring at me from his rocking chair. He was a menacing looking character, with squinty and angry eyes, a scraggly beard, and weather-beaten face. He didn't talk at all, and every time I put the bottle to my lips, I could feel his eyes on me.

The following Friday at work Mike asked me if I wanted to sleep over and I agreed. When I got there he was just taking a shower to wash away the grime of the workday, then he took a shirt out of the dirty clothes hamper and asked, "Does this smell?" He held it up to my nose.

"I don't know," I said, moving my head away and trying not to laugh. He got dressed and we tried to think of something to do. It was only five o'clock and the night was young.

"You wanna go up to the Reservoir?" he suggested, with a French twist to the name, making it Rez-ev-wa.

"Ya, it's not that far from here, is it?" I asked.

"No, it's like a ten-minute walk." I always liked the Reservoir; the view of the city opposite of Prospect Hill, the rolling grassy slopes leading down to the cemeteries, the large basin of water gurgling with a pump in the middle, the smell of grass and trees around you.

We walked up Butler Street, passing the long row of three tenements and looking at the people sitting on their porches, them eyeing us as we passed, and made our way to Ames Street. We followed it straight across Haverhill Street to the Reservoir and stood at the top of the hill gazing across the city. I could see the large water tower on Prospect Hill with the word "Lawrence" painted across the top, visible even from this distance. "Let's go down to the cemetery," Mike said. We walked down the steep grassy slope and went around the chain-link fence to the entrance. As we walked along the road, past all the tombstones and flowers, we saw two girls coming the other way.

"Let's talk to these girls," I said, looking at Mike to see if he was up for it.

"Go for it," he said confidently.

I ran my fingers through my hair to make sure it was pushed back, and as they approached us I said, "Hi, how are you doing?" My face blushed a little.

They stopped and grinned at each other for a moment, then giggled. "We're fine." We looked at each other for a moment, us studying them and them studying us.

"You guys live around here?" Mike asked, trying to get a conversation going.

"We live in Methuen," they both answered at the same time, and then laughed because they did. They looked a little alike, with long brown hair and the beginning curves of teenage girls. But one of them caught my eyes. She was cute with a friendly looking face.

"What's your name?" I asked her, turning my attention to only her.

"Jodie Tucker," she said with a smile. "What's your name?"

"Kenny." I smiled back, smiling a little stronger than I normally would, trying to look handsome.

Mike was talking to the other girl and I looked around awkwardly, trying to think of something to keep the conversation going. "Do you guys hang around here a lot?" I asked, after a short pause.

"No, we just went for a walk and decided to come through here." They looked at each other a second, then the other girl said, "We need to get home now. Actually, I was supposed to be home awhile ago. I'm probably going to be in trouble." They started down the road, looking over their shoulders at us and giggling to each other.

"Hey, how about a phone number," I yelled to them.

They stopped, grinned, and Jodie yelled back, "I don't have a piece of paper. But I'm in the phone book. My father's name is John."

"Can we call tonight?"

"Ya. But not too late," she said laughing and they continued down the road out of sight.

Mike turned to me. "This is awesome—two of us, two of them. We can go on a double date or something."

"But they live in Methuen. How is that going to work?" I interjected, with a tone of doubt.

"So what, we can meet them at a movie theater or something," he said optimistically, with a twinkle in his eyes.

"You really like that girl, don't you?" I teased.

"Yeah! She was hot!" he said emphatically, and burst into a grin.

When we got back to Mike's house we waited for awhile to avoid looking desperate, then I called directory assistance and got her number. Mike's whole family was in on it now; he had told his mother and sister, and they all wanted to know if we were going to get a date out of this chance meeting. "Go ahead and call," his sister egged us on.

"Can I use the phone in the living room?" I asked, uncomfortable with the idea of talking to a girl with an audience.

"Go ahead," his mom said, chuckling at my shyness. I went in the living room and dialed her number.

"Hello," a man's deep voice answered.

"Um, is Jodie there?"

"Who's this?" he said, with a strict fatherly curiosity in his voice.

"Um, Kenny."

There was an uncomfortable pause for a second, then, "Hold on," and the sound of the phone being put on the counter.

"Hello," a soft voice answered, one I recognized from only a few hours before.

"This is Kenny. We met at the Reservoir. Is it all right that I called?"

"Yes, I told you it was okay."

"Your dad sounded a little mad, I guess."

"He always sounds like that," she said laughing.

"Me and Mike were just wondering if maybe you guys want to go on a double date or something. Like maybe a movie?"

"Well, not a double date," she hesitated for a moment, "because, well, we both kind of..." and she didn't finish the sentence.

"You both kind of what?" I prodded.

"We both kind of like you," she answered a little awkwardly.

"Oh, I—" I didn't know quite how to answer. I was proud they both liked me and sad for Mike at the same time. I knew I had to go back into the kitchen and answer a dozen questions, see his expectant face anxiously awaiting news of a date with this girl he liked. "I'm at Mike's house. Can I maybe call you back another time?"

"Sure, that's fine. I'll talk to you later. Bye." I hung up the phone and sat on the couch for a minute, wondering how to say this. Was

I supposed to just walk in the kitchen and slap him on the back, "Tough break, old buddy. They both like me," and smile with conceit? No way. That was inconceivable. I would just make something up.

I walked slowly into the kitchen and sat at the table across from Mike, his mother and sister sitting to each side. "Well, what happened?" Mike finally asked when I didn't volunteer any information.

"Oh, nothing really, we just kind of talked for a minute. She didn't say much. Her father was kind of strict, you know, she couldn't stay on the phone very long."

"Didn't you ask about the double date?" Mike said, still hopeful.

"Well, kind of."

"What did she say?" he asked with his eyes opened wide.

"She just—" There was no way I could say it. His mother could sense my reluctance, and she studied my face.

"They both like you, don't they?" she asked, point blank. I looked back at her, and nodded, my face burning red with embarrassment, trying not to show any hint of pride.

"So what? You're a nice looking boy," she said with a bluntness that caught me off guard. I thought she would be angry, would take this as some sort of rejection of her son. But for some reason she didn't take it that way at all. And that was the end of it. Mike was just quiet for awhile, didn't ask for any further explanation.

We watched television for awhile, his mother and sister excusing themselves and going off to bed. When Mike was sure they were asleep, he turned to me and whispered, "Hey, you wanna do something fun?"

"Like what?" I leaned forward curiously.

"Wanna take my mother's car for a drive?"

"I can't drive. You're joking right?"

"I can. I do it all the time," he said, grinning slyly. He went into the other room and returned with her keys dangling from his finger. "C'mon."

We went out to the street and hopped in her car. It was a big old tank of a station wagon; rust colored, and made of heavy solid steel. He turned the key, and winced as the engine roared, as though the sound might wake his mother. He pulled away from the curb with the confidence of an experienced driver and headed up the street, flicking on the headlights and illuminating the dark neighborhood. He looked comical to me, a fourteen-year-old behind the steering wheel of this large car. I chuckled. "You're pretty good at this."

"I told you I do it all the time," he said proudly, leaning back comfortably in his seat.

We drove around the block a few times and up past the Reservoir, then looped back down Essex Street. He pulled into a large parking lot across from the Essex Project and put the car in park, then turned to me, "Do you want to try?"

I looked at him with astonishment. "I told you, I don't know how to drive!"

"That's why I came to this parking lot. Just try it here. It's easy. The gas is on the right and the brake is on the left," he said, showing me with his foot where everything was. I looked around. It was a huge parking lot, empty with the exception of some cars by the street, and in the back a department store called Stuarts and a supermarket called Demoulas.

He climbed out and came around the passenger's side, opened the door and I got out. I nervously climbed into the driver's seat and looked at the controls before me. I grabbed the stick shift on the side of the steering wheel and maneuvered it over to the right, gently pressed on the gas, and tensed up expecting the car to jump forward. The engine revved a little but the car didn't move. "Mike, there's something wrong with your mother's car," I said, feeling incompetent.

"No, bonehead, you have it in neutral!" he said pointing at the little red arrow resting on the letter N. He pulled the shift over to the letter D and the car jumped forward a little. "Okay, just lightly press on the gas and go in a straight line across the parking lot." I did as he said and I felt powerful as we cruised along, me at the wheel controlling every move. "Turn right," he instructed, and I turned the wheel a little too much, the car tilting slightly to the side as we cornered. I turned just a little back to the left and the car continued back in a straight line. "Hey, you're getting the hang of it," Mike said, slapping me on the shoulder.

The car cruised forward and we were getting closer to the department store. "All right, you better slow down a little," Mike said, with just a hint of nervousness in his voice. My foot searched for the brake pedal and I began to panic, unsure of which one was right, the brick wall of Stuarts closing in, and I stomped my foot down. It was the wrong choice; the engine roared and the car shot forward. "Hit the brake!" Mike screamed desperately, and I felt the front wheels of the car go over the sidewalk, "Hit the—" *Ssmmaasssshhh!* The front of the car struck the brick wall of Stuarts and my head whipped forward, smashing my face against the steering wheel. My ears rang loudly, drowning out any background sound. Mike's mouth was moving, but I couldn't make out a single word.

I felt blood rushing from my nose and mouth, and my senses snapped back. "Are you all right?" Mike asked, distressed and nudging my shoulder.

"I don't know," I said vaguely, confused and having trouble focusing on his face. The blood was flowing from my nose strongly now. I took off my shirt, tilted my head back, and stuffed it against the bottom of my nostrils.

Mike looked over his shoulder, scanning the project across the road to see if anyone had witnessed this, then looked at the front of the car embedded into the brick wall. "Oh shit, we better get out of here." He slid me into the passenger seat. He turned the key anxiously, and when the engine started, he breathed a sigh of relief. "Whew. Thank God."

"What are you going to tell your mother?" I murmured through the rolled-up shirt, pressing it hard against my upper lip and nose.

"Nothing. I'm going to park in the street and act like I don't know anything. She'll think someone stole it." He parked the car close to the curb and we went into his house as quietly as possible, not thinking that car thieves don't usually steal a car, smash it up, and then return it to the exact same spot it was. Mike got some ice from the freezer. I wrapped it in my shirt and held it against my nose, just a trickle of blood coming at this point. "You're going to be okay, right?"

I nodded silently, and tilted my head back again.

"I put a blanket on the couch, you can sleep there. Remember, don't say anything in the morning. We know nothing." It had been a very long day, and as I lay back on the sofa, I felt the exhaustion sweeping over me. Under the circumstances, I should've had trouble sleeping, but was out almost instantly.

I awoke somewhat confused, brought on by the strange surroundings and deep sleep. Voices carried to me from the kitchen, "I can't believe this, what happened to my car?" his mother asked, sounding bewildered and angry at the same time. Mike must have just awakened, because he groggily asking with a feigned curiosity that could have fooled anyone, "Something's wrong with your car?"

"Go look at it." I heard the sound of the door opening and a moment later Mike coming back in the kitchen.

"Oh my God! Someone must have smashed into your car and took off!" he said with exaggerated shock. He must have put some thought into it overnight and abandoned the idea of car thieves.

"I hope the insurance covers this. I wonder if I can even drive the damn thing. This is just great. I need the car to get around."

I heard his mother coming into the living room and I closed my eyes as though still asleep. I could sense her standing over me for a brief moment, and then I heard her going back to the kitchen. "What happened to him?" she asked, matter-of-factly.

"He fell down at the reservoir," Mike said quickly, and by his tone, I knew he had made this up instantly, not having thought this over like the car. I thought she would come bursting into the living room at any second, screaming at me, "Get up you little shit! I know you smashed my car." I lay there tensely expecting it. But for some reason she never put two and two together, or had just decided not to confront us. I ran my hand across my face and could feel my upper lip grossly swollen. I lay there as long as I could, not daring to enter the kitchen and face a round of questioning. When I heard his mother go into the bedroom, I quickly made my move. I crossed into the kitchen and said to Mike, seated at the table eating cereal, "I'm gonna get out of here. I'll see you at work Monday."

I looked at the car briefly as I passed it in the street; the front was dented in a little, the metal chewed up around the headlights, but it wasn't as bad as I envisioned. If this car wasn't such a tank, it would have been much worse. I made my way out to Haverhill Street and started the long walk home in the already hot morning sun, wearing nothing but the shorts I had slept in. I didn't even take the time to put my sneakers on, avoiding Mike's mom at all costs, and had discarded my bloody shirt in the garbage. I became acutely aware of how stupid I looked as I walked down this busy road; my upper lip swollen out like a duck's bill, dried blood in my nostrils, and next to naked. I decided to run all the way home—get it over as quick as possible—and turned my head the other way every time cars passed.

I was glad it was the weekend and I wouldn't have to show my face for a few days. I sat at home all of Saturday and Sunday putting ice on my lip, and by Monday the swelling was just about gone. I went to work as usual, scooping up piles of dirt from the curbside with a shovel and throwing them into the back of a city truck. When no one was around Mike came over and whispered, "You know they had a display of televisions against the wall in Stuarts. When we crashed it knocked some over and they smashed on the floor." I felt a sense of panic come over me.

"Oh, man, we're screwed. We're in big trouble!"

"No, no. Nobody knows anything. Just keep your mouth shut!"

And I did. I quietly and nervously shoveled away in the blazing sun, sweating and covered in dirt. When I got home, I showered and sat back on the couch, hoping and praying we didn't get caught, that the Department of Social Services never caught wind of this. I leaned back and felt a cool breeze blowing through the window and was glad to be resting my weary body.

I was close to dozing off when I heard someone knocking on my door. Irritated by this interruption, I crossed the kitchen and swung it open. My social worker, Don Silva, was standing there with a blank look on his face and I was sure he knew. He was a well-dressed man, wearing a green alligator shirt and his dark hair neatly combed, his dark mustache neatly trimmed. "Can I come in?" he asked solemnly.

"Sure, come in," I answered, pulling out a seat from the table for him to sit.

He sat across from me, and after a moment of hesitation said, "Did you hear about Ron June?"

"No, why? Did something happen?"

"Ron's dead. He died two days ago. He drowned. He was trying to swim across a big lake with another guy, the other guy turned back around but Ron wanted to prove he could make it to the other side. According to witnesses, he ran out of energy about halfway and just sort of went under. He never came back up."

I began to feel dizzy; my senses numbed like someone had slapped me really hard. "What...I can't believe...I just don't under—" the words came out of my mouth, sounding distant like someone else was speaking them.

"I know you and Ron were good friends. I just wanted to tell you."

I sat there stunned, and Don said something as he was leaving, but I couldn't hear anything. I sat in the living room and stared out the window for a long time, unable to think clearly, my mind racing with scrambled thoughts. He was only fourteen and had his whole life before him. I had never known anyone who died before—no grandparents, no relatives, no one. I couldn't grasp the concept of someone I knew ceasing to exist. Andy had disappeared, but I always felt he was out there somewhere, would come home some day. Hours passed and I was still sitting there in the darkness, staring out the window at the distant lights of the city. Then I just got up, sat at the kitchen table, and wrote this poem:

ODE TO A FRIEND
'Twas this summer he passed away
and it will take forever to forget this day
His life was filled with sadness and sorrow
not much to look for in his tomorrow's
I know I too must someday die
and my soul will be happy to ascend through the sky
When I come to those big pearly gates
if I don't see my buddy, forever I'll wait.

I didn't plan on writing anything, was never much of a poet, but it just came out. The next day I brought it down to Key program and showed it to Patty. She read it over and asked me if she could put it in some magazine for social workers, but I asked her not to. Don Silva saw me there and told me Ron's wake was that evening, offered to pick me up at five o'clock if I needed a ride.

I didn't have any dress clothes so I put on some corduroy pants and a collared shirt, then stood in the road out front to wait for Don. The wake was being held in that small town where Ron's father was a sheriff, and it took over an hour to get there. When we arrived, everyone was already inside the funeral home. Don opened the door slowly. We walked past a few people talking quietly in the hallway, Don nodding politely as we did, and an elderly woman directed us to a room in the back. There was a large, heavyset man sitting outside the door and he stood to shake our hands without saying anything, just introduced himself as Ron's father, and sat down again quickly. He wasn't crying, just had a flat and expressionless look on his face while he stared ahead.

We entered the room and I could see a casket toward the back, the top part left opened and Ron's blond hair partly visible over the side. A woman knelt before him with her head bowed, as though saying a prayer, and when she walked away I went forward and knelt down alongside the casket. Ron's hair had been neatly combed to the side, and he was wearing a gray suit. His face looked white as a sheet, fixed and expressionless like stone. His hands were folded neatly together across his stomach and he appeared puffy and twenty pounds heavier than I remembered. I felt a shiver shoot up my spine. This entire moment unreal—unreal and unjust. He was only fourteen years old. It wasn't supposed to go this way. I didn't like seeing Ron in this altered state so I went outside and smoked a cigarette on the stairs.

Don came out shortly after and we both walked quietly to the car, digesting what we had seen. We barely talked the whole drive back, me turning once to Don and asking, "Why did Ron look like that? He was all puffy and swollen."

"Because when someone drowns and their body isn't found for awhile, they absorb water," he said stoic and clinical, and stared at the road ahead. "Are you going to be all right?" he asked, pulling up in my driveway.

"Yah, I'll be okay. Thank you for the ride."

I got out and watched him drive away in the darkness. I stood there for a moment looking up at the bright stars scattered across the night sky, and I wondered if Ron was up there somewhere.

I walked up the three flights of unlit stairs, and as I entered our apartment, I could hear the sound of my mother's little black and white television coming from her bedroom. The door was closed and she didn't come out, might not have even heard me. It was just as well. I didn't feel like talking about anything. I changed into some shorts and went to bed for the night, lying there with my eyes wide open for a long time. There was never any feeling of sleep coming over me, no heaviness of the eyes or anything.

Then I was standing there looking out into an enormous field of tall yellow grass. In the distance, right in the center of the field, was a big tree with a massive trunk that split into a V, two trees coming out of it and rising in separate directions. I thought I could see someone sitting in it, and I began walking in that direction. The grass crunched below my feet and a spring-like smell filled the air.

When I arrived at the tree, I stood speechless for a moment, my mouth open wide. Sitting there in the tree, right where it split into a V, was Ron June, with his back leaning against one side and his legs propped up against the other. I looked up at him and smiled. "Ron, what are you doing here? You're dead."

He looked at me very seriously, then reached down and touched my shoulder. His hand felt like a cold piece of stone, and he said, "I know. I just came back to tell you change your ways or you're going to hell."

Then I was just lying there wide awake; right after he touched my arm and said that, I was just laying there, not a sudden snapping-to like after a nightmare. I felt strange, not afraid but deeply disturbed, and I wasn't quite sure if this was only a dream—wasn't sure if something much more significant hadn't taken place this night.

9

As the school year came upon me, I grew more and more nervous. I would be a freshman in high school and Lawrence High seemed enormous to me; thousands of kids from every part of the city and the building looked vast and intimidating. Mike was going to the Greater Lawrence Vocational School so I wouldn't even have him to hang around with. I had used my money from work to buy a lot of brand-name clothes, wanted to fit right in from the start.

On the first day of school I walked all the way; took the long set of cement stairs to leave Prospect Hill, passing Lawrence General Hospital and cutting through the old Italian neighborhoods, finally entering the North Common which led right to the high school. I saw hundreds of kids making their way along and going into the steel double doors on the Haverhill Street side. I felt a mix of excitement, like I always did when starting something new, and a feeling of apprehension at the unknown. I was really hoping to meet up with some old friends, at least have some familiarity in completely unfamiliar surroundings.

I mingled in with a large crowd moving down the sidewalk and followed them through the double doors that everyone seemed to be using. There were signs that freshman would report to the cafeteria for orientation. Having no idea where the cafeteria was, I followed a group that looked as confused as me. We went through another set of double doors and walked down a long ramp into a huge, wide-open room with tables everywhere. It had the smell of a cafeteria, a faint scent of tater-tots and green beans. There were hundreds of kids milling about, cliques already being formed, or being continued from middle school.

I stood to the side and scanned the area hopefully, looking for an old buddy or two. After awhile of searching faces, I saw an old friend from the John Breen School sitting at a table with other boys I didn't know. There was one empty seat.

I crossed the cafeteria self-consciously and walked up to the table. "Is this seat taken?" I asked, looking at my old friend. It took a second for him to recognize my face, the years and puberty changing my appearance.

"No way, Kenny Tingle. I haven't seen you in years," he said with surprise.

"What's up, Kevin? Long time no see," I said sitting down, the seat unclaimed.

"I thought you moved away or something," he said, more like he was making small talk than a genuine interest.

"I was in Salem for awhile, but I came back in the spring." He introduced me to the other kids at the table, and there was a little more small talk. It became sort of awkward, like I was the odd man out. He was a good friend when I was in the third grade, but it was foolish for me to just assume we would always be buddies, to just walk up and sit at this table, to ignore the years that had passed and all the changes they brought. There was that cool distance that comes when you haven't seen someone for a long time; that makes you wait until they come and say hello first, almost pretending you don't know them.

I just went through the motions that year, taking the easiest classes I could to avoid any real work. I did see old faces from the past, talked to them a little here and there, but there were all these little groups that had formed in my absence. You basically fit into one of two groups: a "jock," which meant you played sports and dressed a certain way, or a "burnout," which meant you smoked pot and wore leather jackets and work boots. I didn't really fit into either one of them. I drank beer with my friends when I could get it, but I was pretty athletic, too. I loved to play basketball and had started to lift weights, although the latter was mostly for appearance.

One spring morning I was walking home from school and questioning my future—whether I should stay in school and try my best, or just quit school and get a job. There were other kids who quit and they seemed to be okay. They found full time jobs, bought cars, and seemed to have plenty of spending money. I was so deep in thought that instead of traveling up Haverhill Street the way I always did, I cut through the North Common and wound up on Common Street. By the time I realized what I had done it was shorter to just keep going and take this different route home. When I got close to the corner of Newbury and Common Streets, a sweet smell of fresh pastry filled the air. I stopped on the corner and looked at the sign above—*Pappy's Bakery*.

I looked in the window and saw a girl behind the counter, her head looking down as she organized different baked goods inside of a glass counter, putting some things on one shelf and others on a different one. She was unique looking; dark wavy hair that was cut above her shoulders, showing her thin and graceful neck, her sharp features complimenting her warm and pretty face. She had on a little gray baking dress with a white collar. I stood gazing at her for a moment, lost in her beauty, and I thought she was the closest thing to an angel I had ever seen. She must have sensed me looking and began to lift her head. I turned as quickly as I could, hoping she didn't catch me staring—and I continued walking again.

I thought about her all the way home, day dreaming of holding her close as I made my way up the long flight of stairs to Prospect Hill. Thought maybe I could go in and talk to her some time, or maybe I would run into her one day at school. I didn't care if it was longer, I took that route home every day after that and looked hopefully in the window of Pappy's Bakery, looking for my angel. She wasn't there all the time. Most days I didn't see her and I passed in disappointment. But when she was there, I would steal a quick glimpse of her and felt my heart dance a little every time I looked at her face. There were times she looked up quickly, or caught me as I looked longingly at her, and I wondered if she wanted me to enter.

On my walk home one afternoon, the smell of spring intoxicating me, I decided that if I saw her at Pappy's then I would go in and talk to her, pretend I wanted a pastry, and find some excuse to strike up a conversation. I walked down Common Street like a man with a purpose, confident and eager to see her. As I came to the corner, I could see her behind the counter in her little baking dress, smiling at a customer as they paid. But just as I went to grab the door handle and go in a feeling came over me; something deep down inside—in that place where you are completely honest with yourself. I knew she was too good for me. I thought about going in and just ordering a pastry, at least I could stand face-to-face with her. I wanted to hear the sound of her voice, to look at her eyes and the delicate curves of her face.

I started to open the door and saw an older woman calling her to the back room for assistance. I stood at the counter waiting to order, trying to catch a glimpse of her out back. Then the older woman saw me and came to the counter, "Can I help you?"

My heart sank. I stalled a little, hoping she would come back out. "Um, hmmm, let me see," I said, looking the case over carefully. A moment passed and the woman began to tap her fingers on the counter, as though saying, "Make a decision!"

"I guess I'll have an apple turnover," I said, looking over her shoulder into the back room, making one last effort to see her. She wrapped the turnover in a piece of waxy paper and I paid her. I walked out slowly, as though she might come out and see me, and suddenly say, "Wait! You're the boy who looks in the window. What's your name?" But there was only the sound of the little bell ringing as I opened the door and closed it behind me.

I still walked by when I could, sometimes seeing her but mostly not. I couldn't find the courage to go in again, felt it was too obvious. I began to feel a little foolish. If I continued to walk by and look at her then she would eventually think I was some weirdo, and I decided to stop for awhile. She was too good for me anyway, so I settled on just dreaming about her.

By the end of freshman year, I had completely lost interest in school. I had made friends with a kid on Prospect Hill and he had already quit school at age fourteen. I decided to do the same. I lied about my age, claiming to be sixteen instead of fifteen, and got a full-time job at Demoulas Supermarket, right next to the department store where I crashed the car. I worked as a stock boy under a young manager named Tom Gelinas. He was a company guy, always boasting, "Let me tell you, I'm moving up in this organization. I'm going to be a store manager, you just watch. I'm just the stock manager right now, but I have a house already. I'm telling you, I'm moving up."

He was a modern-day slave driver. No matter how quick we stocked the shelves, it wasn't quick enough. "C'mon, let's bang them out," he would bark over my shoulder as I shoved cereal boxes on the shelf. Timing me as I pulled a 500-pound pallet full of sugar down the aisle, using all my strength just to wheel it, then standing over me as I stacked the five-pound bags in their place. "Done with the sugar? We got a bunch of juice out back. Done with the juice? C'mon, frozen foods are behind. Get to aisle three, canned goods are in. Done? Good, there's a truck out back, go help them unload it. A fifteen minute break? You people and your breaks ... Go ahead!"

I slowly began to hang around with the kids on Prospect Hill. They all wore leather jackets and would hang around a convenience store playing video games like Space Invaders, Donkey Kong, Pac man, and Missile Command. They fed quarter after quarter into these machines in an attempt to beat the high score. All anyone cared about on Prospect Hill was marijuana, motorcycles, and video games. I was friendly with them but never completely fit into the crowd, avoiding the daily pot-smoking rituals and the more serious habits that it led to. But I did save my money and bought a Yamaha 350. It was a small black and orange motorcycle with a high torque, capable of doing a wheelie with just a few quick turns of the throttle, popping the clutch unnecessary. It was more than fast enough for me, capable of eighty or so on the highway. I rode it to work every day, locking it with a chain out front in case someone from the project across the street got any ideas.

After work I screamed through the streets, the small engine surprisingly loud, and rode around Prospect Hill like a madman; doing wheelies half way down the street, feeling invincible as the wind rushed past my face. The rubber cover had come off the footrest on the right, exposing a sharp piece of silver metal below. As I went down Woodland Street one afternoon, I saw my friend's sister sitting on the front porch and decided to show off. I twisted the throttle and did a wheelie, riding it past her house, but the back tire must have hit something. The bike twisted to the side and fell to the ground with me on top. When I stood up there was a light red scratch going across the right side of my neck, crossing my throat and jugular vein. Had my neck gone down a fraction more, instead of just grazing the peg, it would have torn my throat completely open. Just a fraction more—I had escaped death by a thread.

I stayed up late that night watching television for awhile, but grew bored and lay on my bed listening to music. A feeling of melancholy swept over me. I turned the radio off, walked to the front room, and stood at the window, looking out at the dark silhouette of the city. I knew where the smokestacks were by the flickering lights placed on their tops, and I looked at the bridge crossing the Merrimac River. It was actually part of the highway and all night I heard the soft humming of trucks in the distance. They sounded so close, but were really miles away.

To the right of the highway, on the banks of the Merrimac, was Bay State Gas. I had an almost bird's eye view of it from our apartment; not only were we on the third floor, but we were also up on the hill. I could see the big white gas tanks in the compound and the little building by the front. Could see all the little blue and white vans parked in neat little rows, those vans I had been familiar with my entire life. My father had worked for Bay State for many years, fixing and installing furnaces. It was a good job and a hard company by which to get hired. When I was a little boy and I saw one of the vans going by, I always assumed it was my father and chased it down the street, yelling, "Dad! Dad!" The vans never stopped. I figured he couldn't hear me, or someone else was driving it. When I did see him, he seemed larger than life to me, stepping out of his company truck in his blue uniform.

Bay State was less than a mile from my house, but years would pass and I wouldn't see my father. When I did, he would stop by for a few minutes and ask, "So how you kids doing? How's your mother?" He never stayed long, and I would watch his van drive away until I couldn't see it anymore. I couldn't understand it. He was so close, yet so far from my life. He never told me he loved me, and I never said it to him either.

I stood at the window wondering why he never came to see me. Even now, I got a glimmer of hope whenever a Bay State van was in my neighborhood. Thought maybe he was stopping by; would maybe give me a fatherly hug or something. That would have made me feel important. I wondered why he didn't love me. Wasn't a father supposed to love his son? It seemed to defy nature itself—he was just supposed to love me. Looking over the lonely silhouette of the city, I felt a deep and empty feeling, infinite and painful, indescribable.

10

I began to realize the bad decision I had made. I saw kids walking to and from school, in large groups, laughing and joking as they pushed each other around. I missed being with kids my age, had grown weary of stocking shelves with men twenty years older. I decided to return to school in the fall. I left Demoulas, and on the advice of a friend applied at an upscale Lebanese restaurant. He pulled a roll of money out of his pocket, and smugly said, "These are just my tips. All cash, no taxes." That was all it took to convince me, so I gave his name as a reference and got the job.

Bishop's Restaurant was a landmark in Lawrence, known for many miles for their steaks, seafood, Arabic cuisine, and enormous French fries. People drove from all over to eat there—Maine, New Hampshire, south of Boston, everywhere. It was started years back by the mother in the first floor of an apartment building, and was now run by her children who were all well into their fifties and sixties. She had them make a deal: if any of them married, they were out of the business. They all remained single, except one daughter who worked as a maitre d' sometimes. There was Abe, who made his rounds back and forth from the kitchen to the dining room all day, shaking hands and talking to people, seven days a week. Joey, who ran the lounge downstairs and helped himself to plenty of drinks, gaining a reputation as a skirt chaser. Bishy, a short man who ran the kitchen like a general, ordering the cooks around and testing the food for preparedness. Then Vicki, a woman less than five feet tall who sat in the cash booth out back making change and taking money from the waitresses and waiters all night. All four of them were married to Bishop's Restaurant.

It was a good place to work. There was always a light heartedness amongst the busboys as we cleaned and set the tables; jokes made as we passed each other with heavy trays on our shoulders. There were kids from every high school in the area: Lawrence High, Methuen High, Central Catholic, and Andover High. Most of them were from well-to-do families, and I always felt a little inferior. When people gave me a ride home I would have them drop me off at the bottom of the cement stairs of Prospect Hill, telling them, "I live right up these stairs. It's a lot shorter for you. It's a big pain in the ass if you have to go all the way around." But I really didn't want them to see my humble neighborhood. Didn't want them to look down on me.

It was summer so we often went to someone's house after work and played cards until sunrise, the room filled with smoke as we gambled our tips away. I had good luck with this card game called forty-fives, which was only played in the Merrimac Valley. To the dismay of the other busboys, I usually left with more money. For a little while, gambling fever came over the busboys, and there was always a deck of cards in the pocket of someone's red jacket. "Has anyone seen Dino Privitera?"

"Ya, he's in the coat room for a few quick hands of Blackjack with John Lucey."

"Where is Mike Quintana?"

"He's in the downstairs bathroom for a quick round of seven card stud."

One night poor John Lucey had lost all his tips before he even left the building. Walking out with a phony grin on his court jester-like face, making a futile attempt to mask his outrage.

As I came to work one afternoon, I saw a face from the past standing in the kitchen, wearing the black pants and red jacket of a busboy. It was Timmy Boutin, a friend from the fifth grade with whom I had gotten into some mischief. He was standing to the back trying to be inconspicuous as he smoked a cigarette, looking at people out the sides of his eyes. I didn't talk to him right away. Time had passed between us and I figured I would let him come and talk to me first. It wasn't until I gave another kid a ride to his house that we started talking again. A buddy of his, Jimmy McGlaughlin, asked me for a ride and I took him to Tim's house in

Methuen. We stood in his driveway for a long time talking about my new Suzuki 450 and then became good friends, hanging around together constantly.

Tim was from a good family. His father was a firefighter in Lawrence and he also taught at a community college, his mother a secretary at one of the schools. They had a nice little house in a quiet neighborhood, sent Tim to an expensive private school that he didn't appreciate at all, and I was always a little envious of him. But his mother treated me as one of her own and I liked the Boutin family a lot. Tim was three or four inches shorter than me and had a thick mane of brown hair, and right down the middle of the tip of his nose was a line, making it look like a little bum.

I re-entered school as a sophomore and applied myself as I promised I would, taking regular classes instead of the easiest thing I could find. In my one easy class, metal shop, I met a kid named Daryl Lorenza who wore a leather jacket like me and had the same general attitude I did—give a good effort, but don't kill yourself. Daryl was spoiled rotten, getting anything he wanted from his parents. When he saw I had a motorcycle, it wasn't long until he showed up on Prospect Hill with his very own. Cruising up to the curb casually, grinning as he removed his helmet. There was a joke amongst the guys, "If someone had a helicopter, then Daryl's parents would run right out and buy him one."

It was through him that I met my high school girlfriend. He was dating a girl named Lisa and she had a good friend named Kim. Kim had thick walnut brown hair, was very well developed, and big blue eyes. We were driving around with Daryl's cousin and they turned to her street. Lisa got out of the car and returned with Kim, who slid into the back seat across from me. She was wearing silk shorts and I couldn't help but notice her smooth, tanned legs. A love song was playing on the radio, "Inside you the time moves and she don't fade, the ghost in you she don't fade...stars come down in you and love you can't give it away." Every time I snuck a peek at her, she was sneaking one of me. Before I knew it, she was my steady girlfriend, always at my house, or me always at hers. She lived in a three tenement like I did so I didn't feel quite so self-conscious. We took long rides on my motorcycle, her hugging me tightly from the backseat and whispering in my ear, talking on the phone constantly, to the point of aggravation, inviting me over to her house for dinner or to just spend time. She called me so many times one afternoon that I actually snapped at her, "Oh my God! We just talked ten minutes ago. What could possibly be new?"

After awhile it became a lopsided relationship; she wanted me completely, all my attention, all my affection, to occupy every corner of my heart. I didn't love her the way she loved me. I cared about her, would never purposely hurt her, but she saw a future down the road with wedding bells and the pitter patter of little feet. I didn't. So when she called and I couldn't be with her, there was the long sad pause. Then came the carefully thought out guilt trips, making sure I heard the guilty music playing on her stereo in the background, "I guess I thought you'd be here forever, another illusion I chose to create … la, la, la."

Managing my time became difficult; between school, working three days a week until eleven pm, finding time with Kim, and working out at the YMCA. I was playing basketball and lifting weights, proudly flexing my growing muscles in the mirror, enjoying the camaraderie of the guys in the weight room. I loved pushing myself to the limit, leaving the gym saturated in sweat, and then running a few miles home.

As busy as I was, I still found time to occasionally walk by Pappy's Bakery, peeking in the window and longingly looking for my angel. She was never there anymore when I passed, and I wasn't sure if I was just missing her or if she had quit the place. I always kept an eye out when I walked the halls of Lawrence High School, hoping to see her one day walking by or sitting in a class. At least then I could ask someone her name, find out about her. Did she have a boyfriend? What was she like? Was there any chance for her and me? But I never saw her there or anywhere else. Many nights I lay awake remembering the beauty of her face, wishing I had just one chance to talk to her, wishing even more to feel her close to me and kiss her lips.

One Saturday morning in October of my junior year, Tim called and asked if I wanted to go to the Topsfield Fair with him and some of the guys. I was surprised because it wasn't the kind of thing we normally did. We used to take field trips every year from the John Breen elementary school and spend the day there, and it was always a favorite amongst the kids. The candy apples, cotton candy, rides, games where you could win a prize, crowds of people and the smell of horses which was so foreign to a city boy like me. I hadn't been there in about eight years so I told him I'd go.

I got ready and went out front to wait, knowing that he would be at least fifteen minutes later than he said. But I didn't mind. It was a brisk autumn morning with the sun shining brightly, so I sat on the wall looking at the changing colors of the trees and enjoyed the fresh smell in the air. It seemed autumn had a cleansing effect. No matter what your mood was to begin with, it always got a little better when you went outside.

Like clockwork, Tim showed up fifteen minutes later than he promised, pulling up in his mother's big green Torrino with that insidious, "I know I'm a little late," grin on his face.

Another friend of his, Barry Brussard, was already sitting in the front and he opened the door so I could slide into the backseat. Barry was a big lug of a guy, standing about six feet four inches and heavily built. Not muscular in any way, just big. He was a heavy smoker and was always determined to ride in the front seat, yelling, "I got shotgun," whenever we were heading to the car. As we drove off, he opened the cooler and tossed me a beer, "Suck it down!"

"Man, it's not even noontime yet," I said, laughing over the loud rock music Tim was playing. He liked that thrashing heavy metal, where people were always screaming and guitars sounded like chainsaws. "Turn that down!" I yelled from the back, my eardrums ringing.

"What's a matter, can't handle it?" he joked, twisting the cap off a beer bottle, making a loud *pssstt* sound as it opened.

"So what have you guys been up to?" I asked, more in an effort to keep the blaring stereo down than a legitimate interest.

"Same old shit, you know."

He went to turn the radio up again, but stopped as though remembering something. "Oh yeah, we need to pick up McGlaughlin."

"Oh, not him. I hate that fricken kid," I protested from the back seat. I never really liked Jimmy McGlaughlin. I considered him to be a sneak. He was the kind of kid that always talked about people when they weren't around, switching loyalties to whomever he was with at the moment. He could sense I had him figured out, and because of that didn't like me much either. But we were both good at keeping it hidden. "Why not? He's okay," Tim said, over the music he had turned on again, but a little quieter this time.

"He's a sneak. I just don't trust him!"

Tim just grinned and drove on without saying anything. He had known Jimmy a long time; had lived right next door to him before his family moved out of Lawrence.

He stopped in the south end of the city to get him. We got on the interstate to head for the fair. Jimmy cracked open a beer, the radio so loud again that conversation was almost impossible, having to yell to each other just to be heard. Jimmy tapped Tim on the shoulder signaling him to turn the music down, "Hey, you know it's five bucks to get in?"

"Ya, I know," Tim said, taking a sip of beer.

Jimmy sat back again, not having to yell over the radio. "That place is expensive enough. I didn't bring that much money, let's just sneak in."

"How the hell you gonna do that?" Barry interjected. "The entire place is surrounded by a chain link fence."

"Don't worry, we'll figure it out," Jimmy said confidently, finishing what was left of his beer.

After awhile we turned off the interstate and traveled down a long country road that continued straight for miles, passing through large open fields surrounded by little rock walls, or wire fences, cows sometimes grazing in a pasture. I quietly looked out my window as we passed through a corridor of trees in the peak of their color changes, hoping someday to live in a place like this. It was so calm and serene, like watching a painting that had come to life, so different than the chaos of Lawrence.

As we got closer to the fair, the traffic grew heavy and we came to an almost complete stop. Drive a few feet, stop. Drive a few feet, stop. Drive a few feet, stop. We could see the entrance to the fair way in the distance, and at the rate things were moving we knew it would take awhile to get there. "This is great guys," I said breaking up the silence. "I just finished a beer and I really gotta go!"

"You! I've been holding it for the last ten miles," Barry said with a sense of urgency. "Yah, me too, I'm dying back here," Jimmy chimed in.

"I'd say hop out on the side of the road but there's too many cars around. You're just gonna have to suffer," Tim said, trying to maintain order. "Besides, there are cops all over the place."

The fifteen minutes it took to get to the parking lot seemed like an hour, the painful urge to go to the bathroom constant and unmitigated. The parking lot was really an enormous dirt field that was converted for this purpose, and we hurried to the back corner as fast as the flagmen would allow. We searched desperately for a port-a-potty, but there were none. As soon as Tim parked, the four of us burst out and relieved ourselves behind the car. Of course, an old woman had to drive by and see us, shaking her head in disgust as she searched for a spot.

We headed to the entrance and when we got there saw a large sign above the gate—*five dollar admission charge*. We looked back and forth at each other, and then Barry suggested, "Let's just tell the cashier we were already inside. That we just went to your car to get something."

"Yah, like that's really gonna work. They're stamping everyone's hand," I said sarcastically, pointing to a woman getting her hand stamped.

"Well if you're so fricken smart then you come up with an idea," he snapped back, insulted.

"You know what we're gonna do?" Tim started, "We're going to walk along this fence until we find a quiet spot and then climb over. Is everyone up for that?"

We all nodded and began to walk the perimeter of the vast fence, getting disappointed by the constant presence of people right inside. As we went on, we came to a dirt road that ran parallel to the fence and followed it into a quiet, wooded area. This was just what we were looking for, and as we maneuvered through some bushes and down a small embankment, we encountered a little problem: there was a swamp between us and the fence.

"No problem," Barry said, picking up a long log and placing it across the narrowest part. Barry was by far the biggest one of us and we figured if he could make it across, we all could. Slowly he stepped out on the log, like a cat on a tree limb, and he inched his way along, the three of us watching like it was the seventh game of the World Series. Then about halfway across, the log spun a little and Barry's right leg splashed down into the mire. We tried hard not to laugh, but when we looked at him with his left leg still on the log, his right leg immersed up to the thigh, and him reciting every swear in the English language, we all laughed uncontrollably. This made Barry twice as mad, "Real fricken funny you guys! How about giving me a hand so I can get the hell out of here!"

"I guess we're not climbing the fence around here," Jimmy said, still laughing as he grabbed Barry's hand to help him out. We started down the dirt road again and I was still laughing a little, because every time Barry's right foot hit the ground it made obscene squishy noises. He became two toned; his left leg remaining its natural blue color, the right a nice shade of swamp green. He trudged along swearing and mumbling under his breath.

After about fifteen minutes of walking, it became obvious that there were no secluded areas to jump the fence unnoticed. We decided to make our move, didn't care about the people walking by anymore. First Jimmy walked up to the fence and climbed over it, boldly jumping down in front of a passing crowd, people shaking their heads in disapproval as they watched Tim and I climbing right behind him. Barry took so long to get his big wet body over I thought for sure it was the end of us. But security must have been busy elsewhere, or perhaps saw the drawn-out spectacle of Barry struggling over the fence and just let us go out of sympathy.

Inside it was exactly as I remembered it: one road leading to the horse shows and things like that, another road leading to the rides and concession stands, the smell of horse manure hovering in the air. I remembered that the best candy apples in the world were made here and went to a stand and bought one. As I removed the wrapper and bit through the hard red coating, I had a flashback to a field trip long ago, standing here as a little boy doing the exact same thing.

We spent the afternoon walking around, going on rides, playing those games that no one ever wins, like the one where you try to knock down a stack of cans with a beanbag and they all fall down except the last one. Jimmy attempted to climb a rope ladder to win a prize, but only made it a few feet when the ladder twisted and he flung off onto a cushion below. "Let me show you how it's done," I boasted, paying the worker and starting up the ladder myself. I climbed slowly and cautiously, balancing my weight carefully, but just as I neared the top, it twisted and flung me down. "Nobody ever wins this thing," I complained, getting off the cushion frustrated.

Whenever a pretty girl with tight jeans would walk by Barry would tap on my shoulder, point at her rear end and say, "Oooh, boy, look at that! Look at it!" He had some of the worst pick-up lines I ever heard. Turning to pretty girls and saying, "Hey, honey, how ya doing," or "Hey, sweetie, where have you been my whole life?" This got him no further than glaring looks or sassy comebacks like, "Go to hell!"

It was amazing how quick your money disappeared in this place, so when it got dark and the cold air rolled in we started for the gate. "It's only 5:30. You guys wanna do something else?" Tim asked as we walked across the dirt field functioning as a parking lot.

"Like what? We have no money," I said, scanning the rows of cars for Tim's Torrino.

"Man, I wish I hadn't spent all my money. I'm starving," Jimmy complained, more to himself than the rest of us.

"I have an awesome idea!" Barry suddenly suggested, and he stopped walking, pulling a cigarette out and putting it in his mouth. "Why don't we—" then he paused as he pulled out his lighter. He always did this. Would start a sentence then go into this little ritual, this pause for emphasis as he lit the cigarette. He lit it, snapped the square Zippo lighter loudly against his thigh to close it, then exhaled a big cloud of smoke before he continued. "Why don't we do a chew and screw?"

"What the heck is that?" I asked, just the sound of it catching me off guard.

Tim laughed, "It's when you eat at a restaurant and sneak out without paying."

"What if you get caught?"

"Then you'll be washing dishes all night," Tim said, and we all laughed a minute.

"I'm so hungry I'll do anything," Jimmy said, holding his stomach.

It was settled. During the drive, we decided on Chinese, Tim saying he knew the perfect place in North Andover. After a half hour or so, he pulled into the parking lot of a nice restaurant called the China Blossom. He turned the engine off and asked, "You guys ready for this?"

"I told you, I'm starving to death. I don't care if they kill me," Jimmy said with bravado. I had never done one of these, and I was playing scenarios over in my mind as we walked in: being grabbed as I attempted to sneak out, being screamed at in front of a hundred dining patrons, being marched red faced through the dining room as they called the police.

A hostess greeted us at the door and brought us to a booth with four menus standing neatly in place. "Let's get a pu-pu platter for four. It has everything," Tim suggested. When the waitress came over that is exactly what we ordered, but Barry as usual had to push things a little. "Can I have a Budweiser, please?"

The waitress took a look at him, "You show me license, I get you drink," she said with a strong Chinese accent.

"Oh, I don't have it. Must have left it in the car," he said, sounding like a fool.

"No license, no drink," she said sharply, and walked toward the kitchen with our order.

"You stupid idiot! What did you do that for? All you did was call attention to us," Tim snapped at him scornfully.

"Hey, I just wanted a beer. Wanted to see if she would bring me one. They don't usually ask for IDs in places like this," he said laughing, and he was the only one laughing.

"Well, don't do any more stupid stuff. We already ordered. There's no way out of this now. Keep it cool!" Tim continued to reprimand, and I could sense he was a little nervous.

The waitress brought a big round dish with flames in the middle and set it down on the table. Our mouths dripping at the smell of egg rolls, chicken wings, fried shrimp, spare ribs, and a steaming side order of chop suey. We devoured everything in sight, like a school of sharks in a feeding frenzy, stuffing egg rolls in our mouths, making sure no one got more than their share, leaving only a few crumbs scattered in the bottom of the dish. We leaned back in our seats with bloated stomachs and began to survey the place for an exit.

"I have to go to the bathroom," Tim said, sliding out of the booth.

"Yah, me too," Jimmy followed along. They crossed the dining room and disappeared around the corner. I knew they were making their move, and had no intention of coming back. I also knew the last person sitting there would have the toughest time sneaking out, and it wasn't going to be me.

"You know what? I need to go, too," I said to Barry as I was standing up, and as I crossed the dining room, I looked back at him. The expression on his face was one of a sudden realization, a sudden panic, knowing that he would have to walk past the front desk without paying the check. I went into the bathroom, knowing it would call more attention to me if I went straight from the dining room to the front door. I killed a few minutes washing my hands, looked in the mirror, then walked nervously through the lobby and passed the front desk unnoticed.

I breathed a sigh of relief as I left the front doors. I looked over to where Tim had parked, but didn't see the Torrino. I started to feel betrayed when I heard someone whistling from across the parking lot. "Pssst, Kenny, over here," Jimmy yelled, motioning for me to come that way. They had moved the car around the corner for a quicker escape if necessary, and I crossed the street to join them.

"Where's Barry?" Tim inquired, assuming that the two of us would leave together.

"He's still in there. When I got up to go to the bathroom, I thought he would come right after me. Give him a minute. He's probably killing time in the bathroom like I did."

After a long ten minutes had passed we realized that Barry must have chickened out, sat there frozen in fear, unable to take that first step toward the door. "What are we going to do?" Tim asked with regret in his voice. He hadn't considered the possibility of this happening and had no back-up plan.

"How much was the check again?" I asked.

"It was like thirty bucks. Why? You have money on you?"

"No, but I have some at home in my drawer. I was saving my tips. This really sucks. But we can't leave him there. I live the closest anyway. Let's hurry up," I said with extreme disappointment. It was all the money I had for the week and I was spending it feeding these guys.

Tim drove as fast as he could, speeding across the bridge and making it to my house in less than ten minutes. I sprinted upstairs, grabbed the money from my drawer, and got back down to the car in no more than a minute. The tires screeched as he raced back to the restaurant. Time was of the essence now with Barry having to fend off the waitress and manager for a good half hour by the time we'd make it back. When we did I took the money and went inside, and there was Barry at the front desk surrounded by angry Chinese people. As I approached the desk, it became difficult to hold my laughter. The manager was saying to Barry, "You pay me now, or I call police. I no believe you come with hitchhiker," angrily, in the broken English of a recent immigrant.

"I'm telling you, I picked him up and he promised to take me out to eat," he pleaded with an almost believable sincerity.

When I got to the desk, Barry looked relieved and the manager could see he recognized me. "So, this one of your hitchhiker! I no believe you! You pay me money and get out. No come back again!" I remained silent while I paid him. I wasn't even going to attempt to back Barry up on his crappy story.

When we got to the car I told Tim and Jimmy what happened inside and we all laughed until we were breathless, even Barry. "You know you guys are all paying me back," I reminded, as we started down the road home. I looked out into the darkness; sad the day was over. I rolled my window down and breathed the exhilarating autumn air, feeling it blow coolly across my face, and with my friends sitting beside me I was sure I would never grow up.

11

It was a sweltering August night and the air conditioner wasn't working well in Bishops Restaurant. The manager was worried about the customers being uncomfortable, too preoccupied with that to think of the employees. We carried our trays through the muggy air, sweating beneath our red jackets, wiping our foreheads with the cloth napkins stacked neatly by the bread bin. The waitresses complained to each other as they took a smoke break in the corner of the kitchen, "This is ridiculous, it must be a hundred degrees in here." The cooks had it worse than anyone. It was always hot behind the line, but tonight it was unbearable. Every so often, they removed their aprons and walked outside to get some air.

Everyone was grateful as the night came to an end, the wait-resses talking about taking cool showers as soon as they got home. There was a particularly rowdy bunch of busboys on tonight and we had a different plan. We were going skinny dipping in the state pool. Summer was winding to an end and we wanted to do one last crazy thing before school started again. It was mostly a Lawrence crowd—Ricky Poole, who was my enemy in the projects but had become my friend in recent years, Tim, the only non-Lawrencian, Chris Parsons, who I lifted weights with occasionally, and me.

Chris was the only one with a car, so we all hopped into his yel-low Cutlass and started toward the south end of the city. He loved Ozzy Osbourne and he cranked it loudly as we crossed the bridge, playing air guitar at traffic lights and doing a terrible job of sing-ing along. We pulled into the parking lot of the Stadium Project. I briefly remembered running around there as a little boy; had pass-ing thoughts of Andy as I looked at the pool across the road. We climbed over the tall chain link fence, our slick, black busboy shoes making it difficult to get a hold, awkwardly sliding across the top and jumping down to the ground inside.

We removed our clothes by the fence and strutted naked across the cement path that led to the pool. Ricky had no problem walk-ing around naked. He had once removed all his clothes at a party and stood there naked drinking a beer, not bothered by all the girls laughing hysterically. We went straight for the diving boards. "Who's first?" Chris asked, his grin visible in the moonlight.

"Me. I'm gonna do a fanny cracker off the high diving board," Ricky boasted.

"If you do it, I'm right behind you," I said, laughing hard, pictur-ing his big butt smacking against the water and him screeching in pain. He was the kind of guy that would go through with it. Ricky was one of the craziest people I knew. You were almost guaranteed a wild night when he was around. Like Chris and me, he had been lifting weights for years now, but was short and stocky, with thick legs and big protruding buttocks. His appearance matched his crazy attitude; that big toothy grin with spaces between his teeth, his blond hair shaved in a buzz cut, and his face was always beet red, coming close to the shade of a fire engine when he laughed hard.

He started up the ladder before me and we all started laughing as we looked up at his naked butt ascending the rungs, his family jewels obscenely visible. He stood at the end of the diving board and looked down at the distance to the water. "Oh, man, this is gonna hurt," he said with that psychotic laugh of his, then bounced up and down a few times and leaped forward into the dark night air. There was the sound of smacking skin as he hit the water, like a belly flop gone wrong, and the rest of us cracking up as he emerged. "Ahhhhh! My ass is killing me!" he howled as he made his way back out of the pool.

I climbed to the top and walked out to the end of the diving board, regretting the deal I had made, hoping that he wouldn't do a fanny cracker naked. I looked down at the distance to the water, the moon's image reflecting back up at me. There always was that feeling of deception when you stood on this diving board. It looked tall from the ground, but when you actually got up there, it seemed even higher. "You gonna go or what?" Chris egged me on from the bottom of the ladder. I bounced a few times and leaped forward, a strange and liberating feeling coming over me as I passed through the dark air, my senses in disarray at this instant, unaccustomed to flying through the air blindly. I hit the water feet first and went all the way to the bottom, feeling the coolness all around me, my knees bending as I hit and my ears popping. I sprang upwards and burst through the surface of the water, looking straight up into a thousand glimmering stars across the sky. At that moment, I felt glad to be alive, but also felt a little insignificant as I stared at the vastness above me—the Milky Way, the Big Dipper, the North Star burning brightly, and the flickering red lights of a jet so far above.

"Hey, that was no fanny cracker," Tim yelled, bringing me back to my senses.

"Yah, well my butt is a lot smaller than Ricky's. I'd have no ass left if I did that," I shot back, climbing the ladder out of the pool. Tim sprang off the diving board and it looked both bizarre and hilarious watching a naked guy fly through the air. He splashed down and reemerged a second later, taking a deep breath and screaming, "Wah-hoo! This is awesome!" Chris followed suit, not attempting a fanny cracker either. He climbed out and joined the rest of us standing poolside in the moonlight.

"You guys are—" he started, then stopped abruptly and stared over our shoulders. We spun around quickly to see what it was, and through the darkness saw a figure coming toward us from the lifeguard shack. I had heard over the years that someone slept in there to watch the pool, but always thought it was just a rumor. I never expected to learn the truth while standing naked by the diving boards.

He walked barefoot toward us, stopping about ten feet away. "You guys aren't supposed to be in here," he said, in a tone that was more informative than authoritarian, like he was telling us something we didn't know.

"We were hot. Just wanted to cool off a little," Ricky said, grinning at the man.

"Well you guys can swim for a few minutes then you need to leave. But don't hop the fence again. I'll let you out the gate." Then he turned and went back to the lifeguard shack, leaving the four of us standing there open mouthed.

"Can you believe this? He's gonna let us swim," I said with astonishment, expecting him to say he had called the police and we better run.

We jumped into the shallow end and splashed around a minute, and then Tim said, "This is a little strange. Why did he let us stay?"

"I'll tell you why, he's in there getting his jollies watching you guys. Especially you Ricky," Chris said, spitting out water and twisting his face into a devilish expression.

"That's it, we're out of here!" Ricky said with disgust and we all grabbed our clothes by the fence and headed for the gate. We put our underwear and pants on, all except Ricky, who stood naked waiting for the man to twist the key and let us out. He fidgeted nervously with the lock, uncomfortable with this nude body standing casually before him. Ricky flashed the man his toothy grin as he passed him and we tried hard to contain our laughter, little bursts breaking through as we walked into the parking lot.

As we crossed the road to Chris's car, we saw headlights coming toward us and we started to run. But not Ricky. He stood at the side of the road butt naked. As the car passed a woman turned her head suddenly, caught off guard by this exposed figure, and the brake lights flashed red as she came to a stop a little down the road. Some instinct to help must have kicked in, her mistaking this as some sort of legitimate emergency. A poor naked man stranded on the side of a dark road. "What the hell is he doing?" we asked amongst ourselves as he walked toward the car. He bent over at the driver's side window and was talking to the woman for a moment, the same way he would if he were fully dressed. "What the hell is he saying?" I asked rhetorically, knowing that Chris and Tim couldn't hear any better.

The car shot off suddenly and accelerated quickly down the road, the woman realizing she had been duped. Ricky walked back toward Chris's Cutlass, the three of us standing there shocked, laughing hysterically. "What were you saying?" Chris blurted out, in between gasps of laughter.

"I was trying to get a date," Ricky answered, matter-of-factly.

"Can you put your damn clothes on?" I snapped, worried that our luck would run out and we'd wind up in jail.

"Not yet. I think I'm in the mood for a little walk," he said, crossing the parking lot and heading down the staircase into the project.

He began to whistle loudly and a voice shot down from a second floor window, "Can you keep it down?"

Ricky continued down the path, naked and whistling loudly, undeterred by the Hispanic man walking his dog. The man turned as Ricky passed and laughed to himself. Despite our violent protests, he went all the way to the other side and returned a moment later. As he approached the car, we saw headlights coming in the distance and we jumped into the car as quick as possible. "I don't think they saw us," Tim whispered from the back, crammed uncomfortably close to Ricky's bare backside, all of us lying down across the seats to hide.

A light flashed around the parking lot and we remained deathly silent. Then a flashlight shone through the window, scanning over the front and back seat, over three shirtless bodies and a completely bare one. The flashlight tapped the glass a few times, like a knock on your door, "Everybody out!" a voice commanded.

"This is just great," Chris murmured beneath his breath as we climbed out.

"What is this, a love story?" the police officer said sarcastically, looking over our four scantily clad bodies.

"No, sir, just a little college prank," Ricky said with that space between his teeth, picket-fence looking grin of his.

"College prank, huh? Everybody against the car, hands on the roof where we can see them."

We assumed the position, standing there and looking across the roof at each other, worried but still trying to keep a straight face. The police officer walked over to the cruiser and another officer got out. The two of them stood talking for a moment, their words undetectable. A car drove past and slowed down considerably at the sight of Ricky with his hands on the roof and buttocks sticking sharply out. The driver craned his neck to look for a moment, and then drove off with a confused look on his face. The police officers turned toward us and started to laugh hysterically. "You four get the hell out of here!" As they slowly drove away, we could still hear their laughter coming from the open windows of the police car.

It seemed that summer was one wild party, and nobody wanted to let it end. So even after school started again, those warm weeks of Indian summer, there was always something happening. I pranced around the hallways of Lawrence High with the arrogance of a senior, looking down at all the lowly freshman and sophomores.

Weekend nights hanging around Riley's Roast Beef with dozens of other kids, standing there looking cool, seeing who would cruise through in their cars. Would it be people I knew, like Mike Armand in his mother's brown Monte Carlo, packed with the usual suspects, or girls from another town trying to get picked up? There were brawls there sometimes; kids from other towns coming through and trying to make a name for themselves, sometimes getting a serious beating—one poor kid almost had an ear bitten off. I did my share of fighting too, but never at Riley's, although Ricky was usually involved in some way—yelling insults at a passing car or mooning someone's girlfriend. Some kids hung out there constantly, were almost like furniture in the place. I didn't like it that much. A quick stop by on Saturday was enough for me.

A few weeks after school started Tim invited me to a party in Andover. It was at some girl's house. Her parents were away for a few days and it was going to be a bash. When we got there I couldn't believe how many people she invited; kids from Lawrence High, the Vocational high school, Methuen High, and Andover High. It was elbow-to-elbow people, bumping into each other, beer being spilled, loud voices and even louder music throughout the house. The girl looked on nervously at all the people roaming upstairs and down. She was a pretty brunette girl, and I could sense she was uncomfortable with the size of the crowd and their disregard for her house. "How come you invited so many people?" I walked up and asked her.

"I didn't. Word must have spread, and people just kept showing up," she said with regret in her voice.

I spotted Jimmy McGlaughlin and some other kids from Lawrence High and went over to talk to them. They were in a group by themselves and looking around suspiciously. "What's up?" I asked, joining the crowd.

"Man, I got a television!" one of them was saying.

Chris's brother, Dave Parsons, was with them and he laughed and asked, "What did you do with it?"

"It's outside in the bushes. I'm taking it with me."

"I got some jewelry," Jimmy boasted smugly.

"What are you guys doing? She's all right, cut the shit," I said in defense of the girl. I figured she was nice enough to let us into her house without even knowing us.

"What do you care? She's just some rich Andover Jew," they snapped back at me.

"Yah, she's a Jew," they repeated with conviction, as though this fact justified what they were doing.

"This is why people think Lawrence kids are nothing but scumbags," I said, hoping this fact would trigger some kind of proud reversal, giving them the urge to prove people wrong and put the stuff back. But it didn't.

"Screw you! We're never gonna see her again anyways," they said dismissing me and continuing to laugh, looking around for anything else to take.

There was nothing I could do to stop it, would probably wind up in a fight if I pushed it any further, so I found Tim and Ricky and joined them. They were already pretty drunk and challenged me to guzzling contests, which I usually lost. People all around us shouted, "Go! Go! Go!" Then, his inhibitions gone, Ricky took all his clothes off and ran across the crowded living room and up the stairs. Tim lost his senses and removed his clothes as well, then followed Ricky up the stairs. When they got to the top a girl was laughing loudly, and the guy she was talking to got offended at the sight of them.

"What the hell are you doing?" he yelled, and pushed Ricky from behind. Ricky collided with Tim and they both tumbled down the stairs, twisted and entangled with each other, buttocks and every other part flashing back and forth as they rolled.

Remarkably, neither one was hurt. They just got up laughing and ran out to the back yard, sneaking around the swimming pool and running into the woods. I saw Tim lying behind a log, his arms stretched out like he was holding a rifle, taking make believe shots at Ricky who was standing behind a tree. The girl who held the party watched this entire fiasco, speechless, wanting to laugh, but too astonished to do so. "I can't believe this," was all she could come up with, staring at them with disbelief.

Bit by bit people had left, and there were only a small handful of us remaining. Tim was way too drunk to drive and eventually passed out in the living room. Ricky didn't make it much longer, winding up on the floor with his mouth wide open. And if it weren't for the bursts of snoring every moment or so he would have passed for dead. I turned to the girl who was standing against the counter in the kitchen, surveying the mess before her and pondering the enormous clean-up job she faced in the morning. "Do you mind if I sleep here too? We'll help you clean if you want."

"Yah, I could use all the help I can get," she said, waving her hand at the empty beer cans and garbage everywhere.

"Can we do it in the morning?" I asked, just wanting to get some sleep.

"Yah, that's fine," she said, and went upstairs to bed.

I woke up acutely aware that I had drunk way too much, my mouth dry and pasty, feeling lightheaded and groggy. I heard the girl's voice in the kitchen, distressed and close to tears, "When my parents find out, I'm dead. That was my mother's. I don't know what to do."

"I can't believe someone would do that," I heard Ricky's voice saying, sounding rough and hung over. I stood up and felt dizzy for a second, then walked to the kitchen.

"Where's Tim?" I asked, rubbing my eyes.

"He left a little while ago. Said he had something to do with his parents," she said, then put her hands on her head. "What am I going to do?"

I looked at her and felt sorry for what happened, thought to myself I should have done more to stop it. "I think I can help you," I said, trying to sound sincere and make her feel a little better.

"What do you mean?" she asked, lifting her head and looking at me.

"I know who took your stuff."

"You do!" she said gratefully, her eyes opening wide.

"Who was it? Do I know them?" Ricky joined in.

"Yah, it was Jimmy McGlaughlin and those guys."

"What a bunch of assholes! What's wrong with them?" Ricky said sharply, shaking his head.

"Can you help me get it back? They took a really important piece of jewelry from my mother. I'm dead if she finds out. My father is going to lose it," she pleaded.

"I'll do everything I can. If you want, I'll tell the police what I know."

"You would do that?" she said thankfully.

She made us a breakfast of cereal and toast, and I realized we hadn't even been introduced. "Thanks for breakfast. By the way, my name is Kenny Tingle," I said, putting my hand out.

"Oh my God, I can't believe I forgot to introduce myself. Julie Witover," she said apologetically. After breakfast, we cleaned for several hours, me mopping the kitchen, Ricky filling green garbage bags with empty beer cans, Julie vacuuming the whole house.

As I cleaned, I remembered what they had said about her the night before, about her being a Jew, and it occurred to me that I had never known anyone who was Jewish. I had heard all the jokes and stereotypes, but had never actually known a Jewish person. I looked around the house, thinking there might be some kind of sign or symbol that said "house of Jewish people" but saw nothing out of the ordinary.

I met her parents when they returned, and although they were furious about the party and what happened, they were grateful for my help in getting their things back. I told the police what I knew, and although Jimmy denied any involvement, the jewelry was recovered. I lost friends in the process, but gained a new one also. Julie and I were close for years to come.

At first, I expected them to act in a stereotypical Jewish way, knowing nothing but the rumors and jokes I had heard. Thought they would look down on me, and, in truthfulness, they would have every right. Her father was a doctor and her mother a business owner. I was just a poor kid from Lawrence who was present when their stuff was stolen. But they never lived up to any stereotypes, treated me well, and always made me feel at home.

That Monday in school, I was heading to the cafeteria for lunch, and as I passed through the double doors, I saw a man heading up the ramp toward me. He was tall with silver hair and was wearing an amazing blue uniform. There were all kinds of badges and ribbons on the left breast of his coat, a white belt around his waist with a shiny brass buckle, brass buttons running down the front, and a red stripe down the side of his blue trousers. When he was passing, I stopped him. "Excuse me, sir, are you from the army?" I asked.

"Hell, no, son, the Marines. The army is for people who can't make it in the Marines."

I was impressed by his boldness, awestruck by this big muscular man and his amazing uniform. I wanted to be just like him. "Staff Sergeant Gary Sodek," he said, firmly shaking my hand. "Why don't you stop by the office on Essex Street and we can talk about your plans for the future?"

"Sure. What time should I come by?" I asked, studying all the shiny ornaments on his coat.

"Anytime, we're there until seven or eight most nights." He handed me a business card and I watched him walk away, confidence and purpose in his step.

I bought my lunch and sat at a table by myself, thinking about what the sergeant had said, about my plans for the future. I had never really put much thought into it. I couldn't afford college so I never even applied. I always felt like the future would just come, didn't require any planning or consideration, would sweep you along with it like a raft flowing down a river. Then one day you would just be married with kids and living in a white house with a picket fence out front. It never crossed my mind that there was a path to getting what you want, a path that required planning and hard work.

Kim slid up on the bench beside me, bringing me out of my deep thoughts. "I saw you talking to that military guy. What were you guys talking about?" she asked, putting a bite of tater tots in her mouth.

"I don't know, the future I guess," I mumbled, sensing a long conversation coming. "Your future?"

"Yah, you know, he wants to talk to me about my plans for the future."

She stopped eating and looked away for a minute, looking around the cafeteria at nothing in particular. "You're thinking of joining the Marines?"

"I don't know. I talked to him for one second. I'm just going to stop by his office and see what he has to say."

"What about us? If you join the Marines then they'll send you far away," she said in a soft voice, as though a decision had been made and I would be gone soon. She looked down sadly at the table for a moment and then lifted her head, looking directly into my eyes. "Kenny, do you love me?" she asked, studying my face, her female intuition knowing that the truth is more evident on a person's face, more evident in things unsaid, body language exposing lies.

"Yah, I guess so," I fumbled, and then tried to lessen the damage. "I mean, yes. Yes, you know I do." She looked a little stunned, her face twisting into a frown and a tear starting down her cheek.

Her voice cracked, "You guess so? Well I love you so much. Why don't—" She wiped her cheek with her sleeve, got up from the table, and walked out of the cafeteria. I cursed myself for giving such a stupid answer. But it was the truth. I kind of loved her, nothing close to the way she felt about me. Over the years I had tried to break it off a few times, knowing that she was looking for something I couldn't give her. But she always came to my house or called me, hopeful that we would get back together. I didn't like to see her cry so I always said okay.

After school, I started to take the short walk to the YMCA, figuring I could lift weights for awhile before heading to work at Bishops. Halfway there I realized I forgot my weight belt in my locker and headed back to Lawrence High. I went in through a side door I didn't usually use, and just as I entered, I saw her standing against the radiator. It was the girl from Pappy's Bakery. She was right inside the door to the left, just standing there as though she was waiting for a ride.

I had never been face-to-face with her. I stopped abruptly, not purposely but instinctively. I was a little off balance, stopping mid step and twisting a little as I looked at her. She stared back at me and her eyes locked with mine. I was lost for a few seconds, lost in her big beautiful eyes. Her expression was neutral, like mine, as though she waited for some kind of sign from me. My heart fluttered a little when I looked over her warm and beautiful face. My mouth opened a little … but nothing came out. I wanted to tell her everything—how I walked by to see her, how much I loved her, how I wanted to spend the rest of my life with her, how my heart danced every time I saw her, how much I wanted to kiss her lips and neck and smell the shampoo in her dark beautiful hair, how much I wanted to hold her delicate body and feel her close to me. But no words would come out.

I turned and headed toward the stairway. To stand there any longer without speaking would cross the line; would have probably scared her. I wanted to stay there with her. I would have stayed with her forever if she asked. I made my way slowly up the staircase, unaware of the significance of this chance meeting, not knowing this moment would haunt me the rest of my life.

Later that week I went to see Staff Sergeant Sodek as I had promised. He went over all the benefits of the Marines—the money for college, traveling the world, the thirty days of paid time off, the prestige of being a United States Marine, how it would open doors when I was finished—and that day I enlisted. I would leave for boot camp next summer after graduation.

In the meantime, Staff Sergeant Sodek became not only my friend, but also the father I never had. He played basketball with me at the reserve station, went running with me sometimes, took me to Marine functions, and was always glad to see me anytime I dropped by the office on Essex Street. He took a legitimate interest in my life; made sure I kept my grades up and stayed out of trouble.

As the school year went on it seemed I got busier and busier. I went to an auction with the automotive teacher, Mr. Matthews, and bought a Mercury Cougar for two thousand dollars. It was a sporty looking car—shiny black with red bucket seats and a chrome stick shift between them. It was an eight cylinder capable of great speed, and if you stomped on the gas pedal, it took off like a jet. You could fit six kids in this car comfortably, and I often did. In order to pay for it my mother took a loan through her credit union. She didn't want to, but I pleaded, begged, and demanded until she finally caved. She made me swear that I would make all the payments, and this made me even busier, picking up shifts at Bishops. I didn't mind the extra work, but the problem with Bishops was you had to stay until the last customer left. There were many nights when the restaurant would empty out, but some couple would just sit and yap on and on; some guy hanging all over some girl, giving her as much wine as possible and hoping it would pay off later. So several nights a week, I was getting to bed close to midnight and then cursing the alarm at six o'clock, my eyes bloodshot as I went for a shower. I had fulfilled most of the core requirements for graduation and took several easy classes to just slide through senior year. Many mornings I put my head on my desk and slept the whole period away.

That became the story of my life—work, school, lifting weights at the YMCA—day after day, week after week, time just creeping. School started in September, then before you knew it October was there, November flying by and Christmas decorations and music everywhere. When I did get out it was usually with the busboys after work for an hour or two on weekends, going out for fast food or drinking some beer that someone had in their car.

New Year's Eve of 1985–1986 came quickly, and I was working at Bishops as usual. I didn't want to be there, but the tips were really good on holidays, and a bunch of my friends were working with me. Chris Parsons came over just before closing and slapped me on the back. "Hey, loser, let's go out after work. I have a case of beer in my car and we can see if any parties are still going." Everyone was referred to as "Loser," and sometimes you couldn't distinguish

204 | Kenneth Tingle

if it was a playful compliment or an actual insult. It depended on who it was coming from. Since Chris was my friend, it just made me laugh.

"Who's going?" I asked, punching him in the arm.

"So far it looks like me, you, and Ricky. But we're going to South Lawrence to see who's around. It's New Year's Eve, I'm sure everyone's still out."

"You get Ricky and I'm going to get my tips from Ann. I hope that cheap old bag gives me something decent," I said rolling my eyes.

Chris laughed, "C'mon, you think Ann is going to take good care of you? She doesn't care if it's New Year's Eve and you busted your ass. She's cheap to the bone and that's it."

None of the busboys wanted to work for Ann. She was the cheapest of all the waiters and waitresses, working you harder than most of them, and we would do anything to avoid her. She was the oldest by far, grew up in the days when kids were "seen but not heard" and "young fellas" would clean the tables without looking for anything. I found her out back at the booth making change with Vicki. As I approached, she reluctantly pulled out a twenty-dollar bill and handed it to me. "Good job," she said with feigned sincerity.

"Thanks Ann," I said, taking the money. It could have been worse. For Ann twenty dollars was good, and that meant she must have made a bundle tonight. My other waiter, Little John, gave me twenty-five, so it was still a pretty good night.

Chris and Ricky were waiting for me by the takeout entrance, grinning as I approached. "What did the old bag give you?"

"Twenty. Hey, it's better than I thought," I said appreciatively. We walked out into the cold air of December, one hour remaining of 1985, and crossed the street to the post office parking lot. The owners of Bishops were regarded highly throughout Lawrence and the post office let their employees use this lot. We passed the neat rows of mail trucks and went to Chris's yellow Cutlass, parked directly below a street lamp, the light shining through the windows and exposing a cluttered mess in the front and back seats. "Man your car is a pigsty," I said jokingly.

"Hey, I'm too busy to clean it," Chris said loudly, trying to cover his embarrassment. He removed the case of beer, "Why don't we take your car. There's more room anyways."

"Yah, no problem. I'll drive," I said digging out my keys.

Chris really was extremely busy. He had been involved with a girl from Haverhill, the daughter of a police chief, and they had a baby together. He had graduated high school this year and was now in a full-time technical program to become a mechanic, and still working a lot of hours at Bishops, getting only five or six hours of sleep each night. He really loved this girl and wanted a future with her.

We hopped in my car and drove over to Broadway, crossing the stone bridge to the south end of the city. "Let's go to Mounir's. I'm starving," Ricky said from the back seat, raising his voice over the music I was playing. Mounir's was a little Lebanese restaurant, a hole in the wall type of place that we often went to because they stayed open late. A lot of the Lawrence crowd would show up there after a night of partying, and as we drove by, we saw a lot of faces through the window. I turned around and parked next door at Dunkin Donuts, and we made jokes about our busboy uniforms as we walked across the parking lot. "Hey, Ricky, nice shoes. Nice pants. You look pretty stupid, you know that?" I teased. He stopped walking for a second and flashed a look of stupidity.

"You're wearing the same thing, moron!"

"I know. But it looks classy on me. You just look like a buffoon." I gave my most scholarly look and tone of voice, "You can dress a swine in pearls, but in pearls it's still just a swine."

"Go to hell! Where do you come up with this stuff," he snapped back at me, amused and aggravated at the same time.

When we got to the front door a passing car honked at us, and a head popped out the window. "Hey, you guys wait up!" a voice hollered as the car pulled to the side of the road. A big guy got out and waved to the car as it drove off. Through the darkness, I could still make out that lanky physique and cocky strut—it was Jay Dion. He was a friend of ours that went to the Vocational High School, a stand-out athlete who wrestled, played football, and pitched for the baseball team.

"What are you guys doing?" he asked, walking up and stopping at the door with us.

"We're going to get something to eat, and then drink this case of beer that Chris has," I said, in a tone that let him know he was invited. Chris sort of flashed me a look. A look that said, "It's my beer, who are you to invite other people?"

"Yah, I'm starving too. You guys mind if I hang out with you?" Jay said, more of a statement than an actual request.

"Of course not, let's go," I said opening the door and appreciating the warm air as we stepped inside.

It was packed. All the barstools at the counter were full of people, eating and joking, and the booths up front were just as crowded. Obnoxiously loud voices filled the air, the signs of intoxication evident in people's mannerisms. We waved to a few familiar faces as we got a booth out back, pushing each other around as we jostled for a seat. "What time is it?" Chris asked, alerting us of the impending New Year.

I stood and looked over someone's head at the clock behind the counter. "Eleven forty-five," I said, sitting back down. We ordered four Shwarma sandwiches, which were an Arabic creation of steak covered in a sauce of crushed chickpeas and sesame, called hommus tahini, and wrapped in pita bread. We ordered large steak fries to go with it and there was little conversation as we chomped down hungrily, quickly devouring everything in sight.

Voices began to count down throughout the restaurant. "Ten, nine, eight, seven ... two, one!" Everyone cheered and whistled, and we screamed along with them, banging our fists against the table loudly. A girl who couldn't hold her liquor began singing with a slur, "May old acquaintance be forgot—" but stopped abruptly when no one joined in, laughing and hiding her face with her hands.

"Let's get out of here. I'm not spending what's left of New Year's Eve with this bunch of losers," Chris said condescendingly.

As we walked out to my car, Ricky suddenly went to the large window of Dunkin Donuts and stuck his face right against it, flattening his nose and creating big steamy spots on the glass when he breathed. He twisted his face and mocked a small group of men drinking coffee, imitating and taunting them. They got up and pretended as though they were coming out to do something about it, but turned back around and went to their seats. "Will you stop screwing around? I want to get out of here!" I yelled across the parking lot at Ricky. He continued to taunt them and some sad-looking character got angry and came out to confront him. He was skinny and much older than us, sporting a long beard and cowboy boots with ridiculously big heels. He had probably come out of the biker bar on the next corner and wound up in the donut shop.

He walked quickly toward Ricky, "You think you're funny?"

"Yah, I do," Ricky said smugly, unflinching. The man kicked swiftly toward Ricky's abdomen, but he grabbed his foot and twisted him around as he threw him to the ground. His friends had come out now and we all wound up in a big shoving match in the parking lot. One of them got aggressive with Jay, and he punched him in the face so hard the man staggered back and fell to the cold concrete. He slowly tried to get to his feet, stunned and disoriented, not knowing what he was up against. Jay was over six feet tall with shredded muscles, a washboard abdomen. He was not only a good wrestler but a skilled fighter also. One of them tried to kick me, so I moved to the side and attempted to kick him with the hard heel of my busboy shoe.

"Break it up! Break it up! I called the police. The whole bunch of you better get the hell out of here," a man in a Dunkin Donuts uniform shouted out the door.

We ran quickly to my car and my tires screeched as we flew down the road, turning sharply onto Salem Street, then slowing again to remain inconspicuous as we turned onto South Union Street. We pulled over for a few minutes in the shadows of the common. We drank a few beers and waited to see if any police cars went by in search of us. It was only a fight but there was a case of beer in my car and I had no desire to start the year in jail.

"All right, man, the coast is clear. Let's go by Riley's Roast Beef and see if anyone's there," Ricky said, his voice ringing with boredom. I took the short drive there and circled through the parking lot, going slowly around the drive-through window as we scanned the area for people we knew. With the exception of a few unfamiliar faces standing at a car and talking, the place was empty.

"I can't believe no one is here. It's New Year's Eve. Where the hell is everyone?" Chris complained, looking out the passenger's side window.

"There's probably some huge party that we don't know about," I said regretfully. "Let's take a cruise by the Pit." I continued, "Maybe there's a bonfire down there." We drove toward the woods, and I decided to take a shortcut on the road between the Stadium Project. I took the left and as soon as I was turning the corner a small white car jammed on his breaks and screeched to a halt inches from my front fender. We were both going too fast and were lucky to avoid an accident.

The car pulled up alongside of us, going in the opposite direction so that their driver's side window and mine were face-to-face. The window went down slowly and a large man stuck his head out and began to yell at us in Spanish. The only parts of that language I knew were the swears, and he recited every one of them. "Screw you! It was your fault," I yelled back at him, and just as I was driving away Jay leaned forward and spit in the man's face. It was a lung deep, disgusting glob of sputum. "What the hell did you do that for? Are you out of your mind?" I screamed at him as I sped down the road. I pulled into the parking lot on the hill behind Riley's Roast Beef. From there you could look down over the rooftop and see all the surrounding businesses and well down the road, giving you a good view of any approaching cars. Behind us was the tail end of the Stadium Project, only a narrow road separating it from the parking lot.

I pulled in front of a clump of bushes and we got out and stood by my car, Ricky passing everyone a beer. I glanced around nervously, harboring a bad feeling about what just happened. It was eerily quiet, particularly for New Year's Eve. "What a bunch of idiots at Dunkin Donuts," Ricky said laughing. Chris distorted his face, and did an exaggerated walk to imitate them coming out of the donut shop after us. I couldn't help but laugh at his little show, these faces that he was able to make, and I felt a little less nervous. There was a brief pause, and I heard the sound of an engine grinding as it raced up the hill, the gears changing as it climbed. The cars parked all along the back of the lot blocked my view of the road. Everyone's face had an alert expression and Chris ran to the edge of the lot and looked down the hill. "It's that guy! It's that guy in the white car!" he turned to us, screaming with urgency. We all ran toward the road, crouching behind the parked cars for cover. The little white car screeched to a halt directly in front of us. The door flew open and the large man jumped out, his frizzy hair accentuating the furious expression on his face. He reached behind him into the car and pulled out a rifle, brought it to his shoulder and began firing toward us. *Pop, pop, pop,* sounding almost like a pellet gun. I cursed Jay beneath my breath for spitting at him, and listened in disbelief to the sound of Chris and Ricky laughing, "What kind of gun is that?"

They began to hurl beer bottles at him from behind the cars, and I heard them striking his car with a metallic thud. Jay stood up beside me and hurled a beer bottle with all his might, just missing the man and it bounced across the grass of the project behind. He cocked his arm to throw again, the man fired toward us. *Pop,* and Jay fell to the ground beside me. The man jumped in his car and started down the road, Chris and Ricky chasing him with rocks in their hands. In the distance, I heard them yelling and the sound of the rocks striking his car.

I crouched beside Jay, "Are you all right? Are you okay?" I said, shaking him, panicked at the sight of him on the ground.

"Uhhh, my shoulder," he groaned softly, rolling over and grabbing his right shoulder. I took his left hand and helped him to his feet. Chris and Ricky came back up the hill, laughing, and saying, "We smashed the shit out of his car!"

"Jay got hit. His right shoulder," I cut in sharply, not caring what they did to his car. A terrifying realization came to me at that moment—I was standing right next to Jay when he was hit, if the bullet was a few feet to the left it would have got me right in the head.

"Are you okay?" Chris asked, apologetically, feeling foolish that he was boasting about the car instead of checking on Jay.

"We didn't even know he got you," Ricky added in guiltily.

"I'm all right, I guess," Jay answered, grimacing and clutching his right side. "My shoulder is killing me really bad."

"Let's look at it," I said, helping him remove his jacket and pulling the right side of his collar down to see. In the rays of the streetlight, I could see a small bloody hole in the front of his shoulder, and another bloody hole on the back. "Son-of-a-bitch, that was no pellet gun. We need to get you to the emergency room!" I said authoritatively, leaving no room for argument.

"Is it bad?" Jay asked nervously.

"It went right through. That must have been a .22 he was using," Chris jumped in with the tone of an expert.

I drove up South Union Street going as quickly as I could without drawing attention to us. The last thing we needed was to be pulled over. How would we explain this one to the police—four eighteen-year-olds with alcohol on their breath and a gunshot wound. As we neared the intersection of Merrimack Street, I saw a woman walking on the sidewalk wearing only a tee shirt, seemingly oblivious to the freezing December air. Her shoulder length brown hair was tossed about messily and there was something all over her face. I pulled to the side and Chris stuck his head out the passenger's side window. "Hey, are you all right?" he asked as she passed.

"Leave me alone," was all she said, looking down at the sidewalk without stopping. Blood was coming from her nose and mouth, and she appeared to have been beaten. "Hey, we're going to the hospital anyways. We can bring you if you want," I said out the passenger window, leaning across Chris so she could hear me. She just kept walking without even looking at us.

"C'mon, we need to get to the Emergency Room. She doesn't want our help," Ricky said with urgency.

"Uhhh, my shoulder," Jay groaned. "Now I can't pitch in baseball season."

"You're lucky you didn't get hit in the head. A foot to the left and the bullet would have hit you right in the face," I reminded sternly, driving across the green metal bridge, the familiar humming sound below as the tires went over the grids. The hospital was right around the next corner and I pulled up to the entrance of the emergency room. I turned to the backseat. "Ricky, you go inside with Jay. I'm going back to help that woman. Chris, you come with me." There was no disagreement, and I watched as the electric double doors parted and they disappeared down the corridor.

I drove down the hill and turned back onto Union Street, wondering if I would be able to even find the woman. As I crossed the bridge again, Chris spotted her. "There she is," he said suddenly, like he didn't expect to see her. I went to the end of the bridge and made a U-turn, going back over in the opposite direction. I slowed as we approached her on the sidewalk.

"Hey, why don't you let us help you?" I said sympathetically, worried that she would stop and fling herself over the rail into the icy river below.

"Leave me alone," she said, with a congested voice that sounded close to tears. She kept walking and the support beams of the bridge kept coming between her and us, preventing any serious conversation. In the moonlight, I could see the dark shade of blood on her face, and I refused to give up.

She was already halfway across and I drove to the end of the bridge and pulled over to the side of the road to wait for her. I could hear the sound of her footsteps as she walked across the floorboards of the walkway, echoing in the empty space between the bottom of the bridge and the river below. I stood on the sidewalk waiting for her to reach me, and a police car turned the corner and came down Union Street toward me. I stood on the edge of the curb and waved my hand to get his attention. The cruiser stopped and a bright spotlight flashed directly at me, prompting me to put my hand above my eyes like you would on a bright sunny day, his face only a shadow amongst the glare. "Officer, there's a woman on the bridge with a bloody face. She won't let anyone help her," I said, walking over to his open window.

He studied me for a moment, this figure that appeared out of the dark. "I'll take care of it," he said, slowly driving on and flashing his light around the bridge, fixing it on the woman when he saw her. He stopped to question her and there was muted conversation between them in the distance.

"We did everything we could. Let the police handle it now. We need to check on Jay," Chris said calmly, resolved to the fact that it was out of our hands. I drove back around the corner to Lawrence General Hospital and pulled into the emergency section, intending on going inside and checking on our friend. But Ricky saw us through the sliding doors and came walking out before I even parked. He strolled casually over to the driver's side window, waiting impatiently for me to roll it down. "Guys, Jay is probably getting admitted. His mother's on her way. We might as well get out of here. He's doing all right, and we can check on him in the morning," he said. I stepped out so he could climb into the backseat.

As we drove down the hill, I heard Ricky shuffling around behind me and the sound of glass bottles clanking together. "There's still some beers back here. Do you want to drink them?" he asked in a tone that told me he didn't want to go home.

I looked over at Chris and he shrugged, "Why not? I'm too keyed up to go home right now anyways."

"What about your car? Do you want to go get it first?"

"Nah, I'll pick it up tomorrow." I turned onto Union Street and without asking anyone, by some sort of blind instinct, made my way back to the parking lot behind Riley's Roast Beef. We stepped out of the car and each opened a beer, standing in the first light of dawn that was slowly breaking through the darkness. I looked at my friends for a moment, and then said in an exhausted voice, "What the hell happened tonight? First Dunkin Donuts, then Jay getting shot and you guys chasing the car with rocks, the woman with blood all over her face. I feel like I dreamed it, like it never really happened."

"I know," Ricky agreed, "it's like it was all a weird dream."

The sun was cresting over the horizon and I was glad to put this night behind me. The three of us were quiet now, deep in our own thoughts as we studied the sky, the dawn of a new year unfolding before our tired eyes. The emerging sun evoked feelings of optimism, feelings of promise in the year to come. But feelings of uncertainty also dangled in the cool air. Where was my life going?

12

Like all new years, the first few months of 1986 just disappeared. There was that transitional period where I wrote 1985 for the date, then frustratingly erased it as I had done a dozen times. As time marched on I felt the Marines approaching. I had enlisted in 1985 for active duty the following summer, and when I signed the papers, it seemed so far in the future. A year's wait—a lifetime in the adolescent mind. But 1986 was here now, the buffer of a year's delay disappearing like the old calendars on the walls. Leaving for the military gave me feelings of excitement mixed with apprehension of the unknown. I had no intention of trying to back out, deep down inside knowing I would never make anything of myself if I stayed in Lawrence.

It wasn't Lawrence itself that was the problem; it was the fact that old habits die hard. There would be the same old routine, the same old wild friends, the same partying in the same places. I could sense other people were thinking the same way, and it seemed everyone was busy making some sort of plan for the future. Tim, Ricky, and even Jay Dion joined the Marines like me, although I would be the only one to finish four years with an honorable discharge. If it wasn't the military then it was some other plan: Daryl already had a job lined up with the city where his father was a manager, Chris was finishing his mechanic's school, and the others were heading off to college.

I was ready to move on, was tired of Lawrence High and those same old faces, the same little nauseating cliques, the same old rumors and gossip. "Did you hear what Sherry did with Billy? She was so drunk!" It got to the point where you didn't even want to walk by certain places, knowing that same old crowd would be hanging out in the hall, and if you walked by they would be sharpening their blades on you. You could be sitting at a table eating with some friends and they would be talking about someone, then one of them would leave for a minute and they would start talking about them. You ended up staying there longer than you wanted, knowing that the minute you left you were next.

Daryl wound up being the conversation for awhile. He was usually a somewhat quiet kid who minded his own business. Then one night at a bonfire party in a place called "the Pit" something came over him, some need to look cool and tough, and he walked up to a smaller kid nicknamed "potty" and just punched him in the face. No provocation, no reason whatsoever. When people grabbed him and asked, "What the hell was that for?"

"It's potty. It was just potty," he said as though this kid only existed for people to randomly punch out. His motive backfired, and instead of looking cool and tough, he was called an idiot throughout the school. I would have expected this from some other guys, like Jimmy McGlaughlin with his endless pursuit of an image, but not Daryl. This made me realize that we never truly know anyone, never really know what passes through the dark recesses of their mind. What did he have to be angry about? He lived in a nice house with parents who spoiled him rotten. Where did this pent-up anger come from? I never could understand what happened, and I don't think Daryl ever understood what happened either. In the weeks that followed, he kept a low profile. I could sense his regret.

I kept a pretty low profile as well. Not because I wanted to but because I continued on with my frenzied lifestyle of school, work, and lifting weights at the YMCA. Tim and Ricky had already left for the Marines, having graduated in 1985, and I hung around mostly with Daryl and another friend named Dave Walsh whom I had known for years. Dave was an interesting character; he always maintained a preppy type image but smoked a lot of pot. He had black curly hair and his legs were a little too short for his body—causing a unique bouncy type walk as he went through the hallways. This stride made him recognizable from great distances. He often went out at lunch and got stoned, encouraging me to go with him. I always refused, not wanting that spaced-out feeling while sitting in class and talking to friends.

But one spring afternoon he caught me in a particularly carefree mood. I was eating my lunch when he slid into the bench across from me, grinning in a mischievous way that I knew all too well. "Finish that tray. Let's go outside and smoke a joint."

"Are you serious? Right now?" I laughed, chugging what was left of my chocolate milk.

"Yah, why not?" he encouraged.

"I don't know. I have a few classes left."

"C'mon. You're a senior. You're on the senior slide, relax a little."

"All right, all right, you win," I said grinning back at him.

I put my tray away and we went outside through the courtyard, passing through the little groups of smokers huddled together for a quick cigarette after lunch. "Where do you want to do this?" I asked, looking at the busy surroundings.

"Don't worry, I have a good place," Dave said confidently. We turned the corner and walked along the back of the school, stopping at the little enclave around the back doors that led to the gymnasium. "Right here!" I asked incredulously, knowing that cars would drive back and forth past us.

"This is where I always go. I haven't had a problem yet."

He pulled a plastic bag from his pocket and carefully removed a thickly rolled joint, put it to his lips, and held a match to the end, the tip glowing bright red as he inhaled deeply. His cheeks were puffed out in exaggeration as he held in the smoke as long as his lungs would tolerate, then passed it to me cupped between his fingers. I took a deep drag. It burned my lungs a little as I held it, and then exhaled an enormous cloud of smoke that lingered. A car cruised slowly by and Dave cupped his hand and bent his wrist in a way that completely concealed the joint. We passed it back and forth a few times and a feeling of lightheadedness came over me; a feeling of hyperawareness, noises seeming a little louder, the sound of a car door closing in the distance, startling me and causing me to spin around and look. He took one more drag and put it out against the wall, then slipped the little piece that was left back into the plastic bag. "Man, your eyes are really red," I said, my voice sounding muted and strange to me, like it came from someone else. "How are mine? Are they really red?"

"Kenny, you look really baked. You better not go back in school," Dave said with a concerned look on his face, but couldn't keep it up, and burst out laughing. "Oh, man, I couldn't keep a straight face. You should have seen the look on your face when I said that," and he continued to laugh until his face turned a dark shade of red.

"Keep laughing, Dave, because you really do look baked," and then I started to laugh with him, the word "baked" setting me off. He looked at the silly expression on my face.

"I told you this was really good stuff. I'm not going back inside. You can if you want."

"You bastard! The only reason you smoked that strong stuff is because you knew you were leaving. I have to go back inside like this."

Dave found this incredibly amusing, loved the idea of me sitting through my classes in another world. "I'm taking off, but I'm going by the office first and asking if I can make an announcement over the intercom. I'm letting the entire school know you're baked." Then he cupped his hands around his mouth and distorted his voice like he was speaking over the intercom. "Attention all students! If you see Kenny Tingle, take a good look at him. He is completely baked!" The word "baked" set me off again and I laughed as he crossed the street and left school grounds, waving as he went around the corner.

I went back through the empty courtyard and without thinking about it walked into the cafeteria. I looked at the hundreds of students sitting at the tables and a sense of paranoia swept over me. Every conversation at every table was undoubtedly concerning how stoned I looked. Every laugh in the distance was surely directed at me, and I walked self-consciously across the wide room, convinced all eyes were on me. The minute it took to get to the other side felt like a half hour in my clouded mind.

I sat through my last two classes with the same sense of paranoia, thinking the teacher and every student around me was quietly aware of my condition, but they were keeping it as a private joke between them. When the dismissal bell rang, I breathed an enormous sigh of relief and left the building without even stopping by my locker. I considered going home and taking a nap, but opted instead to go to the YMCA and play a little basketball. I had the night off from work and I always kept some shorts in my car.

I thought my skills would be diminished from the pot I smoked, but the effects were wearing off and I played a couple of intense full-court games, pouring with sweat and gulping down enormous amounts of water. I left around dinnertime and picked up a sandwich to eat on the drive home. As I entered the stairway I could hear the distant ringing of my telephone three flights above, and I sprinted up the stairs to reach it in time. "Hello," I answered, breathing heavy and sounding winded.

"Hi, what are you doing?" Kim's familiar voice said on the other end. I paused for a minute, not expecting to hear her voice. We had broken up a few weeks before and this time I thought it was for good.

"Nothing, I just got in the door."

"Where were you?" she asked, in that old familiar tone that tried not to sound suspicious, but sounded suspicious nonetheless.

"Down at the Y. I played a little basketball and stuff."

"I guess you don't have to work tonight."

"No, I have the night off."

"So—" she hesitated a moment, and I knew she wanted the conversation to go in a different direction. "What are you doing about the prom? You're going, aren't you?"

"Yah, I guess so. It's not for another month, I haven't really thought about it."

There was a long awkward pause and I knew what was next. "So … who are you taking?" she asked innocently.

"I don't know. Like I said, it's a month away. I guess I'll ask somebody … I don't know."

"You have no idea?" her voice was full of suggestive sarcasm, like the answer was obvious.

"No, I'm not sure. I guess I'll have to figure it out." She was quiet for a second. I heard her phone hitting the receiver and the dial tone rang in my ear.

I really didn't know what to do. I had become more than friends with a girl at the Lawrence Vocational High School, Leanne Liskowski, who was a really nice kid. She had dirty blonde hair and piercing green eyes, was always upbeat and happy, and was fun to be around. She did well in school, but the kids at the Voc said she was "book smart" and otherwise an "air head." I got offended by that, knew she was anything but. I wasn't sure what my relationship was with her. We hung around together on occasion, her standing very close at times, and I once even kissed her. But I never asked her out and I couldn't say she was actually my girlfriend. She called me sometimes, and she had hinted about the prom more than once, so I knew she wanted to go with me. But I also knew Kim was fully expecting me to ask her, and in this way she figured we would get back together. I had been on and off with Kim for years and I didn't like to hurt her.

I went and got fitted for my tuxedo and reserved it, made plans to go with Daryl in his parents' Cadillac, even discussed plans for after the prom, but remained frozen with indecision and hadn't asked anyone to go yet. Kim had her friends ask who I was going with, had them strongly hint it should be her, but as the prom drew closer she gave up and accepted an invitation from someone else. I felt relieved now and with a clear conscience asked Leanne to go with me. She accepted and we spent a lot of time on the phone discussing what color her gown should be to match my tie and cummerbund, joking about who was a worse dancer, talking about what we would do after the prom.

The plans were set: instead of renting a limousine, Daryl was borrowing his parents' Cadillac and picking up his date and Leanne, then swinging by my house and we would drive to Diburro's restaurant where the prom was being held. After the prom, we were renting rooms at the Salem Inn. It started with us, then word spread, and it seemed everyone we knew was getting rooms next to us, resulting in an entire floor of the hotel being reserved by Lawrence High kids. Daryl had a brainstorm: he was buying a few cases of beer in advance and filling the hotel room bathtub with ice, then burying all the beer in it so when we arrived there would be plenty of cold drinks. I commended him on his genius idea.

The day before the prom, Dave Walsh stopped me in the stairwell just as I was leaving school, reaching through the crowd and grabbing my arm from behind. I turned quickly thinking I had bumped into someone and they were looking for a fight. "Hey, Ken, relax it's just me. I was looking all over for you. I need you to do me a favor," he asked in a tone that said he fully expected my services.

"Depends what it is," I said firmly, not wanting to get caught up in some time-consuming escapade that he had dreamed up.

"I just need a ride over by the Tarbox School. I have to pick something up then maybe you could drop me off at my house."

"Yah, that sounds easy enough," I said, continuing quickly down the stairs as though I was in a rush to be somewhere, forcing him to walk faster in order to keep up.

I liked hanging around with Dave. He was one of those people who would do something spontaneous, something bizarre and hilarious on the spur of the moment. He once made a dozen prank calls from my house while talking through a detached vacuum hose. He held one end to his mouth and the other end to the mouthpiece of the phone, creating a hollow and computer-like voice. He looked up phone numbers to several girls in our school then called them with this robotic-type voice. "Hello," they would answer unsuspecting. Dave would say, "This is God!" his voice echoing through the vacuum hose. There would be a baffled silence on the other end, and then the phone would slam down. Just as he was having the time of his life, he dialed a girl named Kathy and waited gleefully for her to answer. When she did, he went into his same routine. "This is God!" he shouted through the vacuum hose and there was the baffled pause again, but this time I heard her voice shouting back.

"Dave Walsh you're so weird!" and the sudden dial tone in his ear. He sat there stunned and embarrassed. "Picked off! I don't believe this. She picked me off. She's going to tell everyone in school!"

I drove up Lawrence Street and followed Dave's directions to the place he needed to be. He had me pull over next to a small park that was across from the Tarbox School. "I'll be back in a minute," he said, climbing out of his seat and walking over to a white three-tenement apartment building. He knocked on a first floor door and waited impatiently on the porch, looked over his shoulder a few times, then knocked again. The door opened slightly and a shady looking character with no shirt stuck his head out and looked around a moment, then took something from Dave and disappeared inside. Dave looked nervous as he stood waiting, constantly looking up and down the street. The man returned a moment later and handed something to Dave, closing the door immediately after. Dave tucked it into his pocket as he leaped down the stairs and headed for my car.

"What the hell did you buy?" I asked as he slid back into the passenger seat. I put the car in drive and headed down the street, wanting to get out of this neighborhood. I waited for his answer.

"Just a little something to make sure the prom is a night we'll remember forever," he said, flashing that mischievous grin of his.

"Curiosity killed the cat you know. What was it?" I prodded, knowing he was going to make me work him for an answer. He kept grinning at me, enjoying the suspense. I turned onto Lawrence Street and made a quick right onto Fern then turned agitatedly to Dave. "All right, enough of the little game. What did you get?"

"You ever do cocaine?" he asked inquisitively.

"You bought cocaine! You're doing cocaine at the prom!" My voice rang with humorous disbelief, like he planned on going naked.

"Yah, I told you it's going to be a night to remember forever."

"You crack me up Dave. Only you would come up with something like this."

"No, actually there's a few of us. I got enough for you too if you want," he said and he turned to me to wait for a reaction.

I was quiet for a minute, my mind playing over the idea of something completely new, something entirely different than anything I had done before. A new sensation on the grand finale of high school—the senior prom. Dave seemed to know that my mind was weighing the possibilities and remained silent a moment as I pondered things, but grew impatient waiting for an answer. He finally asked, "Well, you in or what?"

"What's it like?" I answered, genuinely curious.

"It gives you this totally euphoric feeling. It's like you're on top of the world. Trust me, you never want to come down," he said in the convincing tone of a salesman.

It sounded like the perfect idea—a way to make the prom the best night of my life.

"Yah, why not," I said enthusiastically. He gave a wide grin and slapped my right hand as we drove.

"Way to go, brother! Trust me, this is going to be a blast!"

I dropped him off at his house and he stood at his front door flashing that mischievous look again, making me laugh with obscene gestures as I backed slowly down the driveway.

The next afternoon I spent hours getting ready. Taking a long, hot shower, fussing over my hair until I felt it was perfect, standing in front of the mirror gazing at the gray tuxedo I was wearing. I had never even worn a suit and felt like royalty in this outfit. My mother got dressed up too in anticipation of Daryl and our dates arriving, knowing there would be plenty of pictures. I paced back and forth nervously waiting for them to arrive, feeling self-conscious about my humble neighborhood. Daryl was taking a girl from Andover and I was sure she would get out of the car and think I lived in a dump, but would act polite as she looked around condescendingly. I wished I had agreed to meet at his house.

I heard the sound of dress shoes and heels making their way up the three flights of stairs and I stood with the door open to greet them. Daryl was wearing a white tuxedo with a pink cummerbund and tie that matched his date's pink gown. Leanne looked absolutely stunning; her green eyes brought out even more by her teal blue gown and her dirty blonde hair hanging in soft curls to her shoulders. She smiled at me with her deep dimples showing and I knew I was taking the most beautiful date to the prom. "C'mon in," I said anxiously to everyone. My mother stood smiling in the kitchen.

"Would anyone like a cold drink or something?" she asked cordially.

"No thanks," everyone answered politely.

"Why don't we sit in the living room a minute," I said, ushering them there. The four of us sat on the couch and my mom ran to her room to get the camera. "Everyone smile," she said. She snapped a few pictures. Daryl's date was a brown-haired, serious girl and her expression wasn't much of a smile.

I stood with my mom while Daryl snapped a few pictures of us with her camera, then I kissed her on the cheek and we headed down the stairs. Daryl had left his car right in the middle of the driveway as though a valet had brought it there for us. It was an incredible spring day with the sun shining brightly and birds singing all around, the smell of lilacs and other fragrances permeating the air. I got in the back next to Leanne and we turned and smiled at each other, then she turned shyly away with a cute little grin.

The prom was being held at a restaurant in Haverhill called Diburros, and Daryl got onto the highway at the bottom of Prospect Hill. I was a little nervous but even more excited, the anticipation of this day building for weeks. I was proud to be taking Leanne. I knew that all heads would turn when I walked in with her. And they did. I could see it on people's faces as we walked hand and hand into the hall. I knew they were thinking, "Who's that beautiful girl with Kenny Tingle? She's not from Lawrence High. Man, he sure brought a babe with him."

Daryl, Dave Walsh, I, and our dates sat together. The table was waiting for us with little name cards in front of our seats, napkins folded neatly on the tablecloth and fine silverware to the side of our plates. The disc jockey started with some soft music as people filed in and took their seats. All these people who I had seen for years in the halls of Lawrence High looked so different tonight. The guys looking spiffy in their black tuxedos, the girls adorned with fancy gowns and jewelry. Even the average girls looked good tonight with their little corsages pinned to their gowns, but none of them could touch Leanne.

I looked around at all the different tables, seeing who was sitting with whom. When my eyes crossed Kim's table she was glaring directly back at me, shaking her head with a disgusted look. Dave caught this brief moment between us and laughed, "Man, if looks could kill you'd be dead!" Leanne looked the other way pretending she didn't know what was going on, but I knew she did. I held her hand below the table and she turned back to me and smiled. Kim had come with a junior named Carl Farrington, who wasn't a bad looking guy, and I avoided looking at their table as much as possible. But on the few occasions my eyes crossed that way, Kim was invariably glaring right at me.

224 | Kenneth Tingle

The dinner was served and the pictures were taken, so the disc jockey turned up the tempo with a crowd favorite, "Everybody on board...don't miss the party train." Everyone sat watching for a moment to see who would break the ice, what daring couple would hit the floor first, and when someone finally did the crowd followed right behind and the floor was soon packed with gyrating bodies.

Dave leaned to me and tapped me on the shoulder, "Let's take a walk to the bathroom," he whispered in a way that told me he had more on his mind than relieving himself.

I turned to Leanne. "I'll be right back. I'm going with Dave a minute. Maybe we can dance when I get back."

"Don't take too long," she joked, unaware of our intentions. We didn't tell any of the girls what Dave had brought. We knew they would be upset.

We went into the men's room and waited for a kid we didn't know well to leave. When he did, Dave took out a small plastic bag with white powder at the bottom and poured some on a little cosmetics mirror, the kind girls used to check their lipstick. He chopped it with a razor blade and formed it into a straight line on the mirror. Then took out a twenty dollar bill and rolled it like a straw, sticking one end in his nose and bending forward to the mirror snorting, the line disappearing as he moved his head forward. He stood up and put his head back for a second, looking straight up at the ceiling, then lowered it and looked at me with eyes wide open. "Whoa!" he said excitedly. He put some more on the mirror, chopped it into another straight line, and handed the rolled twenty-dollar bill to me. I leaned forward and snorted it the same way Dave did, my nostril burning as it passed through. It left a dry powdery taste all along the back of my throat.

A euphoric feeling immediately came over me, a feeling of absolute well-being, and the world suddenly became a wonderful place. I could feel my heart beating faster and thumping in my chest. Dave smiled at me, "Awesome, huh?" I just smiled back without saying a word, knowing he was feeling the same thing. No comments were required. We walked back out to the blaring music and loud conversations going on throughout the room, feeling an acute awareness of everything around us with our heightened senses.

I walked to our table and took Leanne's hand. "C'mon let's dance!" We worked our way through the crowd, found an empty spot, and danced close to each other, moving to the rhythm of the beat. "Oak tree! Put you to the test, oak tree when it comes to dancing I'm the best."

The disc jockey played a slow song next. "I've been alone with you inside my mind, and in my dreams I've kissed your lips a thousand times. I sometimes see you pass outside my door, hello, is it me you're looking for?" Even though I held Leanne tightly, my mind was filled with the girl in Pappy's Bakery. They weren't Leanne's eyes I was looking into at that moment. They were hers. I wondered where she was, and what she was doing right now. I wasn't even sure she lived in Lawrence or went to Lawrence High. I had only seen her that one time waiting by the doorway. I liked dancing with Leanne, her smile and her sincere laugh made her so much fun to be around. But my heart was elsewhere. I wanted to dance with the girl from Pappy's Bakery and hold her close. Just like the lyrics of the song he played—*in my dreams I had kissed her lips a thousand times.*

The disk jockey played *Party Train* one more time and everyone formed a big long line, putting their hands on the shoulders of the person before them, creating one big human link across the dance floor, moving side to side and kicking our feet as we went. After that song, I had enough and went back to the table, leaned over and whispered to Dave, "Are you going to do anymore of that stuff? I don't feel anything anymore."

"Yah, that's the bad part. It costs a fortune and doesn't last long. That was just a tease we did, we're really gonna hit it when we get to the hotel," he whispered back, glancing over his shoulder and making sure the girls couldn't hear.

The music stopped and some of the teachers took to the floor with microphones, going on and on about this kid or that kid. Then they concluded the night with the announcement of prom king and queen, the two of them having a private dance in front of the whole senior class, looking awkward and self-conscious as they turned slowly beneath a spotlight. After that, the floor was open for one final slow dance and I went back out with Leanne. She stared directly into my eyes as the music played, her green eyes piercing and hypnotizing, her dimples showing as she smiled warmly at me. She put her head on my shoulder and hugged me tight until the song ended. The lights came on brightly and the music stopped; senior prom was over.

"I hope you brought a change of clothes," Daryl said as we crossed the parking lot to his car.

"Of course I did," I said sarcastically. "You think I want to stay in this monkey suit all night? Leanne, you brought a change of clothes too, didn't you?" I asked, grabbing her by the waist and swinging her around.

"Kenny! Stop it," she giggled loudly. "Yes, I brought clothes. Now put me down!" We hopped into the car and as we pulled out of the driveway, we saw Dave in the backseat of the car ahead of us, turning around and sticking his face against the rear windshield, making obscene gestures with his tongue as we turned onto the highway. "Your friend is such a pig," Leanne said, half laughing and half disgusted.

We pulled into the Salem Inn and went straight to the room. Daryl had the keys on him so we didn't have to check in at the desk. I changed into some jeans and a Lawrence High football T-shirt. Leanne came out of the bathroom wearing a loose sweatshirt and tight jeans that showed off her sexy, muscular legs. We had rented adjoining rooms and I knocked on Daryl's door. He opened it wearing a similar outfit—jeans and a T-shirt. I went straight to their bathroom and reached into the ice-filled tub, my hand freezing as I dug out two beers. I tossed one to Daryl. "Let's see who can finish it first," I challenged, popping the cap off with a *pssst*. He smiled with a competitive look on his face.

"You're on! One, two, three, go!" We stuck the bottles in our mouth and tilted our heads back, making gulping sounds as the beer disappeared, and then both raced to bring the bottles down first. It was close but he had me by a good second, burped loudly, and said, "Lightweight! How dare you challenge me!"

We gave the girls a beer and sat on the bed talking for awhile, Leanne sitting next to me and shyly letting us do most of the yapping. Leanne had the exact opposite of a bad reputation, people saying she was a little of a prude, saying she was not the type to do anything with guys. I wondered to myself; she had rented a hotel room for the night with me—did this mean she wanted something to happen?

There was a knock on the door and I opened it. Dave walked in without waiting for an invitation. "I hope you girls don't mind if I steal Kenny and Daryl for a couple of minutes. I want to show them something in my room," he said as though there was something unique and fascinating to be seen.

"No, go ahead," Leanne said, and Daryl's date just nodded without smiling. I wondered how Daryl got involved with her. She was so serious all the time and barely smiled the whole night.

We walked down the hall, the sound of partying teenagers coming from each room we passed. Dave banged on a few doors along the way but didn't wait for them to answer, a few swinging open behind us and voices saying, "Dave, what do you want?" He looked back grinning. "Nothing. Just making sure you guys are having a good time." We went into his room and he quickly took out the cocaine. We took turns snorting lines off the mirror, and I felt that euphoric feeling again, but much stronger this time. We had barely touched it at the prom; nothing compared to what we were doing now. Daryl boasted that he had some really good pot and the room was filled with smoke as we passed a fat joint around.

We made our rounds to all the different rooms, most crowded with kids smoking joints and cracking open six packs. For some reason the beers were going down like water now, the cocaine having some inhibitory effect, and I downed one after another. Things started to become blurry. Somehow a small group of us wound up outside behind the hotel, standing at the back of the parking lot by a little swampy area. It was one of those things that started as a puddle after a heavy rain, had never drained out, and continued to build up until tall stalks of green swamp grass sprouted up in the middle.

I was standing at the edge of the mud and talking to a kid named Dave Matthews. Like me, he had lived in the Stadium Project when he was younger, but he was from the other end and I never really played with him. The conversation eventually turned to our life there. But it wasn't the good memories he brought up. Instead, he brought back every painful feeling I had from those years. "Man, they were always chasing your brother Tommy and beating him up," he went on, drunk and slurring. "Your family was pretty messed up." I listened quietly, in my mind returning to those days. I walked away from the group, heading back to the hotel in a drug-induced confusion, some deeply repressed anger bubbling to the surface at that instant. All bad memories clumping together as one, meeting in a place where primitive emotion rules and crushes intelligent thought. Then there was blackness.

I came to consciousness a little at a time. My eyelids flickered open, but the bright light hurt and they closed instantly. Then they would stay open a little longer, tolerating the light for a few more seconds before I would fade away again. Finally, they stayed open and I realized I was looking straight up at a ceiling, and my back ached from the hard surface I was lying on. I had absolutely no idea where I was, no recollection of the prom the night before, and I lay there trying to focus for a moment. I sat up and my head pounded painfully. My hands rested on my knees and I could see the skin scraped off my bloody knuckles, both hands burning and throbbing. Past them, I saw my muddy feet. I lifted my head and there were prison bars in front of me. Flashbacks, bits and pieces of the night before began to rush back. There was the prom, then the Salem Inn with a lot of partying... but it ended there.

I began to panic, my heart racing, wondering what had happened. Why was I here? How did I go from the prom to jail? *My God, what have I done?* went through my mind. I began to shout desperately, "Hello! Hello! Is anybody out there?" A moment passed and I screamed again, "Is anybody out there?" A gray-haired police officer came and stood in front of the bars looking at me.

"Why am I here?" I asked, with a quiet and hoarse voice.

He stood staring down at me for a moment, and then said, "You don't know what happened?"

"I don't remember anything except being with my friends," I said, looking up at him through the bars.

He lifted one knee and rested his foot on a bar, then leaned forward with his elbow resting on the same knee so that his face was at my level. "You went on a rampage. Punching holes in walls, kicking doors, and you even went into the room of a couple from France and kicked their phone off the wall. It took five State Troopers to drag you out. You did a lot of damage and you're in big trouble."

I put my head in my hands and wanted to cry at that moment. "What happened? What made you do it?" he asked, almost sympathetically.

"I don't know. I guess I tried something I shouldn't have," I said, looking down at the floor in hopeless desperation. I knew this was serious and there were severe consequences awaiting me.

"Did you ever hear of crack?" he asked, in the tone of a seasoned police officer.

"No," I answered, shaking my head back and forth. "What is that?"

"Pow, one hit and straight to the moon," he answered, slapping one hand and lifting it toward the ceiling to emphasize his point.

"Do I have to stay here?" I asked, hoping I could somehow go home until the court date. "That depends. It's Saturday. The only way is to post bail."

"My mother doesn't really have much money. I guess I'm stuck here."

"Do you have any relatives in New Hampshire that own real estate? In this state a property owner can sign against their house in lieu of bail," the officer asked, legitimately trying to help me find a way out. I could sense he felt bad for me and wanted me to go home as much as I did.

"My father lives in Plaistow. He owns a house but I don't think he'll do it," I said doubtfully.

"Do you know his phone number?"

I shook my head no.

"How about his address?"

That I knew. I had once driven my motorcycle to his house and remembered the pleasant name of his street—Sunrise Terrace—and I told the officer.

He walked out with this information and I lay on the metal bench with my hands behind my head, looking at the ceiling with feelings of humiliation and hopelessness coming over me. I had really done it this time. I cursed myself for being so stupid. Why did I have to try that stuff with Dave? But he was right about one thing—this would be a night I remembered forever. I looked back at all the stupid things I did in my life and they all had one thing in common—some need to fit in and be part of a group, some longing to be accepted, and some insecurity prompting me to act in a way I otherwise wouldn't.

A few hours passed and the officer returned, removed a key from his belt and unlocked the jail cell. "Your father is waiting for you." I followed him out of the jail section and into an office area of desks and typewriters. My father was sitting alongside a desk and he just quietly watched as I walked over and sat beside him. I always wanted his attention, but not like this. I felt a shame deep down inside. I always just assumed that my father dismissed my brothers and me as unworthy of his attention—saw Tommy as a retard, Gary as a lost soul, and me as a punk. Sitting there with my bloody knuckles and muddy feet, I felt like I was confirming it for him.

"What the hell happened, Kenny?" he asked in a quiet voice, no hint of anger—just bewilderment.

"I don't know," I said, looking down and putting my muddy sneakers back on, taking my time to avoid eye contact.

"I know what it's like to go for a drink on Tuesday and wake up on Thursday, but what the hell happened?" he continued, searching for some explanation. I didn't give an answer because I didn't have one. Sometimes there truly is no answer.

He drove me home; the two of us quiet with our own thoughts about the situation. He stopped trying to figure out what happened, and I never really tried to begin, knowing the answer was buried deep inside my mind, in some inaccessible place. "Call me," he said in a fatherly tone as I got out of his car. I nodded and walked slowly up the three flights of stairs, not wanting to discuss this with my mother.

When I walked in, she was standing in the kitchen, looking at my face as I passed her. "This is just wonderful," she began, expecting me to stop. However, I continued straight into my room and closed the door behind me. I lay on my bed face down, a severe depression like I had never felt coming over me. I wanted to be dead, to just not exist anymore. This was the final act in a worthless life.

It was late in the afternoon and I just lay there motionless until well after dark, passing through the entire spectrum of emotion— anger at myself, confusion about why it happened, humiliation at the fact that everyone would know, sadness that I had struck yet another blow to my mother. In the darkness around me, I lost all concept of time. I heard some people mumbling in the kitchen, and then my bedroom door opened, and the light clicked on. Dave came in my room, and behind him, I saw Kim standing in the doorway with a sad, concerned look on her face. Even after I took another girl to the prom, there she was, and I couldn't understand how she still loved me after all this.

Dave tried to make me laugh with a few of his obscene gestures, but I just lay there silently. He said something about feeling responsible, but I was so deep inside myself that I only heard bits and pieces, his voice coming and going like it came through a filter. He went to the living room and Kim knelt beside the bed, whispered something to me and kissed me softly on the cheek. Then it was quiet and dark again.

My eyes opened to the morning sunshine and the sound of birds singing outside my window. I wondered what they were so happy about—didn't they know my situation? It almost seemed like they were antagonizing me, rubbing it in, their singing voices saying, "Oh, it's so beautiful out here. What a glorious day. It wasn't us who wrecked the hotel." I couldn't bear to lie there thinking any longer, so I dug through the drawers of my nightstand hoping to find something interesting to read. I shuffled through muscle magazines and other junk that had accumulated over time, and at the bottom, I came across a brown hardcover book. There were a few small BB gun holes in the cover making the title hard to read—New International Version Holy Bible. A few years ago, Gary and I had a BB gun and we shot up everything in sight—the neighbor's windows, the trash cans, streetlights, and various objects throughout the house. We had put thick books behind soda bottles to stop the BBs from hitting the walls. One of us must have grabbed it without reading the title, too worked up with adrenaline and the thrill of blasting anything we wanted.

I couldn't remember how I got it, had never really paid any attention to it. What did "New International Version" mean anyway? It was this title that piqued my interest and had me turning pages. I soon realized that it only meant it was written in plain English. There wasn't that confusing King James Old English, with words like *thou, henceforth,* and *hitherto.* I read through the gospels, first expecting it to be scholarly and reprimanding, condemning me on every page. But, as I continued, I found it was really about mercy and compassion, about less-than-perfect people who turned their lives around. I felt better reading about people who had made tremendous mistakes and were able to redeem themselves. I spent all of Sunday in my room reading it voraciously, continuing on as I ate a sandwich, rushing back eagerly from the bathroom to learn more.

That night I lay awake dreading the thought of school in the morning, of facing the entire senior class, knowing what happened at the prom would go throughout the building in a matter of minutes. Then there was the court date looming in the near future. It came to me suddenly—the only logical solution to all of this—I would pray that I was never born. It said right in the Bible that whatever I asked for in prayer would be given me as long as I believed. And I did believe that God would answer this prayer; it wasn't for glory or fame, nor riches or luxuries. It was a simple and humble request.

I prayed as respectfully as I could, sincerely asking God to return to April 12, 1967 and erase me from the Book of Life, making it so I had never existed at all. I put forth my best argument, giving reasons why it made no difference to the world whether I was here or not. But it made a big difference to me. If I never existed, there was no project, no broken family, no foster homes, no fear, no insecurity, and no pain. I closed my eyes fully expecting to never wake up again.

13

God never answered the prayer. He decided I should face the consequences of what I did. But He did help me get out of a terrible mess. There were thousands of dollars in damage to the Salem Inn and the management was furious, wanted my head on a silver platter. Then, inexplicably, they changed their minds and never pressed charges. The judge showed leniency, knew I was leaving that summer for the Marines, and let me go with the understanding that the smallest infraction of the law would have crushing consequences.

At the time I was angry at God, figured I couldn't even believe Him. But I made my peace with Him long ago. In the process, I had to learn to accept a few things. God won't do things for me, but if I ask sincerely, He will help. He won't pick the winning lottery numbers for me, and He won't help my son hit a game-winning grand slam in the final inning. I also learned that life does give second chances, but you have to be willing to try. That doesn't mean it will be easy, life is never easy—it took me forty years to accept this last one.

It was a long four years in the Marines, but it was just what the doctor ordered for a guy like me. The Marines specialize in taking headstrong, cocky young men and breaking them—and they broke me. Twenty pounds melted away under the blazing sun and drenching humidity of South Carolina in August. Bad habits melted away with them. There is no tolerance in the Marines for laziness, procrastination, sloppiness; no tolerance for answers like, "I'll do it later," or, "I guess it's good enough." Anything assigned needs to be done quickly and done right the first time.

The Marines was the turning point in my life, when I came face-to-face with myself and didn't like what I saw. I finally realized it doesn't matter what people think of you, it matters what you think of yourself. And, ultimately, what God thinks of you. Never again did I let some need to fit in or peer pressure influence who I was or what I decided to do. I learned discipline, perseverance, and to have faith in myself, to reach down inside and do things I never believed I could, not just physically but mentally. It was this mindset that helped me graduate college with honors—twice. I saw different parts of the world, rode horseback by the Great Pyramid of Giza, took a boat ride down the Nile with some European girls, spent an afternoon walking around Rome, and saw crushing poverty on the streets of Tijuana, Mexico. I was honorably discharged in May of 1990, a few short months before Saddam Hussein invaded Kuwait.

I don't live far from Lawrence now, only a short drive away in a small town where everyone knows everyone and things are pretty safe. Sometimes I take a drive through and revisit all the childhood haunts. First stopping at the Stadium Project and looking across the road to the state swimming pool. That pool that excited us so much as it was being built; where we had so many laughs, so many adventures, so many hot dogs and pieces of pizza. It was the last place that Andy Puglisi was seen alive and I cannot look at it without thinking of him; that tragic incident crushing the happy memories and erasing the little bit of childhood innocence the kids in the project had. It is a sad and morbid place for me now—Andy's tombstone.

A quick drive down South Union Street past the Chinese restaurant I was so embarrassed to live above. Across the green metal bridge that I walked over a hundred times as a boy, to Prospect Hill where I lived until I joined the Marines. I drive slowly by our old apartment, different memories coming back each time I do, and sometimes I pull over at the park on top of the hill. I stand at the edge and look over the familiar silhouette of the city I love; the clock tower, the bridges crossing the Merrimac and all the mills stretching for miles on its banks, the buildings downtown and the tall brick tower on Tower Hill. I turn around and look at the park where I ran wild with friends, the same oak tree we stood below twenty-five years ago still standing tall and untouched by time. A short drive down High Street to where Kim used to live. Her family moved from there long ago. I looked at the three-tenement and remembered all the times we had stood in front of her house talking, or I stole a kiss when her parents weren't looking.

Back down the hill and onto Canal Street, down Essex and over to Common to see Pappy's Bakery. It closed a few years ago, but the owner maintains the building almost exactly as it was. The interior is still filled with the glass cases that used to hold all the different pastries, the same paneling on the walls, and the same counter that I saw her behind.

After more than ninety years in business, Pappy's closed their doors forever—gone like the close-knit Italian neighborhoods that once surrounded it. Gone with it, my beautiful girl behind the counter. Many years ago, these neighborhoods were full of immigrants from Germany, England, and Canada. But the winds of change blew and bit-by-bit they became Italian, with little bakeries and fish markets popping up. Recently the winds of change blew again and they became Hispanic. One day the winds will blow again and someone else will come.

It is impossible to revisit your childhood without a sense of sadness, a sense of innocence lost. But it is also impossible to revisit your childhood and not smile a few times. I'm not sure I would want to go back. I wouldn't want to feel that pain again, but there are so many things I would do differently—try a little harder in school, never buckle to the peer pressure that made me do so many stupid things, to have more confidence in myself and believe that anything was possible—because it was. To be a better son to my mother, to walk into the bakery and talk to a certain girl whose face is engraved in my heart and soul. Only for these reasons would I go back. The rest I can do without. I don't feel sorry for myself. I learned a lot of lessons that aren't taught in the suburbs. Nothing ever comes of self-pity except depression and despair.

I have always thought about the girl in the Italian bakery, from time to time remembering the beauty of her face and the soft curves of her delicate body. Somewhere along the way, I pushed her into a far corner of my mind, believing it was just some youthful wish, some desire that will have to remain unfulfilled. But recently she reemerged stronger than ever and my mind is filled with her day and night.

I tried desperately to find out who she was, refusing to go to my grave an old man without ever knowing her name or telling her how I felt. I decided to send her a letter. I knew it was crazy, but there was an overwhelming need to tell her everything, and for some strange reason I felt she needed to hear it; needed to know that for twenty-five years someone has loved her. I went to the Lawrence Public Library and spent hours in the archive section scanning through every available yearbook. I didn't have a name so I looked at every girl's picture in hopes of finding that beautiful face, looking through every school in the area. But I couldn't find her. I wondered if she went to some other school, if she dropped out or moved, or if her picture was in one of the missing yearbooks. As I opened the cover of 1986, I knew what would happen—and it did. I was back in time twenty years. There were flashbacks as I looked over pictures of old familiar faces standing in the hall or sitting in class, and for a moment I was back in the corridors joking with friends, seventeen again without a care in the world. There was the picture of Daryl and me side-by-side in computer class, and underneath it a clever caption, "Masterminds at work?"

Dave had gotten on the yearbook committee and it seemed his grinning face found its way onto every page. I looked at Kim's picture and the message she had written below it, "For now we'll go on living separate lives. Semper Fi." It was a message to me. *Separate Lives* was a song she liked, and *Semper Fi* was the Marine Corps motto, meaning "Always faithful." I smiled when I saw it. I hadn't seen her in twenty years and she was still getting the last word, her feelings those last few weeks of high school captured forever and frozen in time. At that moment, I realized what a lousy boyfriend I had been to her, and wished I had the chance to tell her how sorry I was.

I went on all those Internet reunion sites searching for any clue as to who she was, but without a name, it was next to impossible. I found out the name of the family who owned Pappy's Bakery, suspecting she was related, and searched unsuccessfully under that. No listings for a girl with that last name. I know she is still around. Several years ago, I was sitting with my wife in a quaint little Italian restaurant having a drink at the bar, when she walked right by in a waitress's uniform. She didn't walk by—she strutted, as though she knew my eyes would fixate on her as she passed. She was right. I couldn't take them off of her. Still as beautiful as the first time I saw her, those high school feelings rushed back. Only a year or so ago I saw her in the local shopping mall. My daughter wanted me to buy everything in sight and I was walking toward the door to escape, my daughter pouting and walking a few feet behind. I came up a small set of stairs and she was right there, sitting with another woman, looking as though they were waiting for someone in a store. I stood at the top of the stairs waiting for my daughter to catch up and tried to take a good look at her, but the mall was crowded and people kept coming between us.

I went to eat in that same little Italian restaurant recently in hopes of seeing her, but she wasn't there. I even stopped by at different times of the day pretending to want take-out menus, looking over the shoulder of the hostess and scanning the place for her, wondering if I had just missed her the night I went. She was nowhere to be found and I have reluctantly given up. I guess I will never know her name or the sound of her voice.

Time is merciless—it trudges forward relentlessly, you can never slow it, stop it or go back; it knows no reprieve. You only get to be sixteen once. There was a window in time when I could have walked into the bakery and talked to her. That window is closed now forever, and I will always wonder what might have been. Did she want me to come in? It would have taken one moment to find out, but insecurity and fear stopped me. One moment! And maybe she would be sitting at the dinner table with me right now talking about our children. Maybe tonight I would be kissing her lips and telling her I loved her, kissing her neck and smelling the shampoo in her hair, bringing her delicate body close to me and feeling her warmth. But I will never know those things. That moment when I stood in the doorway at Lawrence High, the two of us face-to-face, how could I have known that twenty-five years later this moment would still haunt me?

I wanted so desperately to find her so I could look into her eyes and tell her everything. For whatever reason, that isn't meant to be. So I will tell her here:

"My beautiful girl in Pappy's Bakery, I loved you the instant I saw you. I have never forgotten the days I walked by to see you through the window. I thought of you as a boy in Lawrence; I thought of you as a young man in Egypt; and I thought of you many a night as I lay in my bunk in California. Even now on a rainy day, I look out the window and think of you, and you bring a smile to my face. I don't know who you were or where life took you. I don't know if you are happy or sad. But I do know one thing—I hope life treated you well and all your wishes came true. Wherever you are, wherever you go, know one thing—"Sixteen-year-old me will always love sixteen-year-old you." I've waited twenty-five years to tell you this; maybe now I can finally stop thinking of you.

They say that, "sometimes one door closes so another can open," but sometimes one door never opens at all because further down the road there is another with your name on it. My wife is no less beautiful than the girl in Pappy's Bakery, and when she wants to be, she is stunning. As remarkable as it sounds, it never even occurred to me until years later that the two of them bear a strong resemblance—the same dark, wavy hair, the same shape to their faces, similar sharp features, and the same small shoulders. This was not my doing—my wife approached *me*.

She is a good wife; always doting on the children and attending to their needs, their school clothes laid out neatly the night before, lunches made or paid for in advance, a multivitamin waiting each morning by their breakfasts, and the house always immaculate. And even though I ask her not to, sometimes she dotes on me. That same hand of destiny that has always watched out for me decided this was the woman I would spend my life with, and I am grateful for her.

She likes to buy a coffee and drive through Lawrence with me, listening attentively to all my crazy stories while shaking her head at my mischief. Sometimes the kids go with us and I try to teach them something along the way, trying to instill an appreciation for the things they have. I want them to know there are people out there carrying heavy burdens. That we're all in this world together—every single one of us equal in the sight of God. If I had to learn life's lessons the hard way so my children don't, if that was the deal life had for me, then I gladly accept.

My son is a handsome boy. He got the best of both his parents. It seems there is always some interested girl. His life consists of private school, baseball, guitars, and ever-changing and ever-more-expensive electronic games and gadgets. Some people say that heaven and hell are really here on earth. I don't know if that's true.

But sometimes at his baseball games when the spring wind blows the scent of freshly cut grass, and the boys are joking around on the field, I think heaven might be something like this. It is as close a glimpse of heaven as this world will allow.

My daughter is a girly-girl, already learning to navigate her way through the cliques of grade school. Her life consists of Girl Scouts, swimming, and whatever trendy "girl" thing is in at the moment. I have called her "my little thumbkin" since she was a baby, and even when she is a grown woman, she will be, "my little thumbkin."

I try to teach my children not to stand on the sidelines in life, to get in the game; *don't let that little voice of doubt get the best of you.* Give everything your best effort; you may not have that chance again. Believe in yourself; you are no less important than anyone else on the planet. Treat other people the way you want to be treated. Don't look down on anyone.

I still don't see my brothers very often. It is hard for me to look at Tommy. Thirty years of institutions and psychotropic medications have turned him into a shell of the laughing boy I remember. The rotted teeth and incoherent babblings are an indictment of all the failures over the years. Aside from my mother, so many of us failed him, and I die a little inside whenever I see him.

Gary is a decent man. He has never had any addictions or problems that are so common to people who grew up the way we did. He lives his life moment-to-moment, never really applying himself at anything. He never married or had children—a few years with one woman, a few years with another. I will always remember Gary as a little boy, stuck in the middle and trying to fight back against impossible odds; trying to protect a defenseless older brother, and trying to watch out for a younger one too. Those early years define the man he is today, damaging him, so he never really tries his hardest at anything. Deep down he feels he can never win, and somewhere along the way, he quietly surrendered. In my heart he will always be my big brother, fighting his hardest to protect his brothers from a brutal world, knowing he could never win—but still not backing down. No, Mom, wild horses couldn't drag us apart, but life could. I always ask God to keep my brothers in the palm of His hand.

I have no anger or hatred left toward anyone. In the end, it only hurts you, not them. I made peace with my father long ago, knowing that he had his own demons with which to wrestle. Life dealt my mother a hand that would have destroyed most people, but somehow she endured. Yet, for years, I watched anger and frustration eat away at her, like termites gnawing at wood. And just as the wood is reduced to fragments and dust, anger and frustration do something like that to a person, altering them, depriving them of what they were meant to be. I love my mother, and was happy to see her let go of the past.

For years, I believed God had dealt me a bad hand and just turned his back on me. But when I honestly look over my life, I can see he never took his eyes off of me. So many things I took for coincidence were really no coincidence at all—when I was three or four years old, I was drowning behind a dock in a small pond. My mother turned away briefly and into the water I went. Just as I was losing consciousness, bright orange shorts burst through the water beside me. The lifeguard carried my semi-conscious body and placed me on the blanket by my grateful mother. I was out of sight, so how did the lifeguard suddenly see me in the nick of time?

My mother didn't have much money when we lived in the projects so she never went away and we never took vacations. During those hot summer days, we were always at the pool with our friends. The one time she suddenly feels she must visit home, tragedy strikes at the pool and Andy is never seen again. I wasn't supposed to be there. The years I spent in foster homes were for a reason. I was headed in the wrong direction and a change was needed.

The night I rode my motorcycle down the highway with Timmy Boutin on the back; the rear tire hit a wet piece of metal and the motorcycle twisted to the side, then came right out from beneath us, sending us into the air. We hit the road and slid across the concrete for a good distance, the motorcycle bouncing and sliding alongside of us, sparks shooting as the metal scraped against the concrete.

There were holes worn all the way through our leather jackets from the coarse surface of the road. My motorcycle was destroyed, yet Timmy and I walked away without a single scratch on our bodies.

My drug-induced disaster on prom night happened for a reason, and taught me a valuable lesson the hard way. I've seen many people's lives destroyed by drugs, and since prom night, I never even considered using them. And why did the hotel manager suddenly change his mind and drop all charges?

While in the Marines, I took college classes at night, so my commanding officer recommended I apply for a ninety-day school cut, which meant I would be discharged three months early so I could register for the fall semester back home. I took his advice. Instead of being discharged on August 3 like I was supposed to be, I was discharged in May. On August 2, 1990, Saddam Hussein invaded Kuwait. Had I not been granted the early release, my discharge would have been cancelled and I would have had to fight in the war. I wasn't supposed to be there.

The night I happened to be in Haverhill, Massachusetts, and decided to get a sandwich at a place called Pizzaland, a pretty young woman kept looking at me and giggling with her friend behind the counter. As I was leaving, she smiled at me and waved in a flirty sort of way. I didn't have the guts to go back and talk to her, although I really wanted to and for days regretted my cowardice. The following Saturday night I ran into her miles away at a nightclub. We talked a little, danced a little, and walked out the door together. I have been with her every day for the last seventeen years. I didn't get the girl in the Italian bakery, but I did get the one in the pizza shop. On and on the list goes; God's fingerprints are all over my life.

Even still, I have my moments of doubt. I have worked in the medical field for twelve years now, and I've seen a lot of things I wish I hadn't—the look on a woman's face when she heard that someone she loved was dead, lives ended before their time, and the grieving families left behind, a mother cradling a baby with bones so brittle that any wrong move could fracture them. Suffering, misery, the intractable pain of cancer, and I can make no sense of it.

Sometimes I just want to lie down and quit, to just not exist at all. I have sworn a hundred times that I would never pray again. But I still do all the time, hoping that someday I will be given the answers to the questions I have struggled with: *Why do these things need to happen? Why all the suffering? What happened to my missing friend Andy? And why was it allowed to happen to an innocent ten-year-old boy? Why all these wars and massacres? Why do children starve to death in the deserts of Africa while one man has enough money to feed a country? Why so much injustice in the world? Why do we even go on, and continue this struggle day after day? Why?*

It's all about unconditional love for our children, our wives or husbands, our mothers and fathers, our sisters and brothers. Where there is love there is always hope. So we hope someday we'll live in a world where children don't disappear. That one day we wake up to a world free of wars, where everyone has enough to eat. We hope that diseases will be cured and loved ones made whole. We hope one day we're reunited with our mothers, fathers, brothers, and sisters; that somehow our broken families are brought back together. We hope someone will accept us and love us—no matter how messed up we are. We hope our children do better than we did. We hope there is a God, because without Him we know the law of the jungle will eventually prevail. But most of all, we hope there is a heaven, because then it all makes sense. We pay a price now, marching on like soldiers through the chastening of this life. When it is over, we hope to see a world the way God intended it to be—where injustices are corrected and everyone is together again. We see the crippled walking; listen to the joyful laughter of the blind when they finally see. We look on with wonder as lions and lambs lay in the pasture side by side. And somewhere in the distance, in grassy fields, all the lost children play happily together, waiting patiently for their loved ones to arrive. A place where all tears are wiped away, and all questions answered.

Made in the USA
Lexington, KY
26 August 2013